T0196742

KING
OF THE ROCKS

KING OF THE ROCKS

A Memoir

BILL GREEN

KING OF THE ROCKS
A MEMOIR

iUniverse books may be ordered through booksellers or by contacting:

iUniverse
1663 Liberty Drive
Bloomington, IN 47403
www.iuniverse.com
1-800-Authors (1-800-288-4677)

ISBN: 978-1-5320-2214-2 (sc)
ISBN: 978-1-5320-2213-5 (e)

Library of Congress Control Number: 2017907150

Print information available on the last page.

iUniverse rev. date: 06/21/2017

For Liz

Contents

PREFACE

This book began as an effort to pass on to my daughters and granddaughters the story of my father, Jim Green, and the other members of our family: my mother, Elizabeth O'Donnell Green; my brother, Eugene; my sister, Liz; and my aunt, Gene O'Donnell.

Although the book was initially meant for family members, I eventually decided that certain themes contained here might be of general interest. Among these are our reactions to death, our struggle with grief and guilt, the problems of parenting, the dynamics and tensions of family life, and the importance of dreams.

I am aware that the narrative is not linear; rather, it is based on my memories as they came to me in dreams, idle moments, or conversations with friends. Some of these flashbacks to the 1950s and 1960s were clearly suggested by my therapist, Dr. Breslow, whom I saw over the years 1970 to 1974. It was his recommendation that I place my father's life in the larger context of family, and it is evident where I have done this. I have tried at all times to keep the central question of the book in focus: namely, who was my father, and what was his relationship with his family, with me, and with the long stretch of grief that I experienced after his death? Even the chapters set in Tucson and in Dallas, forty-three years after his death, shed light on this question, as does the final chapter, which moves between wakefulness and dream. For this reason I have included them in the main body of the book.

Shifts in tenses from past to present are for the most part deliberate. When describing a photo, I often use present tense to give the image an immediacy that it might not have otherwise. There are other points in the book where present tense seemed more natural and appropriate to me, although this might not be the opinion of the reader.

The last chapter may be problematic for some readers. I believe it derives from a deep and unquenched desire to have had that beer and long conversation of which my father often spoke and even wrote in his later years. It is clearly a wish, or a waking dream, in whose reality and realistic detail I firmly believed at the time. It is a story I ardently wanted to be true. But although I thought there would be time for this—as Eliot writes in *Prufrock*, "Time for you and time for me / And time yet for a hundred indecisions / And a hundred visions and revisions"—there was not.

***

Here is something else that might have had a bearing on my desire to write *King of the Rocks* or, at least, on my perseverance through periods of doubt and skepticism. Not long ago, in fact during a recent Fourth of July celebration, I told my friend Keith that I was writing a book about my father. We were standing on a big lawn that might have been straight out of *Gatsby*, except that it wasn't. It was in Indiana, where that state meets Ohio, and I was looking north into high corn as far as the eye could see; to the east was a copse of willows. Keith said, "So, was your father a prominent man, an admiral, a famous academic from Yale or Harvard, an athlete of note?"

And I just laughed. "Not a chance, my friend. He was an ordinary guy. He was a guy from the Rocks. But he was my father, and I wanted to know him."

He nodded. "Well, you wanted to write about him, and you're doing it."

"That's it," I said. "Not much more to it. And I wanted my daughters to know about him. To know their grandfather."

I was holding a Sam Adams in my hand, sipping it out of the bottle, and as the distant vision of the fields blurred into a single greenness, I remembered a poem I had heard back in Pittsburgh when I was in college. It's called "People," by Yevgeny Yevtushenko, and it made an impression on me right there on the spot. I remember some of the lines today, especially these:

No people are uninteresting.
Their fate is like the chronicle of planets; and

We who knew our fathers
in everything, in nothing; and my favorite

Not people die but worlds die in them.

Not people die but worlds die in them. Whole worlds! Think of it.

What was that world my father carried within him? The ball fields, the rails, the friends who thronged him, the love he felt for our mother, his Dear Bunny, and for our family. How did that world, so private and enigmatic, so lost beneath the rippled currents of his moods and silence, intersect with my own self-involved isolation? I needed to know. And I needed to know why Yevtushenko's lines "We who knew our fathers / in everything, in nothing" so limned an image of a man I knew was there, was mere inches from me at the dinner table, but whom I could not see, as though he lived on a fogbound, iced-in land just beyond my viewing. This was the quest in all the memories, the photos and letters. This was the task I had set for myself. "A book must be the axe," Kafka wrote, "for the frozen sea within us."

***

This is my first memoir, and, admittedly, I have struggled with it over several years. I make no secret of this. It is not, however, my first book. It follows three earlier works, of which one, *Water, Ice and Stone,* won the 1996 John Burroughs Medal and was nominated for the PEN Mary Albrand Award. But without question, *King of the Rocks*, personal as it is, has been the most challenging for me.

ACKNOWLEDGMENTS

I would not have written this book without the encouragement and editorial assistance of my sister, Liz; my wife, Wanda; and my daughters, Dana and Kate. All of them read parts of the early drafts and made valuable comments and, in some cases, provided memories that markedly added to the clarity and richness of the work. Steven Bauer of Hollow Tree Literary suggested a number of changes that I believe have greatly improved the book's quality. I went back to Steven's comments often when I had doubts about some particular construction. My friend Don McMullen refreshed many of my memories that had either faded or become lost altogether, and our trips to the Rocks brought places and events to life.

I also wish to acknowledge the fine work of my editors at iUniverse. Sarah Disbrow was editorial coordinator for this project, and she did an excellent job keeping everything on schedule. Her extensive knowledge and her willingness to answer, in detail, my many questions were greatly appreciated. Michelle (developmental editor) made some important suggestions for moving paragraphs and whole sections from one place to another in the book. I believe these changes in location improved the flow of ideas and aided in simplifying the text. Allison Gorman (content editor) completed an extremely careful reading of the book and informed me of inconsistencies and awkward phrasing. I made virtually all of the changes she recommended, and I believe that these changes added immeasurably to the quality of the text. Without her careful attention to detail—which, in my opinion, far exceeded editorial requirements—this book would not be the one you hold in your hands. Finally, Elizabeth D. and Andrea Andonis were extremely helpful in putting finishing touches on the book. Andrea suggested possible arrangements for the photos and for the layout in general.

To all of these people, I am extremely grateful.

The Rocks (2013) Photo of tombstones at St. Mary Cemetery. This overlooks McKees Rocks and, in the distance, the City of Pittsburgh*

1

THE ROCKS (2013)

I am back in Pittsburgh. Back in the Rocks, for a reunion with McMullen, my old childhood friend from age six. He's staying out in the suburbs with his sister. I'm staying in one of the hotels in downtown Pittsburgh so I can look at a few of the sites the great photojournalist W. Eugene Smith photographed in the '50s. We meet in the Rocks for breakfast at our favorite diner, with its hot pancakes and crispy bacon and all the coffee you can drink. There's a big sign celebrating fifty-seven years in this very spot, and I remember it from back when I was a kid.

McMullen has an omelet. I have my usual oatmeal with cinnamon. I sprinkle on some of the almonds I have in my pocket. The waitress remembers us from last year, smiles, and says, "Here again, huh?"

"No way to get rid of us," McMullen says. "We love it here. Fond memories, ya know?"

He's right. This is it, my chance to put it all together: the puzzles of my father's life and my family's life. Their solutions have eluded me for years, despite the analyses, the memories, the handwritten letters, the photographs. I am finally ready for this task. Diving too deeply into the past feels convoluted and dangerous. Who knows where it will lead?

We head first for the Bottoms, the low-lying flood plain near the Ohio River, where a rock outcrop once sheltered the log cabin of Alexander McKee.

When we arrive at the outcrop, we find it much as the explorer George Mercer described it in his writings more than 250 years earlier. Now, however, there's the blight of a gravel operation at the steep eastern end of the hill and a rail line running close by. We park the car and walk along the rails, from which we can see the western tip of Bruno's Island and, beyond, on the opposite shore of the Ohio, the gray, forbidding walls of Western Penitentiary. Just below us, near the shore in the still waters of the river, a few small fishing boats move beneath the leafy trees like an impressionist painting.

The hill appears overgrown, as though no one has climbed it for decades. At the far western end, there is a thin trail, which leads to the top and the ancient Adena burial ground. We start up, but a rusty barbed-wire fence strung across the trail makes climbing difficult, so we decide to return to the car. Another day, perhaps. Or maybe never.

Rocks Rangers Field is nearby. It too is cluttered with grass and weeds, but I can see the outlines of a football field where Joe Vitelli once played and a ghost of the old clay infield I remember. My father would hit me ground balls on this field on days when he had business with some of his friends who lived down here in the Bottoms. On the dust and stone of this ground, I spun my dreams of someday playing second in the "Bigs," maybe even for the Pirates.

McMullen and I drive up to 134 Amelia Street. I want a few pictures of the old place, whatever I can get from the street. I have no idea who owns it. I'm snapping away with the point-and-click when a heavyset guy walks out the door.

He asks, "Whatsya doin', buddy?" and I say, "Reminiscing. Memory lane. I lived here for many years." He shakes his head and smiles. He's friendly enough, in that gruff, tough-guy, Rocks kind of way.

I look around at worn sofas, chairs, clothing, and drywall piled at the curb. "What's all the stuff?"

"Cleanin' the damn place out," he says. "I rented it to the wrong person, a real slob. It's a fucked-up mess."

"I'm sorry to hear that," I say. "You don't mind if I take a few pictures, do you?"

"Hell no," he says. "Go in. Look around. I don't care. Hell, you grew up here. This was your place."

McMullen and I go up the front steps, where we once sat on hot summer days. The same steps I threw a ball against to practice grounders when my father wasn't home. The guy was right, the place is a mess, but I can see he's working to get it back in shape. There are two older guys seated on the floor in the living room. They tell us they're helping him. They're his buddies, both retired. One collected garbage for the city for twenty-five years; the other worked in shipping at FESCO until it closed.

The FESCO guy and I exchange memories of the factory, and I tell him I worked on the line in enameling. "Sinks," I say.

"Enameling," he says. "It was hot as hell over there."

"I remember lots of sweat," I say. "Salt pills all day."

"Yeah," he says. "Shipping was better. You got to go outside, breathe some fresh air."

"Okay if we go downstairs?" I ask.

"Sure," he says, "he won't mind." He lifts his head in the direction of the owner, who is still outside with the piles of trash.

The basement is dark and cool. It is much smaller than in my memory. At the bottom of the stairs I almost run into the wall, the same green wall my father made Eugene kick until his feet bled. "That'll teach him," my father said. "He won't kick anyone again."

McMullen says, "Here's the fitting for your speed bag. They never took it out. And check this: it's the hook for the sandbag we used to punch." I run my fingers over the hook. Only McMullen would remember this.

Off to the right, up against the wall opposite where my mother had her washer and dryer, are three polished desks. They glisten, even in the dim light. The bookshelves my father installed rise above them, almost to the window. It's all one piece—desks and shelves, wall-to-wall mahogany—beautiful construction. Careful work. I close my eyes and see him over there in his white, ketchup-stained T-shirt, bent over the middle desk, holding a beer he had gotten from upstairs. No music, just the silence of a sweltering August evening with only the two of them at home: Jim and Bunny, my parents. He believed in me more than he believed in himself, more than he believed in his own future. It was 1967 and he had less than three years to go. Three years before he'd fall asleep and never wake up.

Just being in this place is haunting. I can well up tears with each step if I don't stop myself.

McMullen wants to go back up to the kitchen. There he extends his big basketball hands parallel to the floor, his fingers spread wide. "Here's where the kitchen table stood. Remember?"

"Sure," I say.

"Remember the kitchen conferences we had after school with Aunt Gene? She was real smart. She had a lot of good advice."

"She did," I say. And I look down at the floor, recalling the warmth of the kitchen and the smell of fresh-baked bread she has pulled from the oven. A smile lights her face as she turns her wheelchair toward us. Her withered legs are pulled up, folded beneath her body. "How was school?" she asks. I put my hands over my face so McMullen can't see. For a second I'm not certain what decade it is, how old I am.

In the dining room, where the six of us once gathered for dinner each evening—steaming mashed potatoes, peas, and pork chops—there's nothing now but the big floor sander. The curtains are gone, and I can see the red bricks of the house next door. I hear my brother's deep voice offering grace. My mother walks slowly toward the table with a bowl of creamed corn.

Gradually, though, I stabilize. I've held the tears back. "I'm okay," I say to McMullen. "Let's go upstairs"

I can't recognize much up there except the shape and small size of the rooms. There's the room where Grandmother O'Donnell died; later I slept in a bed in this room, near the window. When it stormed and there was lightning over the hills to the west, I could see the crucified Jesus in the painting of Golgotha. He appeared to move with the storm outside, and I thought he might come down from the cross and walk over to my bed. I was terrified of him.

This is the same room where Liz and I recovered from measles the year the *Andrea Doria* sank. The news went on all day on the radio, and we couldn't stop listening until it was over and the fog had cleared off Nantucket, fifty-two people had died, and more than a thousand had been rescued. I run my hand across the empty space near the window. "You remember the *Andrea Doria*?"

"No," says McMullen.

There is a pile of stuff blocking the entrance to the "little room" and the attic or we would have gone in and then up the stairs to where all the trains were once stored and the baseball cards packed beneath the rafters. My mother tossed the baseball cards, just like a hundred thousand other moms across the land had thrown away their kids' collections.

In my parents' old bedroom there isn't much to see, but in the adjacent bathroom I can see the pink tub my father installed in the '50s as a major update to the house.

In the living room we say good-bye to the guys, who are back to sanding the dining room floor, but not before the owner gives me an update I didn't necessarily need to hear.

"Damn mess, isn't it?" he asks rhetorically. "The place was a whorehouse. Guys coming and going all night, strange shit on the walls, all those weird little dolls in the basement ... I still can't believe it. And I rented it to her. I trusted her."

"Well, I'm glad you're taking care of the place," I say. "It looks good outside."

After a moment's silence, I say, "It's been great talking with you guys. It's too bad about the mess. But what can you do?"

And we shake hands all around. I slap the owner on the shoulder and tell him I appreciate getting to see the house again, and when I ask if we can take their pictures, they line up, the three of them in their work clothes and floor dust. Before we get to the door, I hear the big sander going again.

As we walk out, I realize how small the place is. I realize that had there been anger, arguments, shouting, displays of temper, I would have known. I would have heard my parents. I would have heard my father yell at Aunt Gene. Heard him complain bitterly to my mother about how Gene could talk with us—Eugene, Liz, and me—and he couldn't. The rooms were close; the walls were thin. Sound traveled. But I heard nothing—no fights, ever. The place seemed a haven of dinner smells and conversations and, at Christmas, the big, tinseled tree with the lighted angel on top that touched the ceiling.

"Let's look at the garage," I say to McMullen, a little shaken. But then I say to myself, *We lived here a long, long time ago. Anything can happen, and besides, it's all over. It's finished*. But in my heart, it sure as hell doesn't feel that way.

We walk out back and I get a few more shots: the window still taped from where I hit it with a baseball one summer practicing grounders; the singed place on the eaves where Liz set a little fire doing something I can't remember with beetles. On the other side of the fence, in what had been Uncle Frank and Aunt Mary Cel's yard, there's a bamboo forest: fifteen-foot-high shoots break into the blue sky like something from South China. Right here in the Rocks.

"Ya gotta love this," I say to McMullen.

"Yep, feels crazy. Like home," he says.

***

There are other places: McKees Rocks High, where my mother once taught Latin. Abandoned now, crumbling—large yellowing blocks of marble lying on the ground, weeds eating into them as if they were the stones of Rome, windows all boarded as if a hurricane were imminent. There is bright-red graffiti scribbled across the fallen blocks. From the school, the hill drops steeply down onto "the field" where we once played football and baseball, the yearly cycle of life.

Up here we can see Pittsburgh more clearly through the smog-free air. With the mills gone, it is easy to spot the tall bank buildings whose construction McMullen supervised—coruscating works of perfection rising straight and high above the Point, gleaming against the hills and rivers. I know he's proud of them, but he'll never say so. I imagine fireworks bursting over the city, the Fourth of July, our own private showing from this vantage point. You can barely hear the sounds, but the green and red pinwheels, launched from a barge on the river, turn silent and mystical, as though the galaxies of the universe were visible and whispering secrets in the darkness.

The once-manicured lawns of the terraces to the south, now mantled in thick weeds, trip over one another right down to Chartiers Avenue, one hundred feet below where we stand. McMullen says, "Remember ..." and I know exactly what he is thinking. "Remember the big tire we rolled down here? We expected the German shepherd to stop it. Tiny the miracle dog."

And I say, "Don't remind me," but he does anyway.

"It went all the way down, crossed the sidewalk, crashed into that parked Chevy, took the passenger door right off." We are both thinking what it might have done if not for some kind of divine intervention: killed anyone walking—kids dawdling on their way to the ice cream shop—or casually taken out a passing car on Chartiers. "Stupid kids," McMullen says.

I nod my head in agreement. "We were more than stupid," I say. "I wish that was the worst thing we ever did."

★★★

Inside the thin walls of the house, in the gas-warmed kitchen, in the stained basement with its broken window, in the fallen stones and weed-eaten terraces of the high school, in the angry words of a stranger, it is all coming back. A great torrent I cannot stop.

Looking down over the old field, I feel a deep sadness that seems a natural part of the atmosphere, of the nitrogen-oxygen mix. I sense it as though it has always been here, not as an annoyance but as a palpable, undeniable presence. It runs through the air above the steeples and domes of the old churches, above the roofs of the houses, above the dirt and grass and weeds of the yards and abandoned lots.

I know for certain it is time to leave.

Belfast. Author at the gardens near Queens University.
Statue of Lord Kelvin is in the background

2

BELFAST (1969–70)

Sometimes the arc of life appears in flashes, in dreamscapes. Of these, the mind makes a continuum. In memory we move so easily through time. We leap across whole decades only to return to visit them with clarity. Travels in the cold isolation of the Antarctic valleys. Psychotherapy. The clack of palm fronds beyond the left field fence.

***

In October 1969, after I finished my doctorate, I set off for England on the *QE2*. My father had purchased the ticket, and as we pushed off from New York Harbor into the evening Atlantic, I was looking forward to my first adventure at sea and to all that would follow.

When we said good-bye at the train station in Pittsburgh, he said, "Have some fun. Meet someone. Get away from those damn books for once in your life!" He shook his head wearily. His son, he was certain, was wasting his youth. Maybe he was right. And yet he had reportedly said, "It makes me proud that my kid did this," to all his friends at the local bar, where he'd passed around a copy of my dissertation, *The Interaction of Nonpolar Gases with Alkali Nitrate Melts*. "Hey, Jim!" someone shouted across the darkness. "What the hell is this cr … stuff?"

The *Queen Elizabeth* docked in Southampton. I took the train up to London and from there flew to Belfast the following week. It was autumn. The whole country of Ireland sprawled below me, a lush carpet of emerald partially hidden beneath wispy gray clouds. Traces of nature ran straight up to the gates of the city, encircling Belfast down to the sea.

In 1969, the city seemed a broken place. There was a sense of confusion, disbelief. What had Belfast become? Why did it seem on the verge of rage and despair? Soldiers, portentous armored vehicles, rifles, bayonets, and Makrolon face shields were common sights. The place was an armed camp, a war zone on the verdant sea-edge of Europe.

By spring though, everything had changed. I was no longer uncomfortable with the roiled political situation; I took it as a barely audible hum to which I paid scant notice. Each morning the streets glistened silver with light rain, there were daffodils flowering in private and public gardens, and the hedgerows were bright yellow with gorse.

The Kier Chemistry Building, where I worked, smelled of the familiar organic solvents—hexane, benzene, acetone, isobutanol. But there was also a welcome hint of sausage roll and tea and asparagus wafting down from the cafeteria above the lab.

I had pleasant conversations with my colleagues, Small and Jamison, about the polymer research we were doing, and on the weekends there were dances in the Student Union. The lovely, dark-haired girls there had impossibly tiny waists, and the deejays played the Beatles and American rock, and for a time I felt a little homesick. Outside, near midnight, a food truck by the curb dispensed fish and chips wrapped in oily paper and seasoned with vinegar. Walking home to Adelaide Park in the chill mist, I pulled my tattered sports coat around me for warmth.

By early spring, I had already been down to Dublin and

Trinity College and to the flat, volcano-laid basalts of the Giants Causeway. The sheer cliffs of Donegal, the Mountains of Mourne, and the Glens of Antrim, which before I'd known only from legend and song, were sources of wonder. Looking out over the Atlantic, I could see the earth's gentle curve in the far blue distance.

My life was improving. There were new friends. There were the girls in colorful skirts hiked tight above their knees, some of whom I invited, after dances, back to my flat at Adelaide Park for a little bourbon and some talk of Yeats. Somehow we rarely got to Yeats. I loved the neighborly din of the pubs, the clink of glasses, the constant flow of Guinness and Harp. The pubs became an evening ritual after work. My research was coming together too, to the point where I could envision other prestigious conferences and papers published in the best journals. Life had momentum. Belfast was becoming my home.

In the lab, I had my pipe lit. I smelled the sweet aroma of the Kentucky Club my father had sent me. Smoke was blossoming all around, filling the space near my desk, then thinning and drifting off. In that elevating cloud of blue sweetness, I was getting lost—as though I were Stubb aboard the *Pequod*—in grand visions of how the future might play out. I flipped languorously, with scarcely a thought, through the pages of a book on kinetics. I took a few notes on the rapid rates at which "living polymers" grow, so lightning fast as to be unmeasurable. Until next week, when our new equipment would give us the vision of condensed time we needed—a curving streak of light breaking instantaneously on a phosphorus screen.

***

The letter arrived early at the Keir that morning. It was addressed in the formal, respectful way my parents had adopted after I received my PhD.

Dr. Wm. J. Green
Chemistry Dept.
Queens University, Belfast, Northern Ireland

I was holding it in my hands. It was dated March 30, 1970. As always, the note was short and my father was not concerned about punctuation. He rambled from subject to subject, and he hadn't asked my mother to read it for corrections. This was his creation, probably written in the basement at night, with a beer in one hand, at one of the very desks he had made for his three children. It was written in his own way, in his own voice, and damn the pretentious rules of grammar, which he'd never bothered to learn.

Dear Bill:

I hope you had better weather on Easter Sunday than we had … It is getting close to Little League time, don't you wish we could go back about 17 years …

We stayed home all day Easter, did not want to go out in the snow. Saw where you had a lot of rock throwing in Belfast during Holy Week. You should see your mother now, I got a Cadillac Fleetwood and she rides around with a big cigar in her mouth and she made me buy a chauffeur's uniform for weekends.

Love
Dad

My eyes focused on a few of his words, and as I read them over and over—*Don't you wish we could go back about 17 years*—they took off into what seemed another life …

It is 1953, he is a young man of forty-four, and I am a boy of eleven. It is really the summer of his life. When he slapped out infield practice with the long, thin fungo bat, he looked like a kid and still threw with the fluid grace and perfect overhand motion that marked him as a former outfielder. I played second and could smell the leather and spit in the pocket of my glove, and the linseed oil. He wanted me to hustle and turn two, or backhand one off to my right side, leap and spin at the same time—perform a ballet in the dirt—and throw hard to first. He never tired, even at six in the evening when the sun hung low over the town and he'd already had a hell of a long day with the trolleys that he scheduled on their runs through the city.

It was his second year managing our team, the Indians, and my second year at second base. It was the year before we went to Williamsport for the Little League World Series, when the whole town was filled with pride. Nothing like this had ever happened, and none of us had ever played on a smooth-cut infield, where the bounces were true and clean, and none of us had ever had a real wooden fence and grandstands or a pastoral outfield where the grass was green and thick and evenly cropped. Beyond the arc of the colorful fence, in legendary Williamsport, lay the loveliness of the Susquehanna Levee and then the broad, shallow, winding river itself, with the long, mellifluous name that I loved to speak even as a kid.

I folded the letter carefully and placed it in my book. I smiled at the thought of my ever-so-proper mother—starched white collar over blue dress—smoking a cigar, and my father serving as her chauffeur. Not likely. No, not in this world!

***

April 16, 1970. The phone was ringing. *It must be someone down in the machine shop,* I thought. Maybe, yes, there was finally good news about the equipment, about the Perspex cell they were crafting for my research—and just in time for our esteemed visitors. Or maybe Professor Ivin was calling to tell me about another European conference like the one we'd attended amid the narrow, medieval streets of Strasbourg. I couldn't wait to get back to "the Continent," as my younger brother, Eugene, always called the European mainland.

But it was none of these. It was the first call I'd received from home in many months. "Bill?" the voice said. "Bill?" It was Eugene.

"Yes, it's me," I answered. *But why this early?* I wondered. It was five in the morning back home. Nothing good ever comes from a call in the predawn hours. A chill suddenly passed through me.

"Bill." There was no hesitation. No pause. His voice was strong. "Dad died last night," he said. "He *died*!" The connection was clear. There was no mistaking what he'd said.

"Died?" I said. "But I just, I was just ... He just wrote me a letter! He just ... It's right here on my desk, Eugene." And my voice trailed off inaudibly into silence. I understood that a letter, even one you can see, even one that ends so lightheartedly, guarantees nothing.

"It was sudden," Eugene said. "He died in his sleep. He was sleeping next to Mother. He was inches from her and she heard him snoring—you know, you remember, those deep, loud sounds he made. The sonorous kind that shook the place. She found him in bed this morning. The ambulance came. They took him up to the hospital, but there was no hope; he was gone. It was a massive heart attack, in his sleep, they said."

"Ah, Eugene." I knew what I had heard, but the letter was there on the desk. I could see it peeking out from beneath the dark cover of a book, near the pipe I had put down. Near the pouch of Kentucky Club.

"I got a Cadillac Fleetwood," he had written. How could he be dead? How could he ever be dead?

The black receiver pressed like a dead weight to my ear. I was shaking my head. Silence. I could say nothing to my brother.

Eugene sensed my confusion. He gave me no more details on

what had happened or how anyone was feeling. "Mother wants you to come home for a week for the funeral and to help out."

"Of course! Of course!" I said. "I'll be right there. I ... I'll be right there."

I spoke as though I could walk a few blocks and be at our home on Amelia Street in ten minutes. I had forgotten where I was. I was standing in a laboratory at a university in Northern Ireland, and that there were planes and oceans and great distances involved. I had no money—not a cent saved for anything.

"It might take me a bit, Eugene, but I'll get there in a day or two. I'll see you then." I didn't know what else to say, so I thanked him for calling and hung up.

My colleague Jamison was sitting nearby, and I told him what had happened and that I would have to leave, and asked him to tell Professor Ivin I'd get back as soon as I could. Maybe a week, I said. Ten days at most.

***

And then I was off and out of the Keir Chemistry Lab, and I can't remember much of anything about what happened or where the tickets came from. I only remember taking off, landing at Heathrow, then taking off again. Except for the pulsing wing light—a tiny beacon of hope—there was biblical darkness over the waters of the Atlantic. The fierce cold lay just beyond the window. I was thinking of those lines from "People," by the Russian poet Yevtushenko:

> We who knew our fathers
> In everything, in nothing

And I couldn't let the lines go. They swirled around in my mind above the vast ocean.

Morning broke. Stab of sunlight. We were on a shallow glide into JFK. By this point I was too tired to worry about the landing.

There was something else, something that I could not understand for years and may still not understand: as I walked through JFK on my way to catch a flight to Pittsburgh, I caught myself whistling—joyfully whistling! It was breezy and lighthearted. I could almost dance to it as I moved through the concourse, the music playing in my head. But then I stopped in my tracks as though I had hit a wall. *"Dad's dead,"* I said to myself. Still, I could not deny a moment's pure pleasure, a moment of euphoria that ran through every muscle and cell of my body.

134 Amelia (1970s) A young Eugene stands before the steps at 134 Amelia.

3

AMELIA (1970)

"You won't always have me," he'd say. "Someday I'll be gone."

***

When I got to our house on Amelia Street, I opened the door of my childhood home. The silence, the smell of lilac, the frayed hallway carpet, the expanse of living room off to the right all would have felt welcoming were it not for the circumstances of my visit. Eugene was there, thin and handsome, priestly in his manner and bearing. He was only three months from ordination to the clergy. He was calm and in control of the moment. We greeted each other with a loose embrace. My hieratic, princely, troubled brother, Eugene. There were no tears. In the narrow hallway, I could smell my mother's perfume.

I caught a glimpse of her at the top of the stairs, standing there about to descend. She was touching her thinning hair as she often did, making sure every lacquered strand was in place. I rushed up and caught her arm and hugged her. I hugged her tightly, and she began to sob. I held her for a long time. I kissed her forehead, stroked her hair.

Then, my face contorted in sorrow, I said precisely the wrong words: "Oh, Mother! I'm so sorry for your loss."

She backed away from me, pushed me aside. Startled. Repelled by my words. In her look there was a sudden coldness, disbelief. I had never seen this before. My amiable, loving, mother. "*You're* sorry. For *me*!" she said. "He was *your* father."

There were no tears in her eyes now, only anger. We looked at each other with mutual incomprehension. I didn't understand. I wanted to hug her again. I wanted to take her in my arms, retrieve my irretrievable words, now seemingly stone-cut into an eternity of granite. I wanted to console her. But a wall had gone up; I could not reach her. She was gone.

★★★

The arrangements for the funeral had been made by Eugene. Everything had been attended to. The viewing was at McDermott's, a few blocks away. I have a hazy recollection of greeting friends and relatives, guys from the Pittsburgh Railways Company, all the people my father had coached over the years. The men, the women, the young kids who had come to offer their sympathies, to tell their stories of the inimitable Jim Green—how he had gotten them into the Elks, found them a job on the "cars," inspired them to perfection on the ball field. How they would never forget him.

When the viewing days were over, Jack McDermott said he'd never seen so many signatures in the big book that stood on the podium by the doorway. "Take it," he said, handing it to me. It was a black binder. "Your father was one hell of a man. It was like … like, I don't know, he was like the king of this place."

The Mass was at St. Francis de Sales. Eugene preached. I have no idea what he said. But my sister, Liz, said Eugene had had a vision of my father standing there at the altar with him. Standing by his side, celebrating the Mass alongside him and the Reverend

William Clancy. Father and son. The way it had never been in this life. But to Eugene, this apparition would forever be a reality, like the undeniable heft of a stone.

The burial in the family plot was at St. Mary's, on the steep, bucolic hill that overlooks the Rocks. Eastward a few miles, the towering structures and mill stacks of the city of Pittsburgh were visible.

***

At home there was quiet. The greetings were over, the guests had gone, the food was cleared up and the house neatly arranged. Eugene had gone back to his rectory, the Pittsburgh Oratory, out by the University of Pittsburgh, and Liz and her husband, George, who had recently arrived in the States from Goias, Brazil, were off to Bloomington, Indiana, where George was studying Portuguese. Only my mother and I remained, and as always we were on good terms. We never spoke of what happened between us at the top of the stairs. To not speak of unpleasantness was our way. We buried our words, buried our feelings. We buried them deeper than any grave.

It seemed like a very long time, the slow-motion largo of sorrowful songs, but I had been gone from Belfast only a week. There was a churchly stillness about the house, as if wax and candles were burning in the dimness and old women genuflecting and whispering in the half-light, fingering their worn beads with arthritic hands. I thought I could hear their thin voices, see the flickering light from the votive candles glowing in their red and blue enclosures.

One afternoon I was seated on the large sofa in the living room, absently staring out of the same windows I had once looked through as a child. The curtains hung motionless. There were no sounds in the room. I could hear my heart pounding and I could not catch my breath, as though a vacuum were forming around me.

I had felt this same fear only once before, when I was six. We had just come from early-morning Mass at St. Francis de Sales—Eugene, Liz, my parents, and I—and were heading off to Cook Forest State Park. The forest was a place I loved. It was moss and flowers, plunging streams, and great pines beneath which fragrant pathways wove amid the fullness of native ferns. It smelled of pine, and pine needles littered the forest floor and tickled our feet, and we could ride horses and buy pine boxes at the gift shop. Our relatives had a cabin there, and we had planned to spend a pleasant week. But from the outset, I felt strange. I had been frightened by the sermon, by the images that had been conjured from the rounded, ornate pulpit. On the drive north, I could think of one thing: death.

I was young—the age of wonder, of newness and discovery, when the world begins to open in its fullness like the petals of a rose—yet all I could think of was death. And in the confines of the forest, which was dense and moist and suddenly making me claustrophobic, as though the ferns and dark trees were closing in on me, forming a tunnel of light-quenching darkness, I began to panic. I told my mother I could not breathe. "Mom, Mom, I can't, I can't, I just can't ..."

She took my temperature and my pulse and said I had never had asthma and there was nothing wrong and that I would soon be fine. But through the next day and night, it only got worse. My breathing grew shallow and then shallower, and I thought my breaths would end and the loud cricket sounds of the forest beyond the cabin would fade and cease. The blackness seemed to be a living, suffocating thing that moved around me.

My parents said we would have to leave for home, see a doctor. "We have to go, Jim," she whispered to him. "We can't stay here with him in this state. Not like this." Within an hour, we were packed and on our way.

★★★

On the sofa in the living room that day shortly after my father's death, it was exactly the same as in that long-ago forest. Something was rising to meet me. It was emptiness, airless and silent, and there was no way out. I felt like I was about to vanish. Was this what it felt like, death? Was this how it felt?

For a second I tried to be rational. I reminded myself that only weeks earlier I had been hiking the Glens of Antrim, had bounded up the Giants Causeway. I was feeling alive in the salt air off the sea-battered cliffs of Donegal. I felt I could dive a thousand feet into weltering surf and emerge above the waves, Poseidon-like, and could not imagine anything but robust good health. But now … none of that mattered. I was gasping. Gripping my chest.

I went to the hospital. I told the doctor everything, told him of my fear of death. His name was Oshieka. He was stocky and powerful, built like a boxer. He looked like a regular guy from the Rocks, someone you could run into at the Wil-Kar Grill and have a shot and a beer with. I had been to his office once or twice when I was a kid.

He listened to my heart, ran an EKG, looked over my body, which was thin and muscular, and said, "There's not a damn thing wrong with you." He was angry, as though I had wasted his time. *Just another damn hypochondriac.* He stared at me a moment and then punched me with his big, meaty right fist in the left arm; he punched me hard, like a prizefighter, as if to make a point. I fell back under the blow, a little off balance.

"I want you to see a psychiatrist. Do it this week." He gave me a sheet of paper with a name scratched on it: Breslow. *Breslow? Who in the hell is Breslow*?

Belfast was my city of silvery rain and fields of golden gorse in the coming spring. I was planning to be back there soon. They were expecting me. Exciting things were beginning to happen. I had finally begun to build a life and could imagine staying on with Ken Ivin for a second year. But first, as a courtesy, I would see Breslow. I would see him once, before I booked my flight.

★★★

Breslow heard my story without comment. He sat there in his striped suit and tie, contemplative, no expression on his face. He looked soft and owlish with those big glasses. I was expecting him to tell me, as Oshieka had, that there was nothing wrong, that I should leave and it would all pass in a few days. What more could he say? We had only five minutes left in the session.

We sat a moment in silence. This whole thing felt so patently unnecessary. I had never seen a psychiatrist, never thought of seeing one.

I had had a perfect childhood, I thought. I didn't need analysis. I had been loved. I was twenty-eight, with a PhD in chemistry. Whatever happened in Belfast, in Pittsburgh, I was looking at a bright future. Psychiatry, with its dreams and possibly fraudulent nineteenth-century mistiness, seemed beside the point. Psychiatry explained everything, but it predicted nothing. In my mind, it was purely discredited pseudoscience. I distrusted it all.

Then the silence ended. For the first time, the laconic Breslow looked at me. His once-expressionless face became animated. He spoke rapidly. "I think we need to talk," he said. "I think you're filled with anger toward him. And remorse. And sorrow that he is gone. And relief—that too. But I will need to know more about your life. Your childhood. Your family, your parents and siblings, even your other relatives. I need to know about your life as a child—not only your father, but the whole setting. I want you to keep a record of dreams. How you feel each day. There's a drug I can prescribe for now, meprobamate. It will calm you down. Take six a day. How would Tuesdays and Thursdays work?"

Tuesdays and Thursdays! What the hell? And six meprobamates!

Breslow said those words so casually. He knew my plans. He knew I needed to be back in Belfast in two weeks at the latest.

"Let me think about it," I said. "I'll call tomorrow." I felt I owed him that much. But I had no intention of seeing him again. I imagined New York, London, Belfast, the coming of spring. Green Ireland. All the possibilities I had created. Freedom abroad: I could taste it.

That night the fear continued. The Void. The emptiness was back. I couldn't breathe. The certainty of death hung in the stale air as I lay under the rafters in the room Eugene and I had shared as children. Faded pennants. A signed baseball encased in a plastic sphere. A small statue of the Virgin Mary. Her long, blue-and-white robes. Everything there, just like when we were kids. My chest ached. My heart pounded; it skipped beats. I felt a great wing pass over me. It cast a slow, dark shadow. I knew that shadow and what it augured. And I knew what I had to do.

In the morning, the bed was a tangled knot. Ropes of wetness lay twisted around my legs and feet.

★★★

Later, I went to see Eugene at the Pittsburgh Oratory. He was doing a lot better than I was.

I said, "What's this all about, Eugene, these feelings I'm having? I never expected any of this when you called me in Belfast. I expected to be back there by now."

He poured me a scotch, and we sat in the big living room in the dim light of the Pittsburgh Oratory. Father Clancy, his mentor and the Oratory's pastor, was upstairs, along with the others. It was quiet, just the two of us.

"Bill, I don't know, but it sounds like grief. You're grieving. The two of you were very close, with baseball and all those summers together on the ball field."

I swirled my glass. The scotch was amber in the evening

light. The fresh ice clinked against the sides, a sweet note of fruit and dry wood rose up, and I settled back into the worn sofa and listened to what he had to say.

"I know you told me the two of you never talked much. But that was his way with us, wasn't it? Emotionally he was far off, somewhere I could never get to. He could not be reached. Liz and I have known this a long time—how distant he was. How cold.

"Sometimes," he continued, "when those we love leave us, especially suddenly, as he did, things have not been resolved." He sounded a little as though he might be speaking to one of his parishioners at the Oratory, not his own brother. He was a little stiff and formal, but I wanted to listen.

He poured us another drink. I was beginning to drift off under the spell of Breslow's pills and the cool blend of whiskeys in my hand.

"Maybe there's something that we didn't say and now we can't. Some unfinished business, Bill, you know? Death closes the door. It beckons us to finality." Only Eugene would say this: "beckons."

"I know, Eugene," I said. "There's no calling him back, and we are left to decipher what remains: memories and dreams. His wallet. The few items he left behind. The letters. But these will never be enough."

We sat for a moment in silence. I felt very close to him, my younger brother, with whom there had been occasional conflicts and rivalries, but also years of searching correspondence in which we advised and encouraged one another and revealed to one another—often indirectly through innuendo or literary allusion—our problems and fears. Our secrets. I respected and loved him.

"I'm seeing Dr. Breslow, Eugene, but I don't know what he can do. Maybe nothing. He wants to know *everything.* My life, our lives. This could last a long time."

Eugene was dressed in black. He was sitting on the sofa next to me, his long legs crossed.

"It may take time, Bill." He reached over and squeezed my shoulder. "It may take some time. I don't know how long. But it could be many years for you. Grief can last, but usually it fades. Slowly, it fades."

"You know," I said, "I was beginning to feel at home in Ireland. I think I could have stayed a long while, another year. The work was taking off. I was beginning to see possibilities in the city and its people. Despite the rain, despite my original discontent, my regret that I hadn't gone elsewhere, I was okay."

"Sad Belfast," he said, with that ironic smile.

We had finished our drinks, and I thought he looked tired.

"I should get back and check on Mother," I said. "Why don't you stop down on the weekend? I want to talk about what you're teaching at the college."

He said he would and said he could use some fresh ideas for a course he was planning on literature and ethics. "Maybe you'd be interested in giving a lecture or two, Bill. I have a few possibilities in mind."

"Sure," I said. "I'll be glad to give it a try."

We walked to the door. I gave him a big hug and thanked him for listening. "You've given me some good advice, Eugene. I'll keep you posted on what's happening with Breslow."

I wanted to tell him how much I longed for the dreaminess I could once conjure, making all the cares of the day, the year, my entire life, disappear among the streaks of light and shadow casually at play around me. "Not a care in the world," Aunt Agnes had said of me. I feared those days would never come again. But I left this unsaid.

I also wanted to tell him what had happened at JFK, but I couldn't.

It was dark in the hills above the University of Pittsburgh. The trees and flowers were in full bloom, and it smelled of spring as I remembered it as a kid. I drove off that night in the big, elegant Cadillac Fleetwood and headed home.

Eugene had helped. Breslow would help. Maybe knowing the town would help.

I drove off that night thinking of the poet Ciaran Carson's words: "What is my name? Where am I coming from? Where am I going?"

★★★

In mid-May, a month after my father's death, I received a letter from Professor K. J. Ivin. It was warm, I thought, if a bit formal.

> Dear Bill,
>
> I was very sorry to learn of the reason for your sudden departure and extend my deepest sympathy in your loss.
>
> It would help me to know whether you intend to return in the near future or whether you now wish to resign your appointment.
>
> Sincerely,
> K. J. Ivin

I never replied.

The Olive Thomas photo shows the Wil-Kar Grill with the spires of St. Mary Church in the background

The Rox Arena Skating Rink (circa 1950)

4

The Rocks (1950s)

A man of the valley is that valley
A man of the mountain is that mountain
A man of the town is that town

★★★

When I saw Breslow again, I told him I was still having arrhythmias and that I had them frequently. During these events, I began to sweat—cold sweat, beaded on my face—and I felt heaviness hang on my chest from one shoulder to the other, just as my father had. I knew then I was going to die just as he had. It would happen in the attic, in the darkness, where I began my youth. It would happen in my sleep. My blood would thicken, and my arterial walls would narrow.

Breslow wanted to know if there was a connection between my thoughts and my bodily symptoms, and I told him I couldn't remember. "It's all random," I said. "I could be thinking anything or nothing at all. I don't know which happens first, the thought or the somatic response, or whether they are even connected."

"Hmm," he said, nodding.

"I feel sorrow like I've never felt it before," I said. "I know that."

Breslow asked me about Belfast and why I went there in the first place, and I told him, sure, it was the wrong end of Ireland, but it was Ireland just the same. I had heard about it all my life—Thanksgiving dinners, Christmases, wakes—whenever the family got together. Whenever they sang their Irish songs, ate their heaped potatoes. I wanted to be the first to go there. Initially though, I hated it, I told him, with all the seeping wetness of the place. The cold, the rain, the overcast, the failing research all added to the misery. Then it changed. It was becoming home. The research was picking up. At the dances at Queens on weekends, I met some beautiful girls, one of whom was Gladys Kennedy, a girl my father mentioned in his letters. As spring came on and the flowers began to bloom and the air softened, I said to myself, *This is all going to be okay.*

"How did you get there?" Breslow asked, his fingers steepled in front of his nose. "Plane?"

"No, I took the ship," I said with some pride. "The new *QE2* over to Southampton, then the train up to London. I stayed in London a few days. I wandered around Soho at night. I visited the Tate and Westminster and Robert Falcon Scott's ship, the wooden research vessel *Discovery*, anchored in the Thames." I thought of that tiny ship pressing through the towering ice floes of Antarctica—the ones I had seen myself only a year earlier when I went to Antarctica to work on a research project—pressing into the safety of McMurdo Sound. "After a week in London, I flew to Belfast."

"How did you pay for the passage?" Breslow asked. "That had to be expensive for someone just out of graduate school." Odd, but he seemed to want to know these details. He was looking right at me. He appeared interested in this everyday stuff.

"My father bought the ticket," I told him. "It was a present for getting the degree. He doubted I'd ever finish. Maybe he thought I was a quitter. That was a big deal for him: being a *quitter*."

Breslow nodded again. "Hmm, your father," he said. He

scribbled a few notes, looked at his watch, and said, "I'll see you next Tuesday." He handed me a crisp, white card with the date and time on it.

***

In a mural that once decorated a wall of the Pittsburgh National Bank on the main street of town, the naked escarpment and the superimposed mound can be seen as a backdrop to a meeting between George Washington and the leaders of the Seneca and Delaware tribes. Between the historical figures and the rocks themselves, you can see the log structure built by Alexander McKee, who was granted this land by the Crown. At the time represented in the mural, 1753, there was discussion of where a major British fort should be erected, whether at the rock outcrop (in today's McKees Rocks) or at the "Point," where the Allegheny and Monongahela Rivers join to form the Ohio. Members of Washington's party who were stationed at the Point referred to the alternate site as "McKees Rocks." The name has lasted centuries.

My father and I did not have that sort of long historical perspective. We lived in a certain narrow slice of time in a certain place, and our years together over the long sweep of life were relatively brief. What we both experienced was a town bordered and shaped by railroads and trolleys, the Rocks of the modern industrial age, the closest of satellites to the coal-and-steel giant that was Pittsburgh. Except for a sign that welcomed you, you couldn't tell where Pittsburgh ended and the Rocks began. I usually told people I came from Pittsburgh. Who had ever heard of the Rocks?

In the '40s and '50s, if you walked from our house along bustling Chartiers Avenue, in twenty minutes you'd come to the noisy, clanging heart of the town, the center from which its industrial life sprang. On our way to the rail yard, we passed

Woolworths with its slanted wooden floor, Jenny Lee Bakery, the pillars of Mellon Bank, Lefkowicz's drugstore, Isaly's, with its Klondikes and skyscraper cones—all of these suggested an unfailing permanency and prosperity. I believed that this was the world as given, and that it would always be so. I thought I'd always be able to get a pistachio skyscraper anytime I walked down Chartiers.

My father liked these walks on Chartiers Avenue. Maybe he was remembering the years he had worked with the P&LE Railroad. The railroad was clearly a source of family pride.

I knew this in part because the only portrait that ever hung in our house on Amelia Street, just above the fat, black rotary phone, was of my paternal grandfather smiling down from the cab of his steam locomotive, his elbow propped against the giant iron machine as if he owned it. God he looked proud of himself! No wonder my father carried his own father's driver's license in his wallet until the day he died. But other than that single picture, I knew nothing about my grandfather. My father never spoke of him; neither did his sisters, Aunt Agnes and Aunt Mary Cecilia. He was a two-dimensional photo and a driver's license. And yet somehow I knew my father loved him, in his wordless way.

The railroad tracks were in my father's blood, in the family's blood. As a young man, by Agnes's account, my father loved to travel the rails with his friends in his free time. These journeys went as far west as Dallas. Of these trips beyond the Rocks, there was always the suggestion of things forbidden or bawdy, but they were never made explicit. As far as I was concerned, my father's early life moved in shadow. He rarely spoke of it. What did I know about him? Not much.

I think of the film *This Property Is Condemned*, with Natalie Wood and Robert Redford. Wooden boarding houses along the tracks. My father walking the rail bed, his arm around a young woman about his own age. She is wearing a cotton dress. I cannot see where they are headed, but I suspect it is private. Just the two of them.

I knew from his sisters that he was tall and extremely thin as a youth and that he was a fine ballplayer and an especially good hitter. He played ball during his high school years and later into his twenties, and he retained a love of the game that would finally manifest itself in coaching and scouting for the Detroit Tigers, an activity that would take him frequently to Florida and the Tigers' training camp. He always had a gimlet eye for talent, and he never lost his love for coaching. "Jim could take a bunch of batboys and turn them into a pennant-winning team," a local sportswriter once wrote.

From what I could tell, the Rocks appeared to have its share of colorful characters. First among them was my father's hell-raising friend and drinking buddy, Joe Vitelli, whose name we spoke with consummate respect; he was a sporting legend during my youth. He had played halfback for the University of Pittsburgh, where he was nicknamed Joe the Horse, and for thirteen years he pitched for at least five minor league teams, including the Wheeling Stogies and the Cumberland Colts. His breakthrough into the majors came during the war years 1944–45, when he pitched for the Pittsburgh Pirates as a reliever. I recall him from the days in the late '50s when he ran summer baseball clinics at one of the large parks that surround Pittsburgh. He was a big guy, six feet one and more than 220 pounds. He taught me the "touch and release" of the double play, and under his tutelage I began to feel a quickness and dexterity I had not known before. Joe V could teach. He'd been around, and I looked up to him. There were other characters too, but it was Joe Vitelli who mattered most to me. One time at a bar, he said something I will never forget, one of those offhanded insights about life that cut right to the heart of things.

★★★

Across the street from us, at 133 Amelia, lived an elderly, irritable lady—this was before the silent, mysterious Lithuanians moved in—whose protectiveness of that tiny sward called a lawn was fierce and unrelenting. Each time a ball I had thrown against our stoop rolled over onto her idyllic postage stamp of heaven, she would burst through the front door, enraged, and threaten me with police or imminent juvenile detention. One summer evening after work, when my father's orange truck had come to a stop in front of our house, she shouted from her porch, shaking her fist in the air, "Keep that kid of yours from my lawn or there will be consequences. What do you think you're doing?"

My father calmly closed the cab door and stood to face this sad termagant. "Over here," he said, "we're raisin' kids, not grass." And with that he tipped the beak of his white-and-black PRC cap, turned toward our house, and with a nod to me, continued up the front steps.

***

It was a minor thing, a memory that had been submerged for decades, but I told Breslow how I remembered the ice-skating. It seemed improbable that my father, who at certain times in his life approached the barrel-girth of a man who had consumed far too much beer, was in all his bulging corpulence so graceful. It defied physics. I recalled for Breslow the weekend afternoons at the Rox Arena, an outdoor skating rink whose presence seemed an anomaly in the heavily industrial setting of our town. I recalled the dance-glide motion of his skates as he and his sister moved across the smooth ice, how he and Mary Cecilia swayed effortlessly to the music, to "The Skaters' Waltz," which resides in my mind as the theme of the arena. Click, glide, beauty, celestial choreography directed and mediated by no one. For me, ice-skating presented an image of perfection.

Some days the world delivers us these moments, these small, gratuitous moments of beauty.

I told Breslow about the games of catch in the spring and summer and sometimes into the fall, when in the cindered back alley we would spend an hour tossing a ball between us. My father and I hardly spoke except for the brief words of instruction: "Get the glove down on that, Bill. Pick it up on the first hop," or, "You should have backhanded the ball. Don't try to catch it with your glove flat. Turn your wrist, like this," or, "Okay, nice pickup." I loved this game. Even though there was nothing shared about my day at school or about his at work with the trolleys, we had "catch," and no matter how tired he was, he was always willing to play. We went out the kitchen door, up the narrow walk along the fence, out the silver gate (click) and onto the flat cinders, where we pulled our gloves over our left hands. The smell of freshly baked bread hung in the air, yeasty and aromatic, from the bakery not far away.

My father never made much of the black eyes that inevitably came from our alleyway game. "Let's go down to Sandal's Drugstore," he'd say whenever I got a big fat shiner. And I'd think, *Oh no, I hate this,* and he'd ask old man Sandal if he had any leeches. Sandal always did. "The kid needs a leech," he'd say. And we'd take the leech home, and I'd sit at the kitchen table and my father would place it on my purple, swollen eye, and I'd stick a little glass vial over the leech and feel it cool and slimy against my skin and let it suck out the blood until it gorged itself senseless. I could feel the wetness of the thing coming right at the big, purple welt near my eye, like it had intelligence beyond anything you'd expect of a segmented worm.

So what of this game of catch, aside from the fact that it was practice? It was practice, yes, but it was far more than that, and I felt closer to my father because of it.

Later Breslow and I talked of family vacations, and I elaborated on Cook Forest and the pleasure I took in the place, everything from the smell of burning marshmallows—the slow browning on the edges and the white goo in blue flame forming under the stars—to the clear-running streams with their endless notes and trills and the gurgling sounds they made coursing through the boulders, to the clank of the rusted pump as we brought up water from deep in the earth for breakfast each morning. And then there were the horses that the three of us—Liz, Eugene, and I—rode each summer. Neither my mother nor my father would ever think of riding a horse, but they insisted that we learn. And of course there was the "episode," which foreshadowed what came after Belfast and had yet to be explained. Why the time journey, the grief, the somatic response to my father's passing? *"There's not a damn thing wrong with you,"* Oshieka had said.

But when it came to vacations, the trips east to the Jersey Shore were the most memorable. For these, my father made his special tomato sandwiches—tomato slices on Wonder Bread and nothing else—and stuck them in the trunk of the car, where the temperature rose to a hundred degrees as we drove down through Philly on the way to the shore. We'd stop at some roadside table and he'd pull them out of their paper bags, hold one in his hand, and say, "Try one—they look great!" They were hot and soggy and red-stained with tomato juice, but we followed his lead and ate them anyway.

When we arrived at a rooming house ten minutes from the beach, we'd race to get to the water. My father, in a white T-shirt, was always first, plunging headlong into the waves until a big roller knocked him off his feet and then he was swimming, doing backstrokes in the calmer depths beyond the surf. We went wild, racing at the sea too, but were knocked off balance by our first contact with the smallest waves. From the boardwalk, my mother, fully clothed and proper, watched and laughed at our aquatic stunts.

We all loved the boardwalk at Atlantic City, with its smoothness, its hundred years of wear and memories, the hotness of the boards under our bare feet, which made us shiver with pleasure. There were the hucksters selling the perfect knives you couldn't live without. "Look at this," my father would say, and the whole family would stop in front of a booth where some fast-talking guy in a white apron was slapping a plastic knife down on the counter to demonstrate that it wouldn't break, no matter what; and then he'd carve up some melons and chunks of beef until my father said to my mother, "Bunny, we need to have one of these."

Farther down the boardwalk, in a piquant cloud of aromas that blended pizza, hot dogs, baked pretzels, and warm sea air, there was a shop that offered a banana split with five scoops of ice cream and all the saccharine toppings you'd ever want, melding into a hopelessly viscous butterscotch-chocolaty mess. If you could eat two of these things, you got them both for free. *Wow, what a super deal!* we thought. But you also got whatever world of pure gut misery was sure to follow.

"Eugene, I bet you can't do this," I'd say, and he'd take up the challenge, and we'd both end up vomiting within hours. Still, we couldn't control ourselves; we were suckers every time.

My mother loved the delicate smell of the sea and the muffled roar of the pounding waves. "Go down to the surf," she'd say to the three of us. "It's great for the lungs. It's great for your health. And get some sun too." She wore a long dress and a broad-brimmed hat and never ventured into the water or even onto the beach. Not an inch of the white skin above her wrists showed.

But my pale Irish-skinned sister always followed her advice, and each summer in Atlantic City she burned herself red and suffered for weeks and then flensed off the flakey skin in strips like some kind of Christian martyr. Oh poor Liz. I felt sorry for her.

When I was fifteen, I'd go to dances at the hall near the end of the pier. Inevitably, I'd fall in love with some girl I'd asked to walk with me on the beach—the moon over the sea; the warm, moist air; her dress floating on a light breeze. On those evenings,

I began to feel things I had not felt before. Another part of the world seemed to be opening up.

These little excursions from the Rocks were a release for my father. He played in the surf with an abandon I rarely saw even on the ball field, and in the mornings he made his signature pancakes—flapjacks, as he called them—and woke us from our deep vacation slumbers to join him in the feast. In the car, he smoked El Producto cigars, which came in an ornate box, the one with the picture of the dark-haired woman with the flared red dress and the golden harp in her hands. And he whistled when he drove, the window open to the ninety-five-degree air and his arm burning and freckled in the sun. It was that special trucker's tan he got every summer. The incessant whistling, the suffocating smoke, drove us all nuts. When the five of us were together, he seemed a different man from the one who so often came and went through the house on Amelia Street like an evening apparition. Here he was a kid again. This was *his* family. This was the family he wanted.

Beyond the ways and traditions of my family, Breslow was interested in my dreams, and I assumed he was gradually putting together some hypothesis about why I was reacting as I was to my father's death. There was one dream that came often to me. It involved a train. The train was leaving the station, gathering speed, and my father was leaning out the window, extending a hand to me, motioning with it that I should hurry. "Run, Bill—you can do it!" And I ran along the platform, trying to reach him, but he was gaining speed and I was falling farther and farther behind. I yelled to him above the train sounds, "Don't leave, Dad! I can't keep up!" I gasped for air, my voice growing weaker, and I realized that I couldn't reach him. I would never reach him. He was gone.

There was another, similar dream of parting, but this time I was the one who was leaving. I was on a plane, an old DC-8, and it was speeding down the runway. I opened the window and saw him running along behind, his big belly flopping in the chase, but we both knew that there was no hope, that he would never catch up. Breslow wanted to know how this dream made me feel, and I told him I wasn't sure. Part of me wanted my father to catch up and sit beside me, but another part of me was experiencing a new freedom; I was about to fly, and he would not be joining me. It was a new feeling. I told Breslow it felt like important things were about to happen.

He listened to me with his glasses slid down on his nose and said nothing but made more than the usual cursory notes. Then he told me my time was up.

In later sessions, I related other dreams that seemed a conflation of times and places and of much that never happened at all. In one, my father entered a bedroom where I was sleeping with a girl, and he stood at the foot of the bed. He told me he wanted her, and I tried to explain the situation to him, but he seemed not to understand. When I woke up, I was confused; I had no idea what to make of this except that it was a dream and I was damn glad it was over.

And so the time went with Breslow, confused and indeterminate. I knew there might be no defined endpoint to this therapy, so I never pressed him about how I was doing or how long I might have to be with him. Besides, I felt that maybe something was beginning to flow, like water locked behind an ice dam in the noonday sun. I could hear crackling and trickling somewhere deep within the frozen structure of what had once been.

It was the last session of the month. Breslow was leaning in toward me. I could see his moon face approaching me like some celestial phenomenon, as though he was expecting something profound. We were nearing the end of the hour, which mostly concerned how I was feeling. I told him yet again about the crazy, inexplicable skipped heartbeats, which at times seemed like sudden storms, like lightning out of nowhere. He was trying to find a rationale, some way to tie these in with the dreams, with the thoughts I was having at the moment. I told him again I saw no connection. I told him these heart-jolts just shivered right through me without warning and they were terrible and frightening. Every time they happened, I reiterated, I thought about how it must feel to die. I popped some of his sedatives or downed a scotch, or sometimes both.

Breslow sat there with his hands in his lap, fiddling with his thumbs. I was expecting that he'd offer some deep insight, but instead he asked me a question that seemed like a non sequitur: "You miss him, don't you?" Suddenly, for the first time, the ice dam broke. I buried my face in my hands. I felt hot tears on my hands. I tried to muffle the sounds I was making, the weeping deep in my palms, but I couldn't. Breslow handed me a tissue but said nothing. We sat there in silence for a minute, and then he said in a low voice, an embarrassed whisper, almost, that our time was up.

He walked me to the door and asked, "Are you okay?" And I nodded my head and he said, "Good." I left and walked down the empty hallway. It was six in the evening. In Pittsburgh it was turning dusk and raining. Raining on the pavement; raining on the trolley tracks. A slow drizzle, as droplet built upon droplet, melding into an iridescent sheen of wetness. I was taken back to Belfast, to Adelaide Park. Memories of rain. The silver of it. Memories of dances. Memories of what was becoming home. Of my good life in a far-off place.

From left to right: Bill Green, Mitzi (the dog), Aunt Gene and Liz. (My parents and Eugene are not shown).

5

SIX OF US (1950S–60S)

It is an idyllic childhood, or so I once believed: my father does important work with the trolleys; he is deeply immersed in the life of the town; my mother has a shy, disarming grace and a splendid education. Yet there seems to be something I am missing—something I can only intuit, a darkness perhaps.

***

Breslow wanted a context in which to place my father. I suspected that through this circuitous approach, he hoped to gain further insight into this man for whom I was visibly grieving. Our conversations for a time, therefore, centered on family; and on this subject I provided him with abundant detail, though in what order and with what accuracy I cannot really say.

There were six of us: our parents, three children, and my mother's sister, Aunt Gene. We lived in a house with three bedrooms, one of which was a utility space that we called, fittingly, the "little room," and later there was a furnished attic for which my father built a low, rectangular bookcase for my mother's many language texts. It was the '50s and '60s, and to me family life was all as normal as it should be.

There was also a basement, which was big and open enough

that at Christmas I could assemble a large train layout there. I made snowy mountains out of sparkly crinkled paper. I created towns with little plastic people, one of whom was the lady in the wide-brimmed hat, her face shaded against the fierce sun of our basement. Through this town of "Plasticville"—where each day the tiny, plastic milkman brought his wire-caged carrier singing with glass and steel, and where the paperboy came spiritedly, hoping for tips—four model trains were running. One sped on an elevated trestle through long tunnels that skirted perilous cliffs; others moved through farmland of tall corn and wheat and towns with lighted storefronts.

Switches like the ones down at the P&LE yards silently shunted trains of the Union Pacific and Santa Fe. There were cars bearing logs and barrels, and there were other cars, round and silver, carrying oil through miles of a vast imagined America, to which the man in the red caboose offered his endless daily greetings, his long fingers extended into the clear air of the countryside.

Hidden beneath the plywood platform, available to the eyes of none, like the levers behind the Wizard's curtain, were the stapled-up wires, flattened red and green and yellow against the wood. It was through these copper conduits that the juice of current hummed and sang.

After Christmas season, when the trains were gone, I could throw baseballs against the cement wall and have space to field them and to practice backhands and bare-handed pickups. To this area I eventually added a body bag, a speed bag, a pull-up bar, and a padded weight bench. And then there were the carefully crafted desks my father had made for the three of us, and the World Encyclopedia that stood in prominence above the desks.

There was a furnace and two small cellars. In one of these, we stored canned fruit and jellies and jams and pickle relish, with paraffin seals to keep them fresh for winter. My mother and Aunt Gene were experts in this business of canning, and I loved the relishes they made and their plum and cherry and grape jams that lasted the winter.

There were old magazines in the fruit cellar with pictures of Marilyn Monroe and Jayne Mansfield and Anita Ekberg, pictures that could raise your pulse in a flash. But they were nothing compared to the stuff up at Benny's place, where I lifted weights. Benny would open up his latest mag and show me the pics, slowly turning the pages and pointing at his favorites. My knees would feel weak and I'd begin to wobble. Benny knew that I was Catholic and gleefully imagined all the sins I might be committing looking at these things. He'd give a sadistic laugh. It was no fun doing bench presses stiff like that.

Near the furnace, where the coal was delivered, there was another small cellar. The coal cellar was black and dusty and it smelled of organic haze, as though there were still a trace of primordial living matter clinging to the air. *Rumble, rumble …* the coal came rolling down the steel chute from the coal truck into the cellar, blasts of winter air swirling amid the dust. The coal cellar was work, large chunks of bituminous fuel ready for shoveling into the fiery maw of the furnace for winter warmth. "Bill, this is your job," my father said. "Make sure the furnace is loaded. We don't want the place to freeze."

On the first floor there was a kitchen with a gas stove, a dining room with the usual long table, a living room with French doors. Upstairs were the three bedrooms, one so small you could barely move in it, and above that the finished attic, a room of dreams and silence my father worked on for a year. Stars and planets moved right outside the window up through the big, leafy maple. Into that room the universe entered, shooting its starlight and moonlight. Vast. Silent. Burning. Mysterious. I felt like Kepler in the fantasies of my youth.

***

I felt wealthy; I wanted for nothing. I had the best mitt Spalding made—deep pocket, big web, and all—and I kept it soft and moist with linseed oil or my own spit. I had gaily colored streamers on my Schwinn. They flew from the handlebars in a bright chromatic display when I rode. At night, an oblong fender light illuminated the red bricks of Amelia Street and guided me safely to the curb.

Of the adults in the house, my mother was the most educated. She had gotten her bachelor's degree in Latin from Duquesne University and had gone on, in her late twenties, to pursue a master's degree in this subject at Pitt. Among men who would one day become bishops and cardinals of the church, she was the only woman. She told us this with the well-earned glow of achievement. We knew that in those years she had worked on Ovid's *Fasti,* a six-volume Latin poem published in the year AD 8. Her thesis was bound in black and stored unobtrusively on a shelf in the attic.

What prevents me speaking of the stars, and their
Rising and setting?

My mother had once read these words in Latin. Had actually read them, had parsed them in the context of ancient Rome. And she had read Marcus Aurelius: "When you arise in the morning, think of what a precious privilege it is to be alive—to breathe, to think, to enjoy, to love." All in Latin. She rarely spoke of these things. Her achievements lay in the dust of the past.

My father had graduated from the same high school that she did, St. Francis de Sales, but unlike her, he had done so without the least interest in formal study and had barely scraped through. I can't recall one subject he ever claimed to have enjoyed. I suspect that there were precisely none. Not literature, not math, not chemistry, nothing. What he did enjoy was the presence and company of one Elizabeth Rose O'Donnell, the blonde, blue-eyed girl who seemed to know so much and was distinguishing herself as the best student in the class. To her he gave his utmost attention, even though for years it went unrequited. Elizabeth O'Donnell had bigger dreams—dreams that opened far beyond the Rocks, beyond Pittsburgh, all the way to the broken stones of Rome and the tessellated acres of the Vatican itself. Eugene, Liz, and I thought them an unlikely couple and wondered what they could possibly have had in common that would have brought them together.

My aunt, Gene O'Donnell, was my mother's younger sister. She had been afflicted early in life with the most dreaded disease of the time. "Polio!"—as we spoke it with fear in the summers, when we swam in scum-green ponds and sluggish streams, where we were told it flourished—seemed the curse of the age. This was all before the great Jonas Salk and his vaccine, which sadly came far too late to prevent what had happened to Gene.

The disease had affected her from the waist down, so that her legs were thin and atrophied and curled beneath her body. They were entirely useless for walking or even standing. Until we could afford a wheelchair, she crawled everywhere on the floor, using a crab-like rhythm that carried her through rooms, into chairs, and even, with the help of her strong arms, up and down the stairs. She could climb unaided in and out of bed, and she never failed to join us in the morning for breakfast and for meals later in the day. There were never signs of depression or self-pity. "They can take my legs," she once said, "but not my mood." Her mood seemed inviolate against the assaults of polio.

Her parents—my grandparents, whom I never really knew, although I do recall being at the bedside of my grandmother O'Donnell when she was dying—decided that Gene would not go to school and that she would not, at least on any regular basis, go outdoors. In the parlance of the day, she was a shut-in, even though her intelligence and curiosity would have dictated a full array of life activities, including a formal education. But these, like a simple wheelchair, were denied her, and so she learned to read and write at only a rudimentary level.

From my earliest days, Aunt Gene was my friend; later she was my confidant. In my teenage years, I became strong enough that I could carry her upstairs, her arms tight around my neck. By then my parents had finally purchased a wheelchair for her use on the first floor. On many days Eugene, Liz, or I pushed her up and down the street, where she marveled at clouds and sunsets and the sounds of sparrows and robins and the forested hills that rose in the west. Her eyes were opened wide against the light. She breathed deeply. She let her hair down so it drifted on the wind.

It was more a collage, I once told Breslow—a mosaic, bits and pieces drawn from the remnants of memory like random loops of tape from an old projector at the Roxian down on Chartiers, or scattered snapshots strewn about after a fire or flood. There was nothing linear, so I couldn't construct a pathway that led from my earliest days with my father until the end, when the call came from Eugene that morning in Belfast.

For the most part, he was gentle. We had no fear of him physically, and yet he projected a strong, intimidating authority. He had his moods, and for days he could lapse into petulant, stone-faced silence. He simply did not speak to us, and often we had no idea why. There was this sense of unease and guilt that, in his presence, permeated the whole house. I felt it especially on Saturdays when he was home and would pull me into a new project for which I could not feign even a mild interest. He'd be sarcastic and tell me my work was shoddy: the wall was not thoroughly scraped of its peeling paint; the tiles in the basement were not cleansed of the fresh tar that had risen and congealed through the cracks; the tracks for the big Christmas train layout were not degreased to perfection, even with the sweet, suffocating carbon tetrachloride he had given me as a solvent. So often I felt stupid in his presence.

Breslow took particular note of this: "A father who could not see fit to offer his son even the faintest of praises."

Saturdays, I believed, were for play, for being on the street or up in the field not far from the house, or for exploring the hills or the bosky empty lot in the back, where the mantises and grasshoppers lived in a tangle of bishop's weed and bull thistle. (Note to myself: Where have they all gone, these grass creatures and butterflies, this once-abundant ecology?) I had studied too hard, done too much homework, to miss out on a game of touch football or an adventure with McMullen.

In the evening, my father's arrival from work signaled a minor drama. Our dog, Mitzi, would come to the door to greet him. A few feet from his boots, she'd lie on the carpeted hallway floor and begin crawling toward him. Perhaps she expected him to bend down and smilingly pat her on the head. But no such thing happened. Instead he would look down at her servile presence and, scowling, kick her outstretched body until she fled for the kitchen, whimpering in terror. As I recall, this happened many times, and under no circumstances did he lay a welcoming hand on her or speak a kind greeting as though she were a member of the family. In time, Mitzi no longer came to him, and she was reluctant even to be caught in the same room.

When I told him this, Breslow immediately inquired about any other instances of cruelty or thoughtlessness that I had observed. I told him there were probably others, but for the moment only one sprang to mind.

I recalled for Breslow the painting story. One week when my mother was bedridden with the flu, her temperature hovering around 103 degrees, my father for some reason insisted on painting the walls and ceiling around and above the bed. It was a hot day in late spring—we had no air conditioning—and the room was still and humid, and she was sweating. He had his painting clothes on and held a roller and tray and brush that smelled of turpentine.

"Dad, can't you do this later?" I asked. "Mother's sick."

He glared at me, that I should have the temerity to question him. "It has to be done *now*," he said in a low growl. "It's waited long enough."

We were in the room not far from the bed. My mother heard us speaking but never said a word. I felt humiliated.

And so it continued. Paint fumes rose to fill the air, adding miasmic vapors to the humidity and heat of the day. She lay there, facing the ceiling, eyes open, a vacant look on her face, while all around her the painting proceeded according to my father's prearranged plans. There was nothing anyone could do.

I wanted to help her, give her some of my comic books to read—Woody and Uncle Scrooge, Superman, something I was sure she would enjoy—but my Latinist mother only smiled, waved her hand dismissively through the air, and closed her eyes.

Breslow stroked his hairless chin. "Hmm, disturbing. Bullying. He was being a bully. Anything else?" He was poised to take notes.

"Well," I said, "there was the kicking episode."

This memory involved Eugene. When he was younger, maybe ten, his principal means of self-defense had become kicking. It was not punching or wrestling, as those of us in the neighborhood were accustomed to, but kicking people with his feet, shoes and all.

At any rate, my father's anger at this behavior slowly grew with each offense, with each new complaint from Liz or me that "Eugene kicked me."

Eventually he took action. One day he ushered Eugene into the darkened basement, where he made him remove his shoes. He had him face the green wall near the coal cellar, and then he commanded him to begin kicking the wall. Eugene must have been incredulous, must have looked at him warily, with tears in his eyes. My father told him to kick it hard, just the way he kicked people. Eugene did as he was told. With each contact, his wails of pain became shriller. Tears ran down his cheeks. His toes began to bleed, and he pleaded, "No more, no more! Never again!" All this took little more than a minute.

My mother was a silent witness to this, a conspirator in this punishment. It was from her that I learned that it had happened. But from then on, the kicking ceased.

Breslow, the man of family context, was taking notes all along in silence. But with this last revelation, he looked shocked. "That was cruel, malevolent," he said. "Traumatic for Eugene." When he called for an end to the session, his head was down and he was writing furiously in his notebook. I had said enough.

***

I remember one session with Breslow when I tried to use the ritual of our evening dinners to convey some sense of the preeminent role my father played in the family hierarchy. Of course, I had no objection to it at the time, because in those days, that's how it was.

After the nightly prayer, we all said, "Amen." It was not in unison; it staggered off our lips indifferently, we'd said it so often.

My father sat at the head of the table. My mother brought the striated roast she had just gotten hot from the oven. He served himself and passed down to us the freshly steamed peas and the huge bowl of mashed potatoes. Conversation moved to the food. "More potatoes, Jim?" And the answer was always "Yes. And pass the gravy too, please." For a long time, I had no idea that you could eat potatoes, plain and simple and white, and that they tasted damn good. I thought they had to be garnished with pools of gravy and pats of butter and sprinkled thick with salt that glistened like a dried-up lake bed. I thought too that a helping of mashed potatoes must be the same diameter as a giant plate. Was this an Irish thing, some vestigial memory of famine? I emulated him and ate the things until I gagged; my parents told me to just keep on eating, that I'd be okay. They passed me the bread. I was about to throw up.

My father never moved. My mother did all the work—everything. She was in constant motion and rarely sat with us. No one ever thought of helping her. She was dressed in a white apron with blue trim, or sometimes red. My father had a long day in his truck and in the small office out at Craft Avenue. He was out of the house at six in a snowstorm, and she knew it had been tough for him. So she shuttled between the dining room and kitchen like a servant—my mother, master of Latin; scholar of Ovid's *Fasti,* of rising and setting stars; visitor, in her dreams, to the stones and monuments of Rome—shuttling again to the kitchen. I never knew when she ate. He'd compliment her on the meal. He never complained, and they rarely argued. If they did have words, she would end up crying softly, her hand pressed over her mouth, staring out the back door window into the falling night.

Aunt Gene had hoisted herself onto a chair at the other end of the table; or, in later years, she wheeled into the dining room, her hands gripping the silvery rims. She spoke to my mother, who was bent over the stove in the kitchen. Aunt Gene could keep a conversation going if the atmosphere was right, but her remarks were always directed at her sister, my mother, or at one of us. She never exchanged a word with my father. Sometimes my father would talk to the rest of us about work that day, about his friends, Marm and Schuster and Big Red Schlentner from the Pittsburgh Railways Company; or he would have news about what he was doing down at the Knights of Columbus or the Elks, where one day he'd become Exalted Ruler. Sometimes he'd complain about "Uncle" Dave Hershmann, the town mayor and oligarch, but he never talked national politics—Truman, Ike, the Marshall Plan, Korea, the state of the economy, the new national highway program. At the table there was nothing much beyond the figurative island of the Rocks and the City of Pittsburgh.

He never asked about our plans; he seemed prepared to let these evolve in their own, slow time without his meddling.

But he cared about our grades, as did my mother. We were all expected to perform, and report card day was a day of sweating anxiety and stomach pains that could double me to my knees, as if I've eaten a bushel of crab apples. Grades were rewarded not with words of praise—never those—but with a dollar bill or a couple of silver halves. We wanted to please them more than they wanted us to succeed.

These were the early days of black-and-white TV: a twelve-inch screen and big rabbit ears projecting like insect antennae toward the ceiling; wobbly, grainy pictures; and my favorite program, the test pattern, which looked like some Navaho or Hopi sign. I could stare at it for hours. The three of us and Aunt Gene gathered after dinner for a Western—the Cisco Kid, Gene Autry, or the Lone Ranger and Tonto. My father never watched TV with us. Ever. He did not sit with us in the living room and talk. He had a reason to be out at night, every night. We never questioned where he went, and my mother never said, and maybe she didn't know either. Or maybe she didn't much care. That was just the way it was. His life shaded in the evenings into complete mystery. It's what happened: our father disappeared. It was part of the family milieu, like Aunt Gene's polio, like her crawling up the stairs to bed each night, like the meals we ate with their hardy but scant selections, or my father's ubiquitous, acrid cigar smoke; these were the givens of daily life. To my knowledge, there was no other way of living.

***

I told Breslow at one point that my father was no philosopher, that he did not try to proclaim any great wisdom. If anything he was self-effacing, especially when it came to matters of formal academic learning. He had only a few serious words of advice, and these were imparted offhandedly and sometimes only once, but for me they carried a kind of Mosaic heft, if only for their paucity of number and because of the respect he commanded in my eyes. He could have posted them on the refrigerator door, I guess, but in those days the refrigerator was for keeping stuff cold and not for displaying magnets or kid art or the wisdom of Marcel Proust. What he said over the years, discursively, and never as a set of canonical pronouncements, were things like "In this world, you can count on your family. That's all. Family is everything. You don't know it now—you're too young—but later on in life, you'll see I was right."

On the ball field, he made it clear that he hated quitters. "Don't quit," he'd say, his lip curling, "no matter how tough it gets out there. Run everything out. Run like hell. Throw yourself in front of a ball if you have to." In different contexts, I'm sure he imparted this same advice to Eugene and Elizabeth. "Don't ever be a quitter in this world. When you start something, damn it, finish it!"

And of course there was that other piece of wisdom drawn from baseball. It came in handy for me many times: "There's always another ball game. Always another day." Forget Scott Fitzgerald and his no second acts. Hell, American life gave you a bunch of second chances, even if you tended to be a real fuckup.

★★★

He was not a deeply religious man, at least not in any dogmatic way. He was born Irish Catholic, and he certainly played the game like a pro. He went to Sunday Mass. Occasionally he fell asleep during the sermons, which he explained to us as the result of intense concentration (even we could see through that). He was generous in his tithing, reveled in the fact that his son Eugene would one day become a priest, and loved and took pride in his sister, Agnes Louise, who was a member of the Sisters of Charity.

He did novenas, stations of the cross, rosaries. He believed. His belief was not based on Pascal's wager, either, or a fear of hell. No, it was genuine.

He seemed to have a tolerant view of human weakness and fallibility, as he had the capacity to overlook his own failings and those of his friends. He accepted the commandments, but with his own caveats thrown in. I don't know how many commandments he abided by, but it was surely fewer than ten.

He was a man more comfortable on a bar stool than at home, and I never recall him sitting contemplatively in one of the overstuffed chairs by the fake fireplace in our living room with a book, or even a magazine with photographs in it—*Look* or *Life*. He preferred the spoken language, often on the lips of women, with whom, in my limited experience, he seemed to enjoy an easy, flirtatious companionship.

Clearly he did not have a vision of the afterlife, as my mother had. She thought of heaven as a vast expanse of blueness. Like a Cape Cod sky in summer, but taken to the third or fourth power. She threw in some harps and other stringed instruments and fripperies of various kinds, along with the usual winged angels floating above fields of tended grass. In these musings there was never a trace of apostasy, nor did they ever fail to bring a look of seraphic calm to her face.

To me it all sounded hopelessly boring, but to her it was a scene of peace beyond the yearnings and disappointments of this world. Maybe in her heart she was a desert saint, a clear-eyed mystic. But no, I think she loved her comforts too much for that. She was covetous and held in abeyance the tenth of God's commandments. When it came to wealth and travel, she could bend this commandment as easily as a harp string, if only in her fantasies.

Hell to her was also real. She could imagine it as a slight enhancement of what she saw on this earth; she did not have to raise its awfulness to some exponential power. The seas of hell were aflame, like so many pools of kerosene, with the rocks melted all around like Dali's watch. It was an imprisonment of time and eternity, a fearsome tableau altered from the pages of Dante, whose writings she knew intimately and often referenced. And it was this hell, I guess, that she feared for all of us. She made it clear that any one of us might someday be cast into eternal torment. "We never know we go—when we *are* going," she'd say, quoting Dickinson.

My father seemed to embrace a more generous view of the Creator, the one enshrined in the Apostles' Creed, which speaks of forgiveness and resurrection and life everlasting—the forgiveness of the Catholic confessional. The deity was not an implacable tyrant, but much like my father himself, was someone, something, who could understand the irresistible pull of temptation and abject failure and the darkness resident in the human heart. He gave himself lots of running room.

★★★

For at least two years—in the early '50s, when we would have preferred to be watching *The Cisco Kid*—he joined us in the living room to pray the rosary. This was something Breslow himself understood, for he was a Catholic too and clearly remembered this period of what I later called "rosary hysteria."

For half an hour, on our knees, we droned on, along with the sad, droning nuns on the radio: "Hail Mary, full of grace, the Lord is with thee ..."And so on and so on, as the crystalline beads bumped along through our fingers. For a Catholic, this was the equivalent of repeating *om* a million times and entering into a transcendent zone of anchorite peace.

During rosary time, I was kneeling. But what had been my knees, trembling a little as I knelt; what had been at my side, Eugene and Liz; what had been before me, my young parents, and behind, my Aunt Gene in her wheelchair; became one in the sound that was our voices—our six voices and the radio voices of the nuns, whose voices became our voices. And the distance toward which we flowed seemed to reach in toward us, taking us and reeling us in like the fish of God Almighty. "And so it is and ever shall be, world without end. Amen." *World without end. World without* ... The words haunt and perplex and resonate. Then they devolve into perfect gibberish, an echo chamber.

I emerge and realize that, with this prayer, I've missed an episode of *The Cisco Kid,* good guys and bad guys riding around in box canyons on white steeds in the forever-unreachable Far West. For my father, it's even worse: a missed beer or two down at the Wil-Kar Grill, some good laughter with Joe Vitelli, an early start to the evening with the guys.

★★★

I tell all of this to Dr. Breslow as a way of clarifying the past, both for him and for myself. All the talk of dinners and rosaries and family structure, of my father's occasional meanness, of his philosophy of life and religion such as it was, seemed to be of interest and perhaps of some value to him in developing an understanding of my response to my father's death. Just putting these memories—random as they were—into words also had the salutary effect of helping me see my life, as it related to my father, as a possible and yet not fully realized continuum.

We were into our fourth month of analysis in 1970. By this time I'd found a good job with a foundation that had an EPA contract to study pollutants from printing presses. No matter my mental state—my fears, my grief, my growing awareness that my father was gone and would never come back—I could not imagine not working. That's what you did; that's what a man did, as my father had made amply clear. This work involved climbing smokestacks, taking grab samples of the emissions, and visiting web-fed offset presses and metal-decorating presses from Chicago to St. Louis to Philadelphia. It involved talking to tough-looking typesetters and plant managers, speaking about the environment and air quality at big printing conferences in Atlanta and elsewhere, and doing a bit of lab work. My partner, Gadomski, and I got along well. He'd been an engineer with the Bureau of Mines before this, and he liked outdoor work as much as I did and could sling the bull with the best of them. So we talked a lot on the rooftops and in the car on the long road trips east and west. This was not exactly what I'd had in mind when I finished my PhD, but it paid well and I liked the travel, and I liked the people I worked with. Breslow's sedatives, the three-martini lunches, and my good boss, Bill Schaeffer, helped assuage the pain. Besides, it was good to get out of an academic setting, where I'd been cloistered far too long.

I still lived at home with my mother, who had retired from teaching junior high—whether from depression or sheer exhaustion—right after my father's death. I greatly enjoyed her company, and after a few months I no longer heard her say, "I just want to die, Bill. I miss him so much. I wish God would take me now."

We could laugh about lighter topics, and we seemed to be keeping each other's heads above the flood. When I'd come home late from the city, smelling of scotch, she'd be up waiting for me and say, "Well, did you meet anyone you liked better than yourself?" And I'd laugh and tell her, "No, not tonight, Mom," and I'd kiss her on the head and notice how her hair was thinning into mere fibers from which, somehow, she managed to create an attractive fullness. And I'd say, "Mom, why don't you go upstairs to bed and get some good sleep?" But she would nod off again in her green chair before the blank TV.

I also had an apartment not far from where I worked, in case I needed the privacy. The place wasn't bad, but it smelled of cooked cabbage and had nothing more than a bed and one of those suitcase-style record players. The smell poured in from my neighbors on all sides, as if cabbage were the only thing anyone in the building knew how to cook. *Who are these people?* Cabbage, I found, can be masked by a few shots of Johnnie Walker or Maker's Mark.

I told Breslow about the place. About why I needed it. About the girl I met at a trashy bar downtown—the girl with the great legs—and how in the mornings we'd have pancakes and coffee and good conversation. Breslow yawned.

***

I played on a couple of softball teams. Out of fear of tachycardia and sudden death, when I felt my heart flipping around with those ominous warnings and intimations, I sometimes made the mistake of self-medicating with Breslow's pills and a shot or two. On these occasions, especially when I played outfield, the ball blurred and became oddly shaped, like a big, fuzzy comet with a long tail. Sometimes the ball hit me smack on the head. Was that a baseball or a chunk of dirty ice from outer space? Who knew?

The manager would say, "Hey, Green, you're playin' like you got a damn snake up your ass. Take a break."

There was time for tennis lessons too, which I took from an old pro on a clay court behind an ice cream shop. He seemed to think I was pretty good and said, "I wish I coulda gotten you into this ten years ago." For some reason, the old guy was a calming presence, and I loved the way a ball bounced on his clay court.

Dances or clubs down on Market Street or in one of the big hotels were favorite hangouts of mine. Everything had the comfortable feel of urban life in the old, familiar settings of Pittsburgh and the Rocks. These were places I knew. I knew these people, even though I'd been away for what seemed a long time.

Breslow knew all this now, and he knew that my heart beat in strange patterns, as though it were on a secret mission to destroy my sense of equanimity and scare the living hell out of me. At times it seemed to stop altogether, bringing me up short with terror. But now, having had many sessions with Breslow, I was beginning to control the fear. The drugs and martinis and alcohol and whatever else I could ingest or inhale weren't hurting either.

Breslow said at one point how impressed he was by my energy.

★★★

Breslow had a number of hypotheses for what might be going on. From all he'd heard, he thought my father was probably not a bad guy, but he was struck again by the fact that I had tried to put so much distance between us. "What is the distance to the South Pole?" he inquired one day, knowing that I'd gone to Antarctica in 1968.

"From here, about nine thousand miles," I said.

"Well, you can't get much farther than that, not on this planet," he said. "And then there was Belfast. You might have gone somewhere closer. You had the opportunity."

Of course I had explanations for these destinations, but he seemed to be looking for something Viennese and subterranean, as though I must have been fleeing, most likely from my father's inscrutable ubiquity.

"It seemed your father was very critical of you," he said. He looked down at his notes. "He never appreciated the help you gave him on Saturdays. *Good work! Nice job!* Those are words fathers often use to encourage their sons. You heard them from your boss, Schaeffer, at Graphic Arts. You heard them from your professor, Paul Field, down at Virginia Tech. But you didn't hear them from him. What sticks in your mind is the criticism, the feeling of discomfort, even fear. It hurt and you wanted to escape it."

He flipped through his sheaf of notes and continued. "I remember the story you told about the baseball game. Your aunt was there at the field, looking on from the car window. You were at bat, the bases were loaded, and you imagined yourself impressing her with a home run. The grand slam would be for her. A dedicated homer for Gene, your beloved aunt."

Breslow was really cutting loose here. Dr. Super-Garrulous. He'd not spoken this much in months. Maybe he had a belt or two of scotch before our session? I doubt it, though. Not Breslow.

"But instead of the home run you'd imagined, you hit this puny, dribbling grounder to the pitcher and were thrown out at first. Worse, you decided not to run it out. You just lollygagged down the base path. Your dad was understandably angry. Any coach would have been. But then he swore at you and called you a quitter. And he created quite a scene. He drop-kicked the water bucket like it was a football, and it went flying down the first base line. That was a public display that was clearly uncalled for." The tone of Breslow's voice and the look on his face made it clear that this was an understatement, just in case I missed it.

"I *was* a quitter," I said in a small voice. "He hated that in his players. He hated it in anyone. I'd given up." For this he visited a display of obloquy upon me, which I now consider warranted. He had his reasons, and I have never forgotten this singular passionate display. *A quitter!*

Breslow hardly noticed that I had spoken. He continued, "Then when you got home, he grabbed you by the seat of your uniform pants and tried to send you flying upstairs." I smiled at the memory of this, of sailing against the law of gravity halfway up the stairs, but Breslow wasn't smiling. "This went too far. Way too far! But it fits."

My smile broke, and I nodded my head in agreement.

"Unknown to yourself, you were always trying to escape him," he said. "In the dream, you were leaving, and he could not reach you. You were gone from him. You were gone from the unease you felt in his presence. You felt lost in his shadow."

Lost in his shadow. I liked that. But Breslow stopped right there, even though it seemed to me he had a lot more to say on this subject. I thought he was getting places. But damn, he would stop midsentence if he needed to. Breslow was very punctual. He stayed to the watch as if he were calling a horse race.

"We can talk about it more in our next session," he said as he rose from his chair and moved toward the door. "How are the drugs holding out?"

★★★

I walked out the door into the same familiar waiting room, into the same dim hallway. We were far along in our sessions. But I realized I had not said anything to him about what happened at JFK. Maybe it didn't seem important enough. It only lasted seconds, minutes, I don't know. Maybe I was embarrassed that I ever had such thoughts, such emotions. Maybe I'd committed a monstrous sin. "Tell me everything," Breslow had said. "You're not here to keep secrets."

I don't know, but whatever it was, I kept forgetting to tell him. Perhaps I needed to write it all down and get it over with.

From left to right: Jack Green, Jim Green, Elizabeth O'Donnell Green and Mary Jo O'Donnell Shrode.

6

Blue Album (1970)

Flood, tornado, hurricane, fire … it's always the same. Scattered wreckage, the houses gone, whole neighborhoods lost in the stench of rising water and rotting wood, the dismembering power and work of the wind. And then, stunned by sorrow and loss, people are trapped in a dream from which they struggle to awaken, wandering in the disbelief of it all—their lives, the what-had-been-but-will-never-be-again-in-this-world, the remains of all they'd made. Then a gold frame peeks out from beneath the soaked cardboard, the charred wood, the randomized pile, and in it there is a photo visible under the smoked glass, preserved as if by miracle; and lower still, in the ruins, the blue-covered album, the kids, their young lives, the weddings and holidays, all those beautiful Christmases when you and your wife were still young. And in all your misery and hopelessness, this is a flower of hope.

***

He kept the photos in a three-ring binder in the bedroom closet. I found it after one of my sessions with Breslow. I could not believe my good fortune.

Plastic covers; faded, sepia-toned, blurred faces; yellowed paper. Over the years since his death, they'd become disorganized.

Some had been removed from the plastic sheaths he had placed them in and were piled in the back in no special order. Others had been turned at odd angles or completely on their heads. Clippings from the *Rocks Gazette*, which had once formed a separate section, were mixed in with the photos. It was obvious that other hands had turned these pages.

We know a photo is nothing more than an image captured, sheaves of light waves gathered from sun, frozen to film, and then printed on paper and put into an album, where it becomes a memory of time past. It's a transient thing, a leaf on the current moving beneath the bridge. It is the *now* we so urgently try to hold on to but cannot. But it is flawed, it is pure surface, it cannot reveal context—what is beneath or what is around. The precedents, the days and years that led to the moment, to the smile, to the look of sadness and toil, to the quizzical expression—these are only to be guessed at.

It was my father who took most of the pictures. I don't remember my mother even holding the old Brownie in her hands. Her relationship to the camera was one of apprehension. It was almost primitive. She did not want to photograph or be photographed, as though something would be stolen from her, one of the multitude of thin laminae that constituted her being and of which there were only so many. Or this apprehension might have been born of simple vanity—one of her countless charms that we all treasured and would never have changed.

She has an image of herself—the young lady of twenty-eight in the white dress, thin and lovely and small of stature, strolling on the avenue with her sister, Mary Jo; or, later, the one who appears with my father in their wedding photo—and these youthful images could not have withstood an encounter, in her middle years, with the camera. Either way, it was my father who took photographs, he who arranged them.

But despite what was limited and flawed in its content, the Blue Album, as I came to know it, told a story. And like the art of those who work with absences and voids, with negative space, with the interstices and gaps, the album spoke with both its polarities—with what was and was not present. Of course, the Blue Album might have been one of many. But over the years, no others have come to light, and given the sedulousness with which we searched the house, it is unlikely that any other exists.

What struck me when I opened it were the first several pages. These seemed to me to be of great importance to him. They had been placed in protective sheets of clear plastic and apparently had never been moved or examined with any degree of scrutiny. To the casual observer, they were nothing. What appeared at the top of the page was the word *Colt* in bold letters, and in the hollow of the *C* was a colt, looking as though it had just burst with vibrancy into the world. It was the insignia for Colt League Baseball Inc., a league comprised of teams from across the nation and headquartered at that time (the year represented was 1959) in Ontario, California. The league motto was spelled out; it read Courage–Obedience–Loyalty–Truth. This was an official, notarized application to enter the Colt League Tournament, and it contained the roster of all eligible players, including addresses and dates of birth. Beneath, listed as team manager, was James W. Green, 134 Amelia St., McKees Rocks, Pa. That year, the states or cities represented in Ontario, California, were Michigan, South Carolina, Florida, Pennsylvania, Washington, Texas, and Ontario and La Mesa, California.

Facing this list, on the following page, was a telegram to Jim Green at 206 West B St., Ontario, Calif., with the salutation Congratulations written in script. Adjacent to this was a pink orchid on a bed of ferns. Then, in caps,

> CONGRATULATIONS ON YOUR EXCELLENT SHOWING WE ARE PULLING FOR YOU ALL THE WAY PS – JIM – EXPECT BIG STORY AND FULL REPORT ON RETURN = MCKEESROCKS GAZETTE

***

This 1959 tournament, which seemed of such great importance to him, was only a vague memory to me. I was seventeen then and had, for a time, lost my interest in competitive baseball. I had discovered the dances at West View Park and had focused my attention on the US Military Academy at West Point, which I one day hoped to attend. My hero was General Douglas MacArthur, whose picture I'd first seen on the war cards I collected years before. I read everything I could find about him, and I memorized his speeches and practiced them before the bedroom mirror. These shifting interests provided a reprieve from baseball, from the need to perform before a crowd—something I increasingly did with great anxiety, to the point, even, of wishing that at game time torrential rains would burst from the heavens.

***

Pictures of the games—some taken by him, others culled from local newspapers—were scattered throughout the album. The Williamsport, Pennsylvania, paper, for example, published a large photo of a game we won in 1954, the very year my father expressed nostalgia for in his Belfast letter. It showed Bill Rudison, our pitcher, crossing the plate after hitting a home run. The names of each of the players rushing onto the field to greet him and shake his hand had been carefully written by my father on the white pant legs of their uniforms. There were smiles and looks of wonder at what I recall being one of Rudison's signature towering drives over the left field fence. Sometimes I actually wished I could *be* Rudison.

There was a full-page entry on our defeat at Williamsport by a team from Masontown, Pennsylvania, which begins "This is how ..." In two dramatic photos, it shows our catcher, Eddy Long, on his knees, attempting to tag out the Masontown runner at home plate. There is no question that he is in perfect position to execute the play and get us out of the inning. But on closer inspection, you can see a blurry sphere spinning off his glove into the air and finally, in the crisp picture below, coming to rest on the ground. Beneath the photos is the caption "Winning Run Crosses for Masontown: Fran Rossini scores as Long drops the ball." I recall this being a painful moment for the entire team, myself included. But seeing it brought to life in the yellowing pages of the *Pittsburgh Post-Gazette,* I wondered why it meant so much to my father, why it deserved such a prominent place in his album. It was the sad flip side of Rudison's home run, of the triumphs he usually chose to display. Beneath the photo, there was the word *Quit.*

Throughout the Blue Book, in random fashion, there are photos of him with the other founding members of the Sto-Ken-Rox Little League. In one he's dressed in a starched white shirt my mother's cleaned and pressed for him at home. He is wearing creased black pants, and his tie hangs crookedly toward his right arm. He looks fit and robust and has a slight smile on his face—a man comfortable with himself and his life achievements. There are other, less formal photos in which he is standing on some field or other, a tool in hand, about to begin work on a Little League project. In one he is wearing a baseball jersey and cap and leaning against the pick in his right hand. He has labeled the men around him—Mike Zavidni, Angelo Pandocchi, and others, each holding a shovel or rake or some implement suggesting hard work. Beneath this is written, "1955—Coke and Chemical Field—Island Avenue."

There is always some construction project. In one photo he is building a backstop; in another he is about to direct the waiting bulldozers as they clear space for his field; in a third he is calling in a cement mixer to lay out a new basketball court just behind our house. Like Robert Moses of New York, he has become the master builder of our town.

Good physical work is part of his life, and he has a mild disdain for the desk and the podium, even though, in time, these become more important as he assumes positions of community leadership. In the Blue Album, there are pages that show him as master of ceremonies or behind a desk at Little League headquarters. A page is devoted to Parent and Son Night, held on November 22, 1954, at Hamilton Junior High School. Along with a list of players who would be "graduating" from Little League and Pony League, the officers and board of the organization are presented. The first name to appear is "James W. Green, Pres."

★★★

Going through his album, I begin to see, in the clear light of my own life, the significance of his letter to me in Belfast: "Don't you wish we could go back …" It is then that so much of consequence was happening for him. There is one entry that summarizes this, namely, "Eagles Will Give Green an Award."

The citation is long and detailed. It goes on for pages in large, celebratory type. Everything mentioned is public service—unremunerated, tedious work done after his long days with the PRC and on the weekends when he might have rested. But then I rarely see him in repose, except for the occasional naps he takes on the sofa at home during his lunch hour. He is a man in constant motion. *Where's Dad?* we often wonder. But then we stop wondering.

I'm vaguely aware of all this when I'm seeing Breslow in the early 1970s. But the extent of the recognition my father had received back in the '50s had escaped me. My appreciation for his achievement then and my pride in his work were absent. I cannot recall ever extending a hand to him, offering my congratulations. So when Breslow suggested that my problems could be traced to an unconscious competition with my father and that I felt guilty for having surpassed him in certain ways—in the extent of my education, my travels, and so on—I simply listened politely and considered this highly implausible. Our career paths had been incommensurable. My father had done enough. I would never be named "man of the year" for anything, nor would I ever assemble the kind of winning teams or community recognition that he did.

Breslow did not pick up on the hint of skepticism on my face. "Your months in Antarctica, your fellowship in Ireland, your PhD—all of these were beyond anything your father could have imagined. And so you are punishing yourself. You are reproducing in your body the symptoms of his illness." He looked down at his hands.

I sat across the desk from him in perfect silence. The room seemed small, and it pressed the two of us into an intimate space. I could not proffer a rejoinder to what he had said. Finally I said in a whisper, "I will have to think about it."

★★★

I told Breslow in one or maybe several of our sessions that in going through the Blue Album, I was surprised by certain things. I was particularly unprepared for the number of photos he had taken of the three of us—Eugene, Liz, and me.

In one of his travel photos, this one taken on a wooden bridge in Cook Forest, he stands behind the three of us. His hand is placed on Liz's shoulder, and the expression on his face suggests familial pride and the joy of being away and of being able to give his wife and children this gift of travel. Trips to Washington, DC, Atlantic City, and the tiny southern Indiana town of St. Meinrad, where Eugene went to study for his priesthood at age fourteen, are all captured in the leaves of the Blue Album.

In 1959, Eugene and Liz accompanied him on his Colt League journey to California—the one to which he accords such prominence—and he photographed them together at the corner of Hollywood and Vine and standing near a trolley on Main Street in Disneyland. They both appear radiant—Liz grinning under a broad-brimmed hat, Eugene smiling in a casual striped shirt—in this newly found Eden of sunshine and desert heat so far removed from the harsh industrial landscapes of 1950s Pittsburgh and the Rocks.

He had pictures of us at church: Eugene as a choirboy in cassock and surplice with a huge, red bow at his throat, gazing down at his hymnal; Liz in the backyard in her white Communion dress and white shoes against the spring-green lawn. And there were pictures taken on St. Patrick's Day—March 17 celebrated as though it were July 4—with the three of us lined up in the living room, singing the greatest hits from the Old Sod:

> Oh, me name is MacNamara
> I'm the leader of the band …

"Danny Boy," "Mother McCree"—we knew them all by heart and often had to sing them, under protest, to the neighbors and visiting relatives.

***

In none of the pictures from trips or family gatherings was my mother represented. The only photos of her—and perhaps the loveliest in the album—were from their wedding. In one of these, she and my father are dressed in white. They are flanked by Jack Green, my father's brother and best man, and by Mary Jo O'Donnell, my mother's sister and maid of honor. Jack is broad-shouldered and ruggedly handsome. He looks cocky, his hair slightly tousled by the wind, his body relaxed and comfortable. Mary Jo is dark-haired and taller than my mother, and she appears, to my eyes, pretty and eminently confident of her own beauty. Jack and Mary Jo have very different lives ahead of them, and their paths from the granite walls and flowers of the garden will diverge in unimaginable ways.

Between these two figures and in contrast to them, my mother and father appear more posed and proper. She has a slight tilt to her head and a demure, becoming smile on her lips. Besides this formal wedding photo, in which she strikes an almost regal bearing, this is one of the few pictures of her. My father has worked toward this day since they were students together at St. Francis de Sales High School, and as she stands close at his side with her small hand linked into the crook of his arm, he has the look of a man who has triumphed over time and resistance.

I told Breslow that it came as a shock to me that, in my father's album, his entire work life—in whose service he had labored through long days and nights, and from whose rewards he had clothed and fed us and made possible our travel and education—was absent. Accented were family and community. There was no trace, even, of those company people who came in the days after his death to pay their respects and offer words of consolation, the very people whose visits at Christmas and other holidays had seemed so important to him. And there was not a single picture of him standing beside one of those classically designed red-and-white trolleys that carried us daily into the downtown.

It was community, it was baseball, it was Jim Green with his family, outside the walls of his own house, liberated—*But from what?* I once wondered—in free flight, generous and whistling, always whistling, in a hellishly smoke-drenched reverie. It was Jim Green down at the Wil-Kar Grill with Vitelli, or Jim Green slapping out grounders, yelling, "Get two! Get two!"

***

From what flood of time and randomness, what entropic cyclone the Blue Book had emerged, I can only guess. There had been so many hands, so much discarding, so little concern, even after his death, for preserving any remnants of memory that lay willy-nilly about the house, that the passage of his album to safety seems a gift of the Fates. I wanted Dana and Kate to know about its existence; I wanted them to know something of their grandfather, a man they had missed by too many years and who would have taken, I believe, such pride in them. And I wanted to hear what Liz had to say and whether her memory in any way coincided with my own, or whether some Rashomon effect prevailed. I suspected that it might.

Whatever the case, he had sorted out his life, placed a frame around it, excluded what was not important in his view. Whatever the case, there was a world in there and I wanted to know it, even as a man yearns to see the soils of Mars, its sunsets and mountains. *No man is unimportant.*

Skippy Tatala and Junior Dean standing
before our California-bound bus*

7

JUSTICE (1958)

What I had not expected was the softness of the air, its fragrance as it swept the fields where we practiced, the clacking of palm fronds in the morning breeze beyond the fence. Our journeys to the Jersey shore, even the vast Atlantic, looked small now. This was a place of dream, the coelum empyreum, whose existence I had once imagined but denied. The girls at the parties wore short white dresses, and on clear days you could see the snow peaks of the mountains. Among the newly arrived, my father was a hero and they welcomed him, and win or lose, there was a lightness to his step. He was champion of the East Coast, after all. I reveled in that. He also had a sense of justice that I had never seen before, but that would soon be revealed.

***

I told Breslow about the role of baseball in our town as I saw it, and how I thought it had been overlooked by our few local historians and members of the newly formed historical society, who were, understandably and to their credit, charmed by the beauty of our area's ethnic churches and by the diverse peoples that had found their way from around the world to our shops and industries. But the absence of sports in the historical record is surprising in light of the coverage our town paper, the *McKees Rocks Gazette*, had given to sports in general and to baseball in particular. There was no evidence of this more striking than Angelo Pandocchi's long and balanced coverage of the "Sto-Ken-Rox Rams California Trip," which appeared on page 1 of the November 6, 1958, edition of the paper. From this account, which my father had tucked away in its entirety in the back of the Blue Book, there was nothing missing, and I believe that my father, the man, was more clearly revealed in Pandocchi's article.

I knew we were good that year, and I wanted nothing more than for my father to have a championship. He had won his share of recognition, but he had never managed a team that had won something big. This was it. When I looked over the roster in the article, it was easy to know why I felt so confident. Rudison was there, not much taller than he had been the year we went to Williamsport, but filled out and muscular. He threw hard, and there weren't many kids of fifteen or sixteen who could get a hit off him. Jerry Opferman, the shortstop, was thin and could move with speed and grace to both sides. He covered a lot of ground. And together, Jerry and I had practiced the double play to a nearly balletic perfection. He was the best partner I had ever had in this pas de deux. Ulysses S. "Junior" Dean played first base, and he could stretch, leap, and dig balls out of the dirt in a way that made the rest of us look good. Dean was the one African American on the team and would be the only nonwhite person in the California series. Eleven years had passed since Jackie Robinson broke the color line, but in California, Junior Dean would be a problem.

We had a strong outfield and a good pitching rotation highlighted by the presence of "Sudden" Sam McDowell. My father had seen McDowell pitch against us when we played North Hills, and he told me, "If we get into the tournament, I want to sign this kid up." He did just that.

McDowell was a tall, thin left-hander who even at fifteen could throw an amazing array of junk. Curves, drops, sliders—you name it, he could deliver it. There was also the legerdemain of the McDowell pick-off motion. What magic! Once, when I played against him, it caught me dead in my tracks. I'd taken my usual big lead off first, thinking that if the opportunity arose, I could steal second. I watched his windup, saw him check first and then pivot toward home. But it was illusion. All of a sudden the ball was in the first baseman's mitt. I was sliding on my stomach, my fingers were desperately outstretched, digging toward the bag, and I was saying under my breath, "Oh shit." It was not even close: I was out. I stood up, dusted myself off, and glanced at my father. He was shaking his head, not so much in anger as in disappointment. I slowly returned to the dugout.

From the first time my father saw him on the mound, McDowell was beyond reproach. He could sit in the front seat of our Pontiac and crank up the volume on "Hound Dog" or "Poor Little Fool" or "Yakety Yak" and my father would say nothing, although his own taste in music tended toward the McGuire Sisters or Patty Page—soft, traditional. In California, McDowell could break curfew without consequence, a transgression that would have earned me a stern lecture on the need to be in top shape for tomorrow's game.

***

Our bus left from the local supermarket in the Rocks. Then it moved on through Chicago, Cheyenne, Rawlins, Salt Lake City, Las Vegas, and finally Ontario, California, thirty miles east of Los Angeles. We arrived at our destination on August 21. I spent my time in a gauzy half sleep that blended inland seas with big skies and deserts and crappy little food and bathroom stops—a distorted dreamscape that lies forever beyond my recall.

But there is no question about my memory of this: once in California, we were feted as heroes from the distant East. I think Breslow was surprised to hear that this was such a big deal. This was back when America felt big and confident and California was remote and exotic and, to most mortals, unattainable. Even Breslow had never been there.

We were greeted by a band associated with the Pennsylvania Society of Ontario and by a small delegation from the Pittsburgh area. We stayed in a dormitory at Chaffey College, in a room filled with army cots. We practiced each morning on the red clay fields nearby.

The practice sessions in the wide, soft dawn, with my dad slapping grounders and yelling out, "Bare-hand it, Bill!" or, "Get two!" were light and insouciant and welcoming of a carefree perfection. I relished these practices and recall them more vividly and with greater fondness than the games themselves. In one of Pandocchi's front-page pictures, I was standing in the grass with a glove folded against my leg and a smile on my face. In California, I was at home. In fantasy, I had lived under palm fronds all my life.

One evening before our first game, there was a lawn party. I remember lush green grass, and palm trees waving in the gentle breezes that blew in from the west and carried with them the sweet hint of orange groves and the distant sea. The slow, melancholy voice of Tommy Edwards—"All in the wonderful game we know"—filled the air as an assemblage of teens danced slowly, dreamily, eyes closed, to the hypnotic rhythms. Were the girls in California really prettier than anywhere else, as was claimed, or was it the magic of place and circumstance that cast its own enchantment, like the light of a thin paper lantern, upon the scene?

On Sunday we played our first game. I was certain that with McDowell and Rudison and the lanky right-hander, Eddy Gregacz, on the pitching roster, San Diego would be lucky to score a single run.

What happened that day is not clear. But in short order, San Diego was pounding the ball. Our precocious outfielders, dazzled perhaps by the late Saturday night party, were allowing balls to fall between them, behind them, and, in two cases, right on their heads. There were collisions, sprained ankles, and risible comedy throws far into the third-base stands. It was a sight to behold out there, a display of court jesters and masked clowns that my father, poised in his usual stoic way on the dugout steps, could only shake his head at with sad incredulity. Could this be happening to his carefully crafted, citywide, pride-of-Pittsburgh team? I contributed to the misery by letting a grounder that had come to me with a perfect, short hop shoot through my legs and on into right field, where I chased it down and bobbled it on the spot as the San Diego runner sprinted for third. I was scratching my head, thinking, *What the hell! How did I screw that up?* If the beginning was bad, the end was worse, and despite my irrational confidence, we lost 10–7. Surprise! These guys from California actually knew the game.

To keep things mercifully short, it was a two-elimination tournament. We won our second game against a team from Canada. In the third game, we were defeated by one of the southern teams, 5–0.

This last game is important to me for a single reason, which has nothing to do with our elimination from the tournament. Before the game, my father was called in by the organizers and told that one team would not play unless Junior Dean was benched. They did not want a black kid on the field, that day or any other. It was 1958, eleven years after Branch Rickey had paved the way for Jackie Robinson to play for the Brooklyn Dodgers. And Robinson, in his greatness and dignity, had opened the game up for Campanella and Newcomb and then Larry Doby, Luke Easter, and the others who followed.

My father considered the problem for a short time and decided that if Dean couldn't play he would rather forfeit the game, bow out of the tournament in protest. It sounded like a move Rickey himself might have made. My father told the organizers that in our town there were many different peoples and they were all treated alike. He would make no exception for Ulysses Dean, who had earned his starting position—had earned it with his glove, his bat, and his speed—and had been playing ball in the Rocks since he was ten. Take it or leave it. It did not take long for the other team to back down. Dean, as he always had been, was right there at first base.

I remember Breslow saying at some point, "You must have been proud."

★★★

In Pandocchi's article, the focus was clearly the social activities surrounding the tournament. We were indeed treated as guests of honor. There was a trip to Mount Baldy, a "patio party" at the home of a former Pittsburgher, an excursion to Lake Arrowhead, a visit to a chicken ranch, an evening banquet sponsored by the Lockheed Aircraft Company, and an outing to Knott's Berry Farm.

I recall only one play, and uncharacteristically for me, it was a hit. It was a totally preternatural event, like a green flash that cracks the sky on the evening horizon off Manhattan Beach or a comet streaking through the desert night. Not only was it a hit, it was a *beautiful* hit. A triple, lyrically touching the far reaches of perfection. The pitcher had thrown a smoking fastball that came in low and inside. I swung. There was that sweet-spot feel when I hit it, that unmistakable sound of wood against cork. Against stretched leather. Solid. No vibrations down at the hand, as though my hand itself were made of ash. The ball shot low over the third baseman's head and fell far to the right of the left fielder, who had shifted toward shallow center. He was nowhere near the ball when it bounced off the left-field wall, ricocheting like a tiny white marble as I rounded second. I easily stretched this hit into a stand-up triple. My father was coaching third, and there was a look of astonishment on his face and then pride, and he slapped me on the shoulder and said, "Way to go. Nice work, Bill!" Before the inning was out, I had crossed the plate, carrying home one of our seven runs.

Had he really said what I thought he'd said? "Nice work." It sounded impossible. It must have been someone in the stands.

I felt this enormous sense of power, a power that comes only rarely and that lives in memory. It is the perfection of a living instant that cannot be improved upon. It lingers and cannot be lost. We are pointillists. We live for the point in time that is joy and convergence, as though heaven and earth have become joined and jolted.

On August 30, the team bus left California for the Rocks. My father and I stayed behind. He had always wanted to go to Mexico and Vegas. We rented a car and drove to San Diego and then across the border onto the crowded mud streets of Tijuana. I remember the barren hills south of San Diego, and a big, neon-lit street with trolley tracks and a taut overhead system of wires. There was a white building with the words *Jai Alai* written on it. I asked my father what that meant, and he told me it was a sport, like lacrosse, that was played at high speed with a big scoop of a racket like the one pictured on the side of the building. That was as much as he knew about this strange game. The Blue Album contains only a single picture of our time there. In the photo, I am standing with my arm around a lovely, dark-haired girl in a black dress and high heels, and I am wearing a white shirt and a big sombrero. I'm sure he had this picture staged, because it would not have occurred to me to approach a stranger, let alone *this* lovely stranger, and ask her to stand by my side.

The next day we were back in Los Angeles at the Santa Fe Railroad Station, waiting for the Super Chief to arrive and carry us east. Of this trip I can recall only a few things. We stopped in Las Vegas and spent the night at the Stardust Hotel, where my father asked if it would be okay if he went out for the night "to play some cards," as he put it. I told him I'd be fine; there were a few magazines scattered around, and I was tired anyway from our baseball and sightseeing marathon and preferred to go to sleep. I have no idea how long he was out or how he entertained himself. But I suspect that he enjoyed the fullness and opportunities of a Vegas evening, probably at more than cards.

On the train—with its dining cars and starched linens and the dome car where I spent much of my time in the thrall of landscapes I could finally see—he introduced himself and talked with everyone in sight. At dinner, we usually joined a table where there were extra seats and he could get to know where people were from and what they did for a living. He had such an easy way with strangers, and he seemed proud to regale them with stories of our adventures in California. I envied him this.

There was only one person on the train that I wanted to talk with, a smiling, dark-haired girl who walked with a fluid motion, her skirt swaying side to side. She sat opposite us and appeared to be my age. But I could think of nothing to say to her, and I could not imagine how I could sustain a conversation, once initiated. I thought of myself as dull and awkward, and she appeared so confident. Why would she want to talk with me?

It is hard to know why I felt this way. When I looked at the photographs of myself in Pandocchi's article, I saw a kid standing with military bearing at Boulder Dam. I had a buzz cut and was wearing a white T-shirt with a western bolo tie around my neck. My arms were muscular, and I looked strong enough to have easily hit a low fastball for a solid triple into left. There was even a whiff of cockiness in the way I was standing, a future (in my fantasies) West Point cadet facing directly into the camera. But it was a lie of photography, a desert chimera. On the train, my father said, as he had before, "Bill, you need to be more confident in yourself." *But how?* I wondered. *How did he do it? Where did his ease with people come from?* He never told me. There were no tips, no secrets disclosed.

Through Wyoming and on through the flatness of the prairie,

I thought, *Any time now I will find something to say to her, something interesting.* But I never did.

***

Breslow seemed affected by these stories. He certainly took enough notes. Then he glanced at his watch. "We should end here," he said.

Truck (1960s) Bill Green at a practice session at Catholic University.

8

TRUCK (1960S)

Evening. It was off beyond the fence. There was a lit cigar you could see through the window and smoke curling up in the cab. Was he judging me? Looking for perfection? Or was he just proud that I was doing this?

***

I related to Breslow my itinerant, seemingly endless years at college. I told him about my first year away, about my uncertainties about what to study and about my deep sense of failure. I had left Pittsburgh to attend the Catholic University of America and was rewarded by a dash of cold, wet reality from which it would take me years to recover.

My time in Washington, DC, was not easy. I had entered as an aeronautical engineering student, but I soon learned that I had difficulty seeing objects in three dimensions, imagining them from the side and the top or turned at an angle. I struggled with mechanical drawing—the smooth wooden board, the T squares and protractors, the plastic triangles—until one autumn morning, in frustration, I stabbed the course textbook with my Swiss Army knife and threw it from the window of my dorm down onto the browning grass. After this outburst of textbook defenestration, I visited the registrar's office and withdrew from the course on the spot. I would never be an engineer.

There was little in the curriculum that interested me. History, calculus (what, exactly, was the point of all those derivations?), freshman composition, with its painful, arterial bloodletting of red ink, became, within weeks, sources of misery and self-doubt. What had those twelve years at de Sales, with their awards and honors, the honor of being chosen class president and valedictorian, really meant? In the context of the Catholic University America, I was beginning to see myself as an irredeemable failure. Only chemistry held the least bit of interest for me. In the sulfurous fumes of the chemistry laboratory, I felt a vague historical kinship with the past. Flames, retorts, bizarre quests into the unspoken mysteries of the world: the cosmos as seen in a flask. It felt a little like the stars and the darkness beyond the attic window, all strange and enigmatic and beckoning into a vastness of things unknown.

It was spring before I found my footing. I decided to major in chemistry, and at the insistence of my laboratory instructor, I enrolled in the honors section of that course.

In early spring, I tried out for the varsity baseball team. I had no scholarship, unlike most of the players that year, and had no reason to think I would be anything but a bench warmer. But after three tryouts, after a beautiful stillness of confidence had fallen upon me—a confidence born of years of practice in cinder alleys and basements and tournaments in faraway cities—it was clear that I would be playing second base for the CU Cardinals. In DC and Virginia and in towns throughout the North and South, I again proved myself a gifted fielder. With Jimmy Hudunich at short, the double play between us became what it was always meant to be—the most poetic of movements on the diamond.

***

Despite the many pleasures of the capital and the proximity

of Aunt Mary Jo, Uncle Irvin, and their two sons, I traveled often to Pittsburgh. I missed my family more than I would admit to myself, and I missed my friend McMullen. I missed Estella, whose voice and touch, whose very presence, filled me with joy. I thought this affection might end when I left Pittsburgh, but it only grew more intense.

Estella and I had met as seniors in high school, when we both attended the Westinghouse Science Lecture Series held each Saturday for teacher-recommended students in the Pittsburgh schools. I enjoyed talking with her from the first time we sat together and shared coffee and cookies in the cafeteria and contemplated the Second Law of Thermodynamics. Later that year we met again, at West View Park's Danceland—a venerable art deco setting of big bands and slowly revolving metallic spheres that cast skeins of romantic desert starlight across the expanse of polished floor. I recall holding her one late evening and fading into some hitherto unknown trance of movement and sound from which all else seemed to disappear. At that moment, I thought I might be in love.

I think I received more letters from my father than anyone that year in Washington. They arrived with the usual advice and the hopelessly mistaken belief that I was incapable of anything but the most dazzling academic success. His short note of December 9, 1960, is an example of what appears, poignantly, to be a naive confidence in his flailing, doubt-ridden son, who at that moment was wondering what exactly he was doing in college.

> Dear Bill:
>
> Your Mother and I were so happy to hear the results of your exams, I know you should like to have done better but you must consider its your first year & everything is new to you, we know that you will improve as you go along, all we ask is that you will give it what you have and not

waste your time and I am sure you will be up with the leaders. We are going to buy you a pen and some writing paper for Christmas so we might get a letter once in awhile. I have been working every evening & Sat & Sun on the new project that's the reason I was in bed when you called, I was tired. I am enclosing a check for $25, you no doubt need some cash, although you have your train ticket, you will have to use it coming home because it is only good from Washington to Pgh. We had several letters from Eugene & he tells us you don't write to him, so get on the ball kid. Our address is

Mr. and Mrs. James W. Green
134 Amelia St.
McKees Rocks, Pa.
Your Dad

In early 1961, after the Christmas holidays, Aunt Gene wrote with phonetic spelling in a light, penciled script, encouraging me to move beyond the foolish destruction I had visited on our Chevy station wagon—a burned-out engine, no less—an act that had caused little but season's grief and a week of sullenness marked by total silence on my father's part. "Do not even attempt to speak to me," his hard face and demeanor commanded. Knowing that sullen countenance, those big, listless hands at his side, the way he brushed by me in the hallway without the least acknowledgment, I could not even hazard an apology, let alone a full explanation for what had occurred. (Driving over a hundred miles per hour! Was there an explanation for that?) Dinners were grueling affairs, and we could not begin a conversation until my father had pushed away from the table.

Of our holiday troubles, Aunt Gene wrote,

Dear Bill,

Received your letter today and was so glad to hear from you. I hope by the time you get this letter you will have sent your Mother and Dad a letter. I am not telling them I heard from you because tha may think you have forgotten thim. I know how hard it is to take at times, but you must buck up and start over again. You now how good your Mother and Dad are to you it may not seem like it to you now but think it over and wright to them. I think you shoud wright to that man at Westinghouse if you have not heard from him. I am send his name and address. See what you can do.

Keep up your hope. I never hard from Aunt Mary. I am going to wright her today.

You had better get back in that ball game. Glad to hear you went to the show. I hard from way back that is a good show. I am glad to hear you like it.

Remember you must get that letter to your Mother and Dad before the weeks end. I am not going to say a word to them I sent you a letter this is between you and me. Please get back in the swing of things and forget all that happened and look forward to your next trip home and do good in your school work. I am with you all the way. The car is going again so dount worry.

Love Aunt Gene

There were letters, too, from my mother and Aunt Agnes. With my mother, there were always the sounds of good tidings and news from the family and the Rocks and the occasional jibe about the brevity of my own letters. Agnes tended to be the advice-giver and the celebrant of my parents, especially my father, whose sacrifices and love, in her opinion, had no limits, and who in her eyes bestrode the world of fatherhood. Whether or not they were intended to, her letters never failed to induce in me a sense of guilt.

At one point, in March 1961, Agnes wrote,

> Your dad has done more for you than many other fathers do. He idolizes the three of you. I know he expects nothing in return except love, respect, and obedience. He has often remarked to me that he has three wonderful children. The only thing that bothers him is that he feels that you should confide in him a little more than you do. Don't let anyone take the place of your mother and dad.

Is that all? I wondered. *Love, respect, and obedience?* Breslow would one day find these expectations of great interest in his analysis. Somehow it always took Agnes to put my father's thoughts into language. He simply could not do it himself.

> Wed. April 12, 1961
>
> My dearest Bill,
>
> Since we haven't heard from you, I presume you arrived safely in D.C. I would like to have a few details on the trip if you are not too busy to supply them.
>
> Things have been moving along rather slowly with the exception of the preparations we are making for our operetta. The matinee will be held this afternoon and then regular performances Thurs. and Fri.

How were your games or were you unable to play because of the bad weather? (We have had too much of it.) Let us know what happened.

The car is again running, but I don't know for how long. That thing is a real mess.

I do hope you are attending all your classes and keeping up your usual good work.

Try to write soon and let us know about your activities.

With lots of love,
Mother

***

In 1961, I left CU behind, returned home, and enrolled at the University of Pittsburgh. I wanted to finish my undergraduate degree in two more years, and Pitt, with its novel trimester system, was the perfect place for me to do it. Why I felt it necessary to rush through college, a time many people consider to be the best years of their lives, is entirely lost on me. I cannot find evidence for my motives anywhere. I had no idea where I was going, but I wanted to get there fast.

By the time I transferred, Pittsburgh had become, even with its smoke- and grime-filled visage and its fetid rivers, a city tinged with romance. It was, after all, the city where Estella lived, where we had met as high school seniors on those cold winter mornings at Westinghouse, where we had discussed viscosity and superconductivity and other deep matters of the heart. And she would be there for another three years before setting off for graduate school. In that time, who knew what might happen.

But there was another motive, and it was compelling. With a fine year of baseball behind me in Washington, and a diminished fear of public performance on the diamond, I wanted to try a more demanding athletic conference with more challenging teams, and I had few doubts that I would end up at second base for the Pitt Panthers. "Just walk out there and show 'em what you've got," I said to myself in my more supremely cocky moments. There was still this vestigial belief that I'd held from childhood that I was destined to play in the Big Show, at least for a time, before I moved on to something that the science of chemistry would magically open for me.

Spring practice began in winter, when it was too cold and the ground was too raw and hard to play outside. So for tryouts we used the Pitt field house, whose smooth wooden boards made fielding grounders a dream. The hops were true, and all that mattered were your range and swiftness and the ease with which you could backhand a ball or charge it and pick it from the floor and release it to first in a single, fluid motion. And the double play felt exactly the same on wood as it did on clay, since the ball came only by air and the art was in the release and the movement of the glove to the hand and the cock of the arm and the touch of the bag, so subtle it was hardly noticeable.

Again there was a scholarship kid on second, but Bob Santini, the senior catcher, said, "I've never seen anyone play the position like you. Coach has gotta give it to you." So despite everything, despite the physics and quant labs, the organic and physical chemistry, and all the lit courses I was coming to love, I felt I could somehow work in the demands of varsity baseball without too much difficulty.

By early 1962, it was warm enough to play intrasquad games outdoors. The field felt rough and hard, the ground was cold, and the ball, when you hit it, sent shivering pulses up the wooden bat right through your hands. Still it felt good to be outside in the real world of wind and dusk and the trademark air of Pittsburgh, in which we would soon be playing.

Beyond the meshed cyclone fence in deep right field, an orange truck would appear in late afternoon. In it sat a single figure dressed in a black woolen uniform and white cap. His gaze was fixed on the spot between first and second, or, at times, on the white, irregular pentagon of home plate. From this position he could see the turn of a double play, or the long run of a figure toward shallow right field, where ball and glove met in some kind of kinematic miracle of timing. From this position, he could see a pair of cold hands with a bat send a line drive down the third baseline, just over the third baseman's head. And perhaps at that moment, he thought of California and the way the palm trees swayed in a light breeze beyond the left-field fence.

This scene with the orange truck played out many times, and at dusk I would walk out to meet it and to greet my father and thank him for coming to pick me up. "I think I've got it made, Dad, just like at Catholic U," I said, sinking into the warm, acrid opulence of his smoke-filled cab. Ahh!

But then the news came. It came from Coach. He called me into his unadorned office at the field house. It looked much like my father's place at the Craft Avenue Car Barn, but without that old, stale smell of cigar smoke. "I hadn't realized you're a transfer," he said. It sounded almost like an accusation. Like, "I didn't know you were a convicted felon, and now that I do, well, that changes things."

I glanced at him with what must have been a quizzical look.

"You understand what that means," he said. "Don't you?"

"No," I muttered, "I … I … I'm afraid I don't." And I didn't. I was completely bewildered. But I knew from the tone of his voice that this was not good news.

He put his hands over his eyes and there was a moment of silence. "It's an NCAA rule I've never agreed with," he said slowly. "But transfers, transfers like yourself, well, you're required to spend an academic year in residence before you can play varsity." He had a frown on his face, as though it pained him to deliver this news. "You understand?"

I nodded my head.

"You're only a sophomore," he said. "So you can plan on playing here for two years if you want."

Then he apologized for not having known of my situation earlier.

The message had not really sunk in, but I had to say something and not just stand there in front of him, slack-jawed, with my eyes averted. "Ah, yeah, right," I said. "I'm sorry about this, but I didn't know. I guess I should have told you."

"Look," he said, "Most people don't even know what the NCAA is. And no one can follow their rules or know the reasoning behind them. It helps to be a lawyer, and I'm not one."

I tried to squeeze out a smile, but I didn't come anywhere close to it. I was staring at my shoes. I felt my lips moving, and then a sound emerged that might have been close to "Thanks, Coach. Thanks for the tryout, for giving me a chance. I'll be seeing you next spring." We shook hands and I stood there for a second, motionless, before I remembered there was a door somewhere nearby.

When I left his office, my glove was folded tightly, pressed hard to my waist, and my head was down. I had no idea what this news meant for the future. Did I still want to get out of Pitt a year early? Did I want to extend my education an extra year just to play baseball? Or was this simply the end of the game for me? Was it the end of something that had begun in the back alley when I was four, when I could smell the fresh bread from the bakery only twenty feet away and hear in the distance the sound of a ball game on the radio? Maybe I should have stayed at CU. Things were simple then.

***

I exited the hissing folding doors of the trolley that evening in the Rocks and stepped onto Chartiers Avenue, where I began the slow, dejected ten-minute walk home. On Amelia, the trees were starting to bud and the orange truck was already parked at the curb in front of the house. I turned from the sidewalk toward the cracked cement steps that led to the porch and then through the front door and into the hallway. The smell of dinner still hung in the air, and from the kitchen I heard the familiar click of silverware being put in the drawer.

Mother and Aunt Gene were cleaning up, and Liz was seated at the dining room table with her advanced algebra book open to a page of word problems. My father was in the living room preparing for a speedy exit to some bar or other—probably the usual Wil-Kar Grill—and Mitzi was asleep on the carpeted floor. In deference to Liz, the TV was off. And there was no music from the radio.

★★★

In the end, I decided to finish Pitt in two years, as I had planned. With a schedule that included so many challenging courses packed into a few trimesters, I knew that trying out for the Panthers and playing a demanding schedule, much of it on the road, was no longer an option. My best bet, it seemed, was graduate school, but before I pursued this, I finally had that talk with my father.

One snowy January evening, when he seemed less anxious than usual to be gone from the house, I said, "Dad, do you have a minute?"

"Sure," he said without hesitation. "What's on your mind?"

"Well," I said, "I'm scheduled to graduate this summer. I'm twenty-one and I can't get baseball out of my mind. It has been with me so many years. What would you think about getting me a tryout with Detroit this spring? Or next spring? Down in Florida."

"You mean talking with Cy Williams?" he said.

"Yes," I said. "I'd like to give it a shot."

He was silent for a moment. He checked his wallet to make sure he had Cy's number. I knew when he looked at Cy's card—looked at it hard for a long time—he must have been thinking of Sam McDowell, "Sudden" Sam, the kid both he and Cy had wanted to sign with the Tigers. But that had not gone well, and in the end McDowell had decided to accept a $75,000 bonus and go with the Cleveland Indians. It was heartbreaking for my father. After all, he thought he had discovered Sam that year we went to California.

After a minute, he said, "Let me see what I can do."

Then he was off.

Indiana Cornfield. (1963-1964)

9

MIDWEST (1963–64)

What I remember is the wind. The early morning cold. The endless rows of corn, tall and waving in the autumn fields. The flatness.

★★★

That fall, bachelor's degree in hand, I decided to try graduate school after all. I accepted a fellowship at Purdue University to begin work on my PhD. I lasted a year and a half before I felt I could no longer take another college course, another equation, another moment in the laboratory, another promising research project that seemed destined to go directly into the annals of failure. I could no longer take what seemed to be the infinite expanse of time that lay between me and the doctorate; that lay between me and what I knew was a mirage. I was giving up my youth for those "damn books."

From that year and a half in Lafayette, Indiana, as eventful as they were, I have found only a few letters—and of course these were found after my father's death, just as all the others were—and not a single photograph. None of the correspondence provides a hint of the turmoil in which I was engulfed; I must have conveyed to my family that all was well and my course was as clear as a ship's on a star-filled night.

Jul. 1964

Dear Bill,

Well, dear heart, I suppose I've waited long enough before adding my entry to the summer mail. Please accept my most humble apologies for not writing sooner, O Holy One. I have no excuse for my negligence. I beg you upon bended knee to forego punishment so that I may fulfill life's duties.

I hope my decision to enter Duquesne University has not put me on your blacklist for life. I looked over both of the catalogs from Pitt and D. and decided that D. had history courses, which would be more beneficial to my chosen field. I realize you never thought too much of the Bluff, but I hope in the next three years I can bring it up somewhat in your eyes …

As things stand now, I suppose I shall be unemployed for the summer. I have tried several places but none seems to need my able assistance. However, I have not been totally lax about my duties around the house. As of today, I just finished washing the walls of the upstairs boudoirs, including that scum-filled hovel of yours. I swear you haven't touched it for two years. I had to hire a dump truck to remove all the dirt.

How has your work been coming along? Still plugging around with the math courses? Believe me, pal, I really feel for you.

Well, I guess I shall discontinue for a while. Please write soon. Good luck with everything.

Needless to say we all miss you very much. Take care!

Love, Liz

Good old Liz. Sarcastic. Irreverent. Filled with secrets about her longing for far-off places. I loved her.

August, 1964

My dearest Bill,

At this point all of us are eagerly looking forward to seeing you at the end of the week. I fully realize, however, that between now and then there looms a certain major obstruction, namely a test for which you are probably making preparations at this very moment. We shall be offering prayers for your success and hope you will do the same. Good luck!

Mary Louise drove me and Sister to Virginia last week in the Lincoln …

Dad went to Cleveland yesterday with Al, Harry, and Red Schlentner and will return home tonight. They went there to arrange for an Elks affair in October and to see a game. I hope Sam McDowell is pitching.

Father Connolly passed his first test and will take the others in November. He wants to see you.

We will be looking forward to seeing you on Saturday.

With lots of love,
Mother

★★★

Sometime in October, my father arrived unannounced in West Lafayette with his friend Bill Marm. They came in a brown Dodge Polara. He said he could only stay for a day. That evening as we sat in my room, he handed me a set of keys and announced, "Bill, the car outside—it's for you. I want you to use it so you can travel back to Pittsburgh. Maybe you'll visit us more often." He laughed. There was a broad grin on his reddish face.

I took the keys. They sparkled in my hand as I shook them to convince myself that they were real. I thanked him, saying I had never expected *this.* I asked him and Marm how they planned to get back to Pittsburgh. "Train," my father said. "You know I love the trains."

★★★

The last letter of the year came from Estella, who by this time was studying in Kansas. It was postmarked December 7, 1964.

She talked about Teilhard de Chardin, whom we were both reading. But more than the popular and celebrated *Phenomenon of Man,* she liked Teilhard's mystical reflections in *The Divine Milieu.* She wondered how the two of us were always reading the same things at the same time, and she concluded that we had a special telepathic ability to communicate across great distances.

She told me I should be with her right now in Kansas, should be there to experience the first snow of the year. "SNOW. Everywhere drifting, deep windy and just SNOW," she wrote. Then she wrote the words that for me will forever define her: "I just love being alive."

She wrote a few weeks later. It was after Christmas. She wished I had been home in Pittsburgh and thanked me for a gift I had sent. She said she felt I was nearby, but then decided it must have been wishful thinking. I folded the letter carefully and put it in my file.

***

I wondered why I was there—lonely West Lafayette, lonely Purdue. Books on inorganic chemistry, physical chemistry, analytical chemistry, and other subjects crowded my desk. I was remembering that the shape of phosphorus pentachloride was trigonal bipyramidal and that phosphorus hexachloride was octahedral. I knew the hybridized orbitals involved and could see them, all fluffy and cloudlike. I kind of liked this stuff, *inorganic* chemistry. Atoms, always moving but linked in different ways, a myriad of forms created in their swift and sundry associations. But the atoms themselves? Ah, these were eternal! Not like ourselves, fleeting and gone in a second. Still, enough was enough. I was exhausted. Everyone'd gone for the holidays: empty campus, cold winds whipping across the unbroken flatness of barren fields. My father's gift, the Dodge Polara, sat out in the parking lot, a temptation. Waiting.

I turned back to my books on instrumental analysis, to thoughts of the upcoming qualifying exams for which, ostensibly, I was studying and for which I was sacrificing the Christmas holidays. But I couldn't concentrate. My mind blurred and wandered. It transited distant landscapes. Barren mountains of umber and russet blended into the endless heaped sands of the deserts. Great rivers carved slowly, inexorably, into obdurate stone, revealing time and time in a micrometer-by-micrometer unveiling. Dissolution. Abrasion. The wearing away of stone. The dissolution of whole continents.

The books before me could not compete, would never compete. One instrument, one technique, faded without distinction into another: ultraviolet-visible spectroscopy, nuclear magnetic resonance, polarography, gas chromatography. Methods of analysis. Who cared?

In the morning I cleared my desk, ran downstairs, shook the silver keys, and started the Polara.

California Orange Grove. (1965)

10

WEST (1965)

There was a deep cold that settled over the Midwest in January 1965. The skies were threatening snow. All I knew was that I was headed west. It was freedom and empty roads and a thin scrawl of snow. It all felt right and beautiful.

***

In my mind, it had been decades since the Colt League World Series, but in reality, only seven years had passed. This was nothing really, a mere drop in time. And yet so much had changed in my life and in my father's life. I had finished a degree in chemistry at Pitt and had gone off to study for my PhD at Purdue. My father's *wunderbare jahre* had gone. He was no longer president of Little League, and his days of tournaments and winning teams had seemingly passed.

"It's a beaut," my father had said when he handed me the keys to the Polara. "A real beaut!" I had a copy of *Travels With Charlie* in my pocket and a pile of El Producto cigars on the passenger seat. These were not the fat, acrid stogies my father smoked; they were thin, with plastic tips, and they burned with the sweet smell of cherries.

It was cold and snowy. Across Kansas, the corn silos rose

and disappeared, the Eiffel Towers of the plains. I was off to somewhere, but I had no idea where. All I knew was I was heading west. I would stop in Kansas to be with Estella, and then I would visit the tiny village of Santa Fe to see her cousin.

Along the way, I napped at truck stops, ate at all-night lunch counters, imagined myself in dim paintings, hunched over coffee and a big burger and some tattered paperback, feeling not anomic or lonely but free and unburdened, with all those historic two-lane highways that might lead anywhere. In Tucumcari, I called home for the first time. I talked with my mother and told her I had decided to forego the qualifying exams for my degree and had opted instead to drop out and see what the larger world had in store.

She sounded shocked. "Where are you, Bill? Where are you calling from?"

I told her I was in New Mexico, in a small town called Tucumcari, and I would let her know where I ended up when I got there. "Tell Dad I'm okay," I said. "I'm okay. I'm tired. I've been driving straight through from my layover in Kansas." I told her not to worry and to tell my father not to worry. "The roads have been great, empty, and I'm feeling good and in good health. It's all just so beautiful."

Tucumcari, I learned, was named after a nearby mountain. The name might have been derived from a Comanche word meaning "lying in wait for someone to approach." Well, I guessed the place had been lying in wait for me all those years, and here I was, so I decided to accommodate the Comanche and stay for a night. I booked a room at the Palomino Motel on Route 66, and the next morning I treated myself to bacon and eggs and had the car filled up by the uniformed attendant at the local Texaco. He was dressed in gray with the red company logo, and he cleaned the windshield, pumped the gas, and even checked the oil. "Looks good," he said, holding up the shimmering dipstick. *God I love 66!* I said to myself.

***

Then I set off across the most desolate stretch of highway I had ever driven, the road from Tucumcari to Las Vegas, New Mexico. Highway 104 passed through sere brown hills with sparse vegetation. There was not a single car anywhere. I had no idea where I was going, but I was driving under cerulean skies, listening to Bach, and experiencing episodic flights of mind and spirit that placed me square in union with the blissful center of the universe. Where did I leave off and the infinite sky begin?

Along the way to nowhere, I stopped in Santa Fe for a day, overnighted in Flagstaff for several hours until the snow on the roads melted, and passed through San Bernardino, and then—either out of sheer exhaustion or a sense of familiarity—I decided where I would I go. It was the only place out there I knew: Ontario, California, the home of Colt League Baseball, thirty miles east of LA. The streets I drove through looked as they had back in the late '50s, and the place seemed hospitable enough, and I soon found a room at the Commercial Hotel, where I paid a reasonable monthly rent, less than a hundred bucks.

Once settled, I called home and told my parents where I had ended up. My father immediately offered me the names of former Pennsylvanians he had met during his two glory summers in the city. I dutifully took down the names and thanked him, even though I had no intention of contacting anyone. He never mentioned the Polara.

By now my mother seemed completely untroubled, as though somehow my childhood had predicted just such a misadventure as this. She was concerned only that I write frequently to tell them what I was doing and what my plans were. She was happy I had crossed the country without incident.

My father obsessed over my hopeless fecklessness with money and, as always, worried that I might not be eating well or that I might be in debt back in Indiana or other states farther west.

"Have you applied for a job yet, Bill?" he asked. "You have all the right education, and you should be able to find something in a few weeks ... California is booming, from everything I hear."

Then he asked whether he could send money and I said, no, I was expecting my last paycheck from Purdue any day. Ah yes, a month of teaching in hot, sulfurous, freshman laboratories on cold winter mornings had rewarded me with the princely sum of $250.

★★★

My father was right. I did find something in a few weeks. In no time, I was picking oranges in the sweet-smelling groves all around Ontario. I was a *bracero*, and even if I wasn't making much money, I was making enough, and I was doing something I enjoyed. Hot sun, physical labor, climbing trees like a kid, pulling fresh oranges off branches, peeling and eating them right on the spot, juice flowing warm down my face in sticky little runnels. I was getting good at this. My hands were quick and certain, the hands of a guy who'd once played second.

More than a strong back, you needed to have dexterity in this business of orange picking. You needed to be able to rush at the ladder, clippers in hand, and when you reached the top rungs, you had to break into the trees, into their fullness and density, and wrest the oranges, hands flying, from the branch to the bag swinging on your left hip. I got dirty and sweaty, and all of this reminded me of jobs my father had found me in the summers, digging trenches and operating jackhammers and tampers and other equipment, but in far less hospitable environments than this, which, when you stopped a second and took it all in, was glorious in its hues and vistas cast into the distant smog-bound mountains.

I knew nothing about migrant workers and their hard lives and the money they had come north to make before returning home. I knew nothing of their dreams, their villages, their childhoods, the dusty roads they had traveled. All I knew was that I was working with people I liked and I was working at my own pace in sunshine and orange-scented air. And I was paying the rent and living on oatmeal and cheeseburgers, and at twenty-three, who could beat that?

It was true there had been job offers over in La Verne, Riverside, and Compton, doing tech stuff at a lab bench, but that was exactly what I didn't want. Weigh, titrate, run stuff through flames—who needed it? I realized I was fleeing all that.

Fleeing those instruments and those "damn books," possibly forever.

The Commercial Hotel was no one's idea of posh living. It was inhabited by old guys on pensions; by people who drank too much or were broken and way down on their luck and spent their days sitting around talking, flipping through moldy issues of dog-eared magazines, or aimlessly walking the streets. Perhaps in the faded pages of *Life* and *Look* they found images of what might have been for them or what might still be. But in the Commercial, the air seemed drained of hope.

Guys wandered around in nightshirts, going nowhere, not even talking about going anywhere. There was no talk of big dreams, just a lot of padding through stale, dim hallways that smelled of booze. The super was a woman I judged to be forty-five or fifty and whom I never saw without a soiled white nightgown and a bottle of cheap wine in her hand. Her name was Pearl, and she owned a dilapidated trailer up in the foothills, where she had once raised her kids, made a tire swing for them to play on, and tolerated a no-good drunk of a husband until she could take it no longer and kicked him out. The kids were grown now, but she kept the trailer as a retreat—memories, she said. When I told her my story one night, she said, "You go get that degree."

The Commercial was not especially well kept, and there were reports from some of the guys that they had spotted rats. I never saw one myself, but I did see plenty of cockroaches. They scurried about as soon as I turned on the one bare lightbulb that hung in eternal pendular motion from the ceiling right above the center of my bed. Outside, in the alleyways, a few women worked the night. Some I found attractive. Their prices were low, and no one much cared who came and went through the dim hallways and rooms of the hotel.

Concerns about cleanliness and all the imagined or real critters moving in the darkness prompted me, unwisely, to wear socks when I went to bed. Day after day they clung to my feet, grafting themselves onto my skin. Within a few weeks, my feet had broken into a full-bloom fungal infection, and I was going slightly mad from the itching and from scratching until my feet bled little rivulets onto the sheets. "Look, kid," Crapo from down the hall said, "always take care of your feet. You're nothing without them." I thought of Aunt Gene, her feet dangling uselessly from the wheelchair, and I had to agree with him. "And watch out for those ladies too."

It wasn't long before I'd developed a bulge in my groin that I mistook for a rupture I had suffered in the orange groves, or maybe something worse. Some dreaded disease. "Oh, not *that*," I said to myself.

Wrongly, I decided it might be time to give up my clippers and ladder and shoulder bag for another kind of work, one that made use of my education. In no time I found a job as an egg picker on a chicken ranch not far from Ontario. The ranch, with its long rows of chicken coops under artificial light, was owned by a Hollywood studio musician. He looked at me quizzically when I told him I was interested in the job he had advertised. I told him I needed the money and really loved good physical labor. So what had I been doing in school all those years, he wondered, and what was I running from back East?

After seeing a doctor, I learned that the lump in my groin was associated with the foot fungus and had nothing to do with orange picking or any of my other activities. When I heard this I was sorry I had given up the trees for the chickens, but the money was better out at the ranch, and I would need money to go wherever I was going next. I told my friend down the hall at the Commercial Hotel, "You were right, Crapo. It was all about my damn feet."

"Yep, kid," he said. "You need any advice, you come and see me."

Kid! I still looked like I was sixteen.

***

At the Commercial I had an address; I could write letters and receive them. The first came from Estella, whom by now I had known nearly six years.

During our time together in Pittsburgh, we saw one another regularly, talked by phone on cold winter nights when the snow was too deep for travel, and enjoyed an easy friendship unburdened by obligation or commitment that neither of us was prepared to make. This continued for years and through great distances that only letters, phone calls, and the occasional road trip could bridge.

She got my new address at the Commercial from my father and wrote, "Dear Bill, happy 23rd, out there." She told me she thought about me often. She commented on the note she'd received from my father and mentioned how much faith he had in me and how much he loved me. "I've been waiting to send it to you and have faith that it will get to you this way."

She talked about a short letter she'd received from her cousin in Santa Fe—"nothing but happiness."

Then she thanked me for stopping to visit her and told me how much I had taught her about love. I found this cryptic, as I often found her words, but I realized how much I missed her and how much I wished I had ended my journey in Kansas.

***

In California, I never pursued a job in chemistry even though

I had a degree in the subject and a year and a half of graduate work at one of the best universities in the country. My father found this perplexing. "You just don't have confidence in yourself, Bill. You're older now, and you need to get some."

But where did you get self-confidence? It had always come so easily to him. So train-ride easily, as if he were the mayor of anyplace he ever went. How had he acquired it? Was it locked up in the spiral towers of DNA that everyone was talking about? Were there instruction manuals for this trait that you could simply pluck from a library shelf? I was at a bit of a loss, and I realized, as did my musician employer, that I was slightly underemployed. But I was happy to have a job sufficiently remunerative to allow me the pleasures of a roof over my head and occasional things to do at night, to say nothing of funds to buy books and travel around the state on weekends and even down into San Diego and the colorful, animated mud-squalor of Tijuana.

***

On this matter of self-confidence, I recalled a conversation my father and Joe Vitelli had one night at a local tavern in the Rocks. It was after a ball game, and I was there even though I was too young to drink anything but Coke. They were talking about me as though I were on Saturn, and Joe Vitelli was saying, "Look, Jim, I think he's a really good second baseman—great hands, you know—but he's not tough enough and he doesn't believe in himself." When Joe Vitelli spoke, my father listened, because Joe had once pitched for the Pirates and he'd served in the Pacific in World War II. He was a man of the world. He could be trusted when it came to issues of character and real life. "And the ground he can cover, Jim. Well, you know that. It's amazing!"

Joe Vitelli was nursing an Iron City Beer, his left elbow on the bar and the bottle in his big right paw. "So here's what I think, Jim." He was leaning in with a conspiratorial tilt, his face, slightly flushed, inches away from my father's. "Jim, you gotta let him go. You're trying to protect him and you can't. You gotta cut him loose. You gotta let him go, be on his own." Then he had a big grin on his face. "Whattaya gonna do, Jim, be in the bedroom on his wedding night?"

My father's face reddened. He knew I was right there, not on that faraway ringed planet at all, and could hear everything.

"Joe, Joe," he said, "not now. Please, keep it down." And they changed the subject and ordered more beer for them and a Coke for me.

***

Antonio Joseph Vitelli, local hero and legend—denizen of a modest row house in the Rocks—died in the VA hospital in 1967, at the age of fifty-eight. You can visit him anytime. You can imbibe his spirit rising from the wet earth, from steep hills in the Rocks more lovely and peaceful than Malibu. He is buried in St. Mary's Cemetery in a grave not far from my father's. Steep hillside. Simple stone. No mention of baseball, the Pirates. No mention of "Joe the Horse." I remembered and stood there a long time in the rain, paying my respects.

***

The letters flew back and forth between the Rocks and the Inland Empire. I told them of my work and of my occasional travels that took me down south, where I visited Scripps and thought that oceanography, with its blend of hard physical shipboard labor and cerebral work, might be just what I was looking for. I drifted across the border, where the caduceus on the license of my secondhand Polara earned me the unearned title El Doctor. *Okay,* I thought, *sure, I'll take it. Why the hell not?* I wrote about Pasadena and Cal Tech and about Pomona, Riverside, and the beaches west of LA. Everything was exotic and new and tinged with romance, and my gaze was riveted on the present as I was living it and not on what was going on in the larger world of politics and historic racial struggles and the distinctive music and culture of the sixties that were beginning to flourish around me. I had no special awareness of anything but my own needs, my own interior wonderment and amazement, as though I had been freshly born. Yes, as Estella had said, *alive*!

★★★

In her letters, my mother, who had never been to California, seemed far more interested in the ambience of place and in the nature of my unfamiliar work than in my living and eating habits or my health. I think she somehow assumed that as long as I was in regular contact with them, I was doing just fine. More intriguing for her were the origins of place names—Santa Monica, Ontario, Riverside, the freeway system around LA (the Ten and the Four-Oh-Five)—the distance of the San Andreas Fault from the Commercial Hotel, and my one and only experience with a surfboard at Manhattan Beach (it did not turn out well). On March 21, 1965, she wrote in her customarily cheerful, newsy voice about events back home. There was even advice, as there always had been when I was a kid, on proper grammatical usage, something involving split infinitives.

Also in March, Aunt Agnes wrote, betraying a hint of skepticism about my situation, redeemed only by her memory of my father's youth and how he had done something similar at my age:

> Dear Bill,
>
> I believe your father is worried about you. He doesn't say much, but you can tell.

Guilt. Agnes, with her black, floor-length habit, her black bonnet and white collar, black bow at the throat. Sisters of

Charity. She could be counted on to induce a sense of guilt. "Your father is … Doesn't say much, but …" Her letters, straight from some convent.

But in his letters, my father never said any of this. He was concerned about practical matters. The laundry of life. He wanted to know about the Dodge Polara. "You need to make sure the tires are good, Bill, especially on those freeways, and that the car is well-lubed." There was never a mention of the fact that he had bought the car for me to get me from Indiana to Pennsylvania, not for some pointless journey into the Far West. That possibility, when he proudly presented me with the gift in October, had never entered his mind. Nor had it entered mine.

Then there was my father's usual obsession with matters requiring paperwork, all of which he knew I disdained: license plates, debts, draft notices. How was I spending my meager earnings? I couldn't have been spending it all on oatmeal, rice, and beans and the monthly rent at the splendid Commercial. So why was I always broke? And he wanted to know about my health and about the athlete's foot, with which he himself had a lifetime acquaintance. As Agnes had said, "I believe he is worried about you."

And there was the prospect of a possible visit. He wanted to see my situation for himself, since no one in the extended family had ever been so impulsive or downright foolish as to give up on a life's plan and a fine education to set off into the complete unknown. After my second month in California, there were only hints that he might do this. But in time I could see (fear!) that his uncertainty was lifting like the morning smog in Ontario.

Several of his letters stand out:

> Dear Bill,
>
> I sent your license plates today and the motor club is going to send them direct to you so if there is any change in address let me know right away. Friday de Sales plays their first regional game

at South Catholic against a team from Erie and if they win I think they go to Maryland. Your Mother had a real bad cold but feels better now. Eugene just finished a retreat and of course is in good spirits. I saw an ad in the paper. Santa Fe Railroad has a round trip to California for $98.00 so after you get settled maybe I'll take a train ride. Cy Williams wrote to me and wanted me to come to Florida but I don't think Ill make it this year. Liz is really hitting the books and doing well in school. I think you have been an inspiration to her and Eugene as far as education is concerned.

Love,
Dad

Dear Bill,

I just came from the R.R. station where I picked up my tickets. I am due to arrive in Pomona at 11:35 Sunday morning April 4th. Pomona is only about 6 miles from Ontario. I want to go to Long Beach to see a friend of mine and maybe over to Catalina of course I would like to see our friends in Ontario and if you want to come back so we are in time to see Eugene maybe we should leave Sat. Apr. 11th or maybe sooner it all depends on how things go, we want to take our time and maybe stop at a few places of interest. I just hung up from talking with Bill Marm he would like for us to stop and see his mother in La Mesa, you remember her, we stopped to see her before in '58. Hope to see you Sunday.

Love,
Dad

***

Breslow knew this story. I had told him of my California adventures, had related them at length. As usual, when he finally offered his interpretation, he focused not on my father's largesse—his purchase of the Polara; his offer to travel, at great expense, to California—but on his meddling, his officiousness, his unwillingness to loosen that continent-spanning, globe-spanning grip. "Even at that distance, even across the country, he was trying to hold you. He was trying to smother you."

I got the point. But hearing it from Breslow over and over was balm to me. I liked the smell, the healing nature of it.

Breslow's story had not changed: the flying water bucket, the bitterness that passed between my father and me each Christmas as we set up the holiday train layout—these and other events seemed to Breslow iconic of our relationship. He listened, and listened at length, to the contradictory evidence I brought to his attention, but he seemed never to weave these threads, bright and colorful as they were to me, into the tapestry that I could see was taking form in the confines of his office. If this selective sorting of data seemed to me a flagrant violation of the fundamental laws of hypothesis formation and testing, I never mentioned it to him. I rarely challenged his interpretation of events, but rather took them as opinions to be considered. He was the doctor.

Arizona Desert Scene. (1965)

11

(EAST, 1965)

In one of our sessions on the subject of California, Breslow asked how it had all turned out, and so I told him the story of my return east with my father and what I had learned on our short road trip. I began with my memory of the week or so prior to my father's arrival.

On one of my last nights in Ontario, I set off toward the coast and drove up the winding hills above Malibu. There I sat on the grass, looking down on the Pacific Coast Highway and beyond at the vast Pacific, out to the horizon. The earth seemed to curve in the distance, a gentle bending arc into the blueness of space. I was aware that I had done few of the things I had imagined doing. I could barely afford breakfast. Had taken the first job I was offered. Stayed in a flophouse. Picked oranges, fed chickens, collected their eggs. I read books on the Great Plains and the history of LA, all under the dimness of the single lightbulb that drifted above the bed. I had written countless impressionistic essays and odd, directionless poems that I'd left wadded in the trash along with greasy wrappers and half-eaten fries. I had really met no one with whom I would ever correspond again.

I wished things could have turned out differently, the way I had dreamed it crossing the deserts and mountains, the way I had imagined it in Tucumcari. And yet somehow I knew that, years hence, I would remember all of this with great fondness.

★★★

As we'd agreed, I met him on the platform of the Union Pacific Station in Pomona, east of Los Angeles. He was smiling and red-faced from the bar car. I thought he looked fine. He greeted me with his usual handshake, oddly limp and passive, and asked me what freeway we should take to get to Ontario. Of course he wanted to drive, as I knew he would, so I handed him the keys and led him to the car. I had repaired the brakes with money I'd made pawning my slide rule. I would never see that precious slide rule—pride and joy of my budding scientific youth—again.

We drove east on I-10 to Ontario and took Euclid Boulevard to the Commercial Hotel. Once inside, he looked around. He walked slowly down the dark hallway toward my room. "So this is where you ended up?" He had a bemused look on his face and was nodding his head in that slow way that suggests incredulity. *Youth,* he must have been thinking. *I remember, I was once young too.* There was not a word of criticism.

I introduced him to Pearl, who greeted him in the same soiled nightgown, a cigarette dangling from her lips. "He's been a good guest," she said. "No problems at all."

We checked out and he got us a room in a nearby Travelodge, which seemed bright and clean. It was pure luxury to me. Then we went out for dinner. "You must be hungry," he said. "You've lost lots of weight. I remember a good restaurant from the tournament in 1959. We can go there."

"Fine," I said. "I could use a big plate of spaghetti. How's that sound?"

So I indulged myself. I ate and I ate as though I had not eaten properly in months, and I probably hadn't. He seemed pleased that I was enjoying myself. He relaxed across from me with a beer in his hand and occasionally threw off a question about the place and the work and how the car had performed for me on the freeways. I told him that everything was good and I had finally gotten accustomed to pushing buttons to shift the Polara into forward and reverse.

I didn't drink much in those days, and we rarely shared a beer, though I wish we had. Maybe it would have made the conversation less formal than it became and the silences less frequent. *Maybe someday, though, maybe someday we would have that beer.*

In the days that followed, he called the Pennsylvanians who had treated him as a hero when he arrived in Ontario with his champion teams in '58 and '59. We met with the Whirls, formerly of Penn Township, and he reminded me that their daughter, Janie, had been a Pennsylvania state princess. We sat in their living room and chatted, mostly about California and its rapid growth since the late '50s, when we were there. They had questions about Pittsburgh, since no one had been back recently, and my father told them how the big GM buses had come in and all but replaced the trolleys, whose tracks had been smothered over with asphalt. "It's a shame," he said, shaking his head. "You can taste the diesel fumes when you drive behind them. And they just don't look as nice."

They wanted to know about the mills, and my father said he could see they were in trouble. "They just look old," he said. "They're beginning to rust out. Ya know, I bought a bar down in the Rocks a few years ago, and I'm beginning to see the guys from the graveyard shifts disappear. I think it might be the mills."

They wanted to know about baseball, and he told them he was coaching a Little League team called the Pirates. "I was elected exalted ruler of the Elks a couple a years ago," he said proudly, "and that's taking a lot of my time." He gave a little smile, as though he was uncertain whether they knew what the

Elks organization was all about. Whirl smiled and said, "That's great, Jim."

I suspected that the Whirls knew all about the Elks, even though I hadn't the faintest idea what they did. I resolved that on our return trip I'd ask my father about this, about what it meant to be exalted ruler.

Mrs. Whirl wanted to know what I thought of California, and I told her that I loved it and had enjoyed the weather and the hard outdoor work once I got the hang of it. "And what are you going to do once you leave?" she asked. I told her that I wasn't sure, but I might go back to school and try again for my PhD. "I think that would be good," she said. "Your father says you're very gifted at chemistry."

She told us that Janie was married now and that they were the grandparents of a little girl. She seemed delighted by this, and my father said congratulations. "How about you, Jim?" she asked. "Any grandkids yet?"

And so it went for two hours or more until my father said it might be time for us to leave, since we had a big trip coming up tomorrow. If he was disappointed that I had not contacted the Whirl family or anyone else from his glory days of the 1950s, he never said so.

***

We left early the next day for San Diego. We visited another acquaintance and then once again crossed the border into Mexico, where my father had a beer called Corona, which neither of us had ever heard of. In Arizona we drove to the edge of a deep canyon and peered over the rim into the dark river far below. My father stood there for only a short time before he backed away and returned to the car. He patiently waited for me while I stood there listening for the sound of water, but I could not hear it over the wind. When I returned to the car, he looked pale.

I recalled something Liz had told me, that he could no longer drive his truck through the tunnels around Pittsburgh. For the last two years, she said, he'd gone out of his way to avoid the Squirrel Hill Tunnel, which was more than four thousand feet long. When I was younger, we had driven through it many times, and he'd had no problem at all negotiating the many tunnels of the Pennsylvania Turnpike. But at age fifty-seven, he had these new fears. He panicked.

We were making good time on our drive to Pittsburgh. On the Great Plains, I told him some things I had learned in my travels about windmills and barbed wire and why they were so important in this treeless, waterless landscape, which was so different from what we knew back East. I told him how Hamlin Garland had written short stories about the wind out here and the haunting effects it had on the early settlers, the way it moaned around the houses. He listened quietly and said, "These things are interesting, Bill. Where did you learn all this?" I was surprised that he actually found my bookish knowledge worth something.

***

I kept only the most meager notes on our trip, and he took no photographs. It seems as though we were trying just to get back to the Rocks, and little else. But I did write a few words in my Purdue Planner, on the calendar pages that reminded me I had gone to a poetry reading in West Lafayette. It was by Brother Antoninus, a poet of the San Francisco Renaissance ("Clack your beaks you cormorants and kittiwakes"), whose images of Northern California had impelled me, on one long weekend journey, toward Big Sur and Carmel. At Purdue, I had also attended a meeting of the Teilhard de Chardin Society, where we discussed *The Phenomenon of Man* and the noosphere and the Omega Point—how the evolved consciousness of man feels itself drawn toward some ineffable cosmic intelligence. I loved Teilhard's ideas. The universe seemed to tremble on every page of the *Phenomenon*.

Riding with my father, I thought that these events and musings, lightly penciled into my Purdue Planner, appeared to have come from another life.

There was enough space in this tattered notebook to jot down that on April 15, 1965, my father and I spent the night in Groom, Texas. The next morning was a Sunday, and he insisted that we go to a nearby church for Mass. We sat in the back pew, where he could unobtrusively rest his eyes as the sermon droned on.

Later that morning, we stopped at a small café. He ate his eggs sunny-side up with a double helping of crisp bacon and a large pile of buttered toast. As I spooned through my oatmeal, I decided to ask him about those events back at Pitt from nearly two years before: the news about my ineligibility to play baseball as a transfer student, our talk about a tryout with Detroit, and his talk with Cy Williams and eventual advice to me.

"You loved baseball all your life, Dad. All your life you managed teams, you won championships, you had an eye for greatness—in the way a kid moved, his spirit, his hustle and flare for the game. You could see something inside him. Maybe it was desire, hunger, I don't know. And you could see it before anyone else could. There was Sudden Sam. Glenn Beckert. Bob Priddy. All of them made it, and you could see it coming when they were twelve, sixteen. Early."

"And I saw some of that in you," he said, crunching on a strip of bacon and washing it down with freshly poured coffee.

"Then why did you give me the advice you did?"

"I saw what it was like down in the minors," he said. "I heard all the stories. I hear them from Cy and the players. I've been down to Florida enough times to know what's going on."

"And what is?" I asked.

"Like I told you back then, it's a hard life. Small towns,

all-night bus rides, lots of drinking and whoring around. Too many ways to mess up your life for good."

"There was something else, wasn't there?" I asked. "There was the weak hitting."

"I didn't worry so much about that. They had the best hitting coaches down there. Guys who could have given you lots of tips I never could. Joe Vitelli couldn't have either. You would have come around." He was mopping up his plate, the running yellow yolk and bits of bacon, with the last piece of buttered toast. He wiped his mouth with a napkin and balled it up. "No, that wasn't it. I thought you had other possibilities. You were always good at science and math. Both your mother and I saw that. Saw it real early. Agnes saw it too, and so did Mary and Irv. You were curious about everything."

"Back then you painted a pretty grim picture of the minors, Dad," I said. "Now, after all the chemistry, all the libraries and laboratories, it sounds to me like a great life adventure. I might have liked it. Maybe I should have taken it, seen what I had. I know I'll always wonder."

"Look," he said, "Cy was ready to set the whole thing up that spring. I told you that. No, you didn't screw up. Right now you just need to get yourself back on track. Get your head straight and get that damn degree. You don't want to be a quitter."

My oatmeal was getting cold, and it was mostly uneaten. I sensed he was ready to move on. He picked up the green check, pulled some cash from his wallet, and left a few dimes on the counter, and we headed for the door. Outside, all the flatness of North Texas lay around us. We had some driving to do.

***

On the way north toward Missouri, he asked me to tell him more about the orange picking. I told him I loved it. "It was like all those fresh mornings back in '58 when we were up practicing, when you were slapping out grounders. At the end of the day, I liked to throw an orange into the sky high above my head and catch it behind my back. The Mexican foreman—his name was Luis—seemed fascinated. He'd say, 'Where'd you learn that trick, amigo?'

"My last few weeks on the job, Luis and I would toss an orange between us in one of the long truck rows. He got really good, and so closing time ended with a little play and a few laughs, and we left the place in our separate vehicles, feeling good about the day's work."

"Good story," my father said. "You know, Bill, you're only twenty-three. You're in good shape. You still want that tryout, I can arrange it."

I smiled at him and shook my head. "Maybe, Dad. We'll see." I tried never to burn a bridge.

My father said he had always wanted to see the Merrimac Caverns. He said Jesse James and his brother, Frank, had used it as a hideout in the 1870s. It was nearby—there were signs all over Route 66—and he wanted to stop. We did not go deep into any of the narrow passageways of the cave (too much like the tunnels of Pittsburgh and the Pennsylvania Turnpike) but instead stayed in the great anteroom and heard a lecture on the history and geology of this spectacular formation: limestone, stalactites, stalagmites, the slow effects of water, drop by drop, over four hundred million years. This cursory exposure to the place seemed to satisfy him, and we were soon on the road.

***

All along our trip, you could see the coming of spring. A lovely blush, like that on a woman's cheek, rose up and flowed across the land, across the rivers—the Arkansas, the Platte, the Red—and into valleys where sunflowers and daisies sprang up in great profusion in fields of long grasses. The full colors of

Oklahoma and the first greenness and shoots up in Missouri and then just the hint of a new season in Illinois. With each mile north and east out of the sere brown desert south came the watered hues of the Midwest. To love the Midwest, you had to have a sense of subtlety. The place wasn't going to knock you over with its serrated mountains and deep canyons or the white silence of its ski slopes. It didn't speak in vast deserts and blue skies that at night put you right in the rounded palm of the cosmos. Nor could you hear from its interior vastness the call of the circumambient seas that washed the coasts.

No. It was grasses and infinite flatness, and unceasing winters where the sun could be hidden for weeks, as though that life-giving sphere were some majestic fiction. "How many words," someone once asked, "do Midwesterners have for 'boring'?" Yet there was beauty, if you could see it. It lay all about in lakes and cornfields, in the seasons that changed, in the fluff and mix of the clouds, in the way the air smelled of growth in springtime, with the soil breaking into new life. And all those cities, too, with their winds and their trumpets, like St. Louis and Chicago, and their river barges—all different, as though the seeds of urbanity had been widely sown by some invisible, far-reaching hand moving between the great mountains east and west. Such an extravagance to those who would open their eyes. Such a rebuke to those who would not.

***

We got to the city of Pittsburgh on April 18. Along the way, there were the usual questions about when to stop for food and when to fill up with gas and what radio station to listen to, if we could even find one. There were the long silences to which I had become accustomed over the years. But there were also some memorable conversations. We had had a pleasant experience, without friction. He was a good companion. I forgot to ask him about the Elks or what he did as exalted ruler and what kind of ceremonial clothes he wore, or whether, as some had said, he could ride off in ceremony into the distant future. I forgot to ask what the Elks meant to him, what they represented. I had sworn that I would ask all these things, that I would learn about this newly important part of his life, this part of which he was so proud. But as usual there were other things on my mind.

West View park, showing from left to right: Eugene, Liz and Bill.(1965)

12

TICKETS (1965)

It was through literature that he dropped the first hint—Isherwood—and I never saw it.

***

I wasn't expecting to learn anything. It was spring, and then summer. A time of rest.

In Pittsburgh, Amelia Street was leafy. The big maple in front of the house was still standing. Eugene was back from St. Meinrad. Neither of us had the prospect of a job, but my father, without ever asking, just assumed that we both wanted to work, and so as usual he set about making inquiries across the city. There was no limit to the people he knew and could call upon for a little favor.

During my three years in college—one in Washington, DC, and two in Pittsburgh—he had found me jobs as a pool guy, as a line worker at a local enameling plant in the Rocks, and as a pipeline worker out in Shadyside, not far from Carnegie Tech, as it was known then. When I was sixteen or so, I carried mail as a temporary extra during the Christmas season, when the bulk of cards and letters far exceeded the capacity of the regular staff. And during my two years at Pitt, I mopped floors in the mornings at the Wil-Kar Grill, which my father had recently purchased. There was always some job to be had, and I knew it wouldn't be long before one of his contacts came through. As for Eugene, he'd gotten the real plum—a summer job in the steel mills—a year or so earlier.

Sure enough, within two weeks my father had arranged work for Eugene and me. "I talked with Jack Hickey this morning," he said. "He wants to see you and your brother at West View Park at nine o'clock tomorrow. You know where the park is, don't you?"

"Sure, Dad," I said, "I've been there many times."

"Good," he said. "You wanna talk with Jack Hickey. He's in the main office right there on the left side as you walk down the Midway." Who Jack Hickey was or how my father knew him, I had no idea. He had nothing to do with baseball.

The year West View Park closed, twelve years after Eugene and I worked there, it was as though a shroud descended and bells of mourning rang out across the city. The *Pittsburgh Post-Gazette* wrote of abandoned rides and ticket booths fading, unpainted, into desuetude. Even the dips, from which screams of excitement once reverberated throughout the park, rose and fell in silence. But in the spring of 1965, when Eugene and I entered Mr. Hickey's office, the park was in its heyday. It was alive. And Mr. Hickey sat there behind his desk, a man in his element and without worries, smiling at the two of us with a tilt of his head and an ease that permeated the room.

"Your father says you need a job," he said. "Which of you is the reverend?" And Eugene said, "I guess that's me."

"So you must be the professor," he said, directing a bemused look at me. I nodded, and he said, "Good."

It mattered not at all to him that neither of us was anything but a student, but throughout our time at West View Park these are the only names the amiable Mr. Hickey would call us. Maybe he was prescient, or maybe my father had convinced him that his two sons were destined for these very appellations. Jack was one smart, perceptive guy. Regardless of their origin, these titles were conferred in good spirits and were always a source of amusement to Eugene and me.

"Okay, Rev, how's the ticket stuff going?" I'd ask Eugene as we drove to the next school to sell tickets to the students for their annual picnic.

***

To the north of the city there is a park where, as kids, we often went with our family for picnics on the Fourth of July or Memorial Day or for no special reason. In the middle of the park was a small lake, and in spring and summer you could rent a rowboat or kayak there. The lake was a narrow thread of water that ran southeast to northwest and was bordered to the north by a steep, wooded hill. There was a large gray boathouse of some architectural distinction, concession stands, and, at the water's edge, a fleet of colorful boats that bobbed gently against the pier. In the early spring, there were few people there to disturb the tranquility.

We both rowed, and as we rowed, we talked. Eugene loved to discuss his studies and comment on the books and poems he was reading. That afternoon he seemed especially intrigued by the works of Christopher Isherwood, a writer I had never heard of.

"What about Isherwood?" I asked. "What do you recommend?"

He gave me a brief introduction to Isherwood, to his life and work, and said, "I suggest you read *A Single Man*. I won't tell you what it's about. You'll see."

We had rowed far up the thread into the northern bay of the lake, and it was time to turn around. The sky was darkening in the onset of early evening, and between thoughts and reflections, we had finished our cheese and tomato sandwiches and sipped our Cokes and were beginning to feel hungry again.

★★★

We agreed that we liked working at West View. We talked about what a great guy Jack Hickey was and how our partners, the directionless "Beagle Boys," were more cheerful and fun than we could have expected.

Our job was to sell long strings of yellow tickets at schools throughout the city. These could be used for the giant dips and the tilt-a-whirl, the laugh-in-the-dark, and the two-tracked racer. The students came to our tables talking excitedly about their upcoming picnic and offering us ones and fives that we placed in a metal box. The days were long, and the three-dimensional landscape of Pittsburgh sometimes made it difficult to find the school we were looking for. "Look, I can see it, Eudge—I just can't figure out how we're going to get there."

★★★

Eugene and I laughed a lot that spring, and Jack Hickey seemed understanding of our directional shortcomings. "It's not an easy city, Professor," he'd say to me by way of excusing my spatial ineptitude. I had a feeling he liked both of us, and we liked him, and it all went by swiftly and ended with warm good-byes. "Give me a call if you ever need a job again," Jack said.

Somewhere around June, I made arrangements to return to Purdue, where I was offered an ongoing graduate assistantship. My father seemed pleased that my hapless adventures in the West had concluded and that I was getting serious about a profession and finishing my degree. When I left, he extended a warm hand at arm's length and we said good-bye, without mention of the two of us having crossed the country together.

I found time later that summer to read *A Single Man*. It was a great book, and I wondered if Eugene had been trying to tell me something about himself through the novel. But what? Something about his relationships that he could not express outright? It was not unlike him to be subtle in matters of personal revelation.

It would have taken so little to ask him, "What did you see in *A Single Man*, Eugene? What did you want *me* to see? Was it LA in the early sixties? Was it how it felt to teach college? Or was it George and his passionate relationship with Jim? Did you want me to see that?" But I could not bring myself to ask, even though I suspected it was the last of these. As with so much else, we did not discuss the novel further, even though I liked it and planned on reading more of Isherwood's works.

We let whatever memories we had of our pleasant lake outing rest in silence.

Dinners

13

Events, Revelations, Dinners (1950s–60s)

It looks bad. Something crazy is going to happen. I can feel it.

***

It's the problem of love. Which child do you love more? Do we have a meter for this? No, of course not. Then how can we possibly know?

Breslow inquired at one point whether my parents had treated us all equally, or whether I had noticed over the years some disparity in their affections. I think at one time or another each of us asked our mother whom she loved most. And at this question, she would simply smile and say, "Well of course I love you all *equally*. You know that." I wondered how that could be true, because to my mind love was an exhaustible resource, much like a precious metal, and surely, I thought, she must have partitioned it in some slightly inequitable way. It seemed to me that Eugene, given his calling to the priesthood and her own religiosity, would have been singled out for her favor. But she claimed that this was not so, and her letters to me, as if to prove the point, were always signed, "With lots of love, Mother." I assumed that she signed her letters to Eugene and Elizabeth in the same manner. Eventually

I had to conclude that my analogy had been incorrect and that love, being measureless, was different from gold or silver. You could not put it on a scale.

***

Of my father, we never asked the question. It was just not the kind of thing he would have responded to—metaphysical, insubstantial. But Breslow was not interested in hearing about some philosophical discussion, in which my father was not wont to engage anyway. Breslow was interested in action. "What things did you *do* with him?" he asked. "I know about the games of catch, but what else was there? Did you go hiking or camping with him, or just walking with him through town?"

I had to give this a little thought. What had we done together, just the two of us? "Well," I said, "there was more than catch in the back alley. He liked to go out with me to some grassy field, maybe it would be the football field at Stowe or the field down on Neville Island. This would usually be in the evening, in the summers, when it was getting cool and the light was beginning to fade and there was no one else there."

"And what did you do?" he asked, as though he had no familiarity with baseball or what a father and son might do in a big, open field.

I said, "What comes to mind first are the fly balls. He loved to have me out in center field. It was just me in a wide-open space, under a blue sky and with the smell of cut grass, and he would hit me these long fly balls. Some off to the left, some to the right, some that made me run in and catch them at shoe-top level, and others that I would have to run deep for and snag with one hand over my right shoulder, back against the fence."

"But you were an infielder. You played second." Breslow seemed curious about why my father wasn't having me practice grounders.

"You know, I loved it. I loved the feeling of open space, the feel of the grass. And I think my father enjoyed using his power to hit the ball as far as he could." I looked directly at Breslow and smiled. "I remember—those were great times!"

"What else?" he asked. "What else did you do together?"

And I told him my father had bought a pitching machine, one of those spidery metal things where a ball rolls down a track into a mechanical scoop of a hand and the hand rears back and throws the ball hard toward the plate. He would stand out on the mound with this spindly aluminum creature and fill it with balls he kept in a cloth sack, and I would be at the plate. Every minute or so, a ball would cross the plate at a good speed, and I would swing and try to hit it as far as I could. Or he would tell me to "lay one down," and I would hold out the bat horizontal to the ground and bunt one down the first baseline or the third baseline. Sometimes he would have me run them out.

"How did you like that?" Breslow asked. His head was down and he was taking notes, as he had throughout the session.

"I preferred shagging flies, but I liked this too. It was good batting practice. It was something I needed, and my father knew that. It probably bored him, but he knew it was good for me."

When we met the next time, I told him about Eugene and Liz. But first I told him about something I had forgotten: the Big Card Drop-Offs on the front porch. When I was nine, ten, eleven, twelve, somewhere in there, I spent some portion of my summer days seated on the floor of the porch with my pinball game. The game was glass-covered, tilted upward at a fifteen-degree angle, and had a variety of slots for outs, singles, doubles, and so on. In the center was a lighted plastic mesa that read Home Run. You shot the metal pinball up a chute, and it rolled into one of the slots. The usual rules of the game applied. Three outs and you changed sides.

I played this game using baseball cards. I arranged the cards for each team to form the lineup I preferred. So if the Indians were playing the Yanks, I had two stacks of cards with Avila, the second baseman, my lead-off for the Tribe, on top of the stack, Larry Doby second, and so on down the order until I got to Early Wynn, who was hitting ninth and pitching that day. I did the same for the Yanks. Then I launched my first ball for Avila and watched it roll down through the maze of hits and outs, and if he was out I noted it on my scorecard. In this way I went through a nine-inning ballgame.

But I had a haphazard way of collecting cards for my teams. It involved stopping at Kramer's corner store after my paper route and buying a pack of cards, opening it, folding the fragrant pink sheet of bubblegum into my mouth, and going through my random purchases. No matter how many packs of cards I bought, there were always players missing, and so much to my displeasure, I always had to put in second stringers.

My father, knowing how much I liked this harmless amusement, and pleased that I was learning all the players and their stats, occasionally surprised me. Sometimes after work, if his route ended in downtown Pittsburgh, he would stop at his favorite cigar store, buy a box of El Productos, talk with the guys for a while, and then purchase an enormous supply of brand-new cards for me. He would greet me on the porch, usually after six, and say, "I got you something."

He'd hand down a box to me on the floor, where I was working my way through a game, and I'd say with great excitement, "Thanks, Dad! Where'd you get these?" And the answer would always be the same, delivered after a pause and a big puff of blue-white smoke from his new cigar.

Breslow seemed bemused by my devotion to this game. He even gave me a little smile and a nod of his head. "What were you feeling when your father did this?"

"I was happy. I was grateful. And I was surprised. I just couldn't wait to see what all those packs of cards had in them. I knew they would complete a lot of my teams. And I liked to stack the bubble gum and shuffle it like cards and smell that sweet aroma and then stuff one of the sheets into my mouth."

"What else?" Breslow wanted to know, and I said, "My father seemed big and important in those moments. That he could do this."

***

Breslow wanted to know about Eugene. I told him Eugene was not interested in baseball, even though for a year or two he played for the Indians. Mostly he rode the bench, but once in a while, when we were far ahead, my father put him in. But eventually he gave up baseball and joined the Boy Scouts, where he became an accomplished naturalist. Our family rarely went camping, and I remember only one trip that involved pitching a tent and sleeping outdoors. This ill-fated expedition lasted exactly one night, during which my mother, appalled at the thought of sleeping on the ground, opted to stay in the back of our station wagon. The other four of us slept in a big tent.

That night it poured for hours, and the rain beat down on the canvas tent, making our sleep fitful at best. But Eugene, who was our guide to the natural world, our Thoreau and our Muir, had had the foresight to "ditch" the tent, to dig deep trenches along the sides so that the streamlets that would have otherwise come flowing in among us instead drained harmlessly into the forest. In the morning, we awoke to sunshine and birds and my father made his flapjacks and my mother prepared coffee and we sat happily at a picnic table, enjoying the sun. When he served Eugene, my father put his hand on his shoulder and smiled down on him and said, "Nature boy!" That was all he said, but it was enough. After breakfast and a game of catch in which we all participated, my mother announced that she would not spend another night in this horrible place, and in the afternoon we packed up and left.

When Eugene went to St. Meinrad Seminary for his first year

of high school, we often drove to that small cathedral town in southern Indiana to visit him. In the winter, he took us down to a frozen pond on the seminary grounds. Wearing skates and his long, black cassock, he would glide out with the same grace that my father and his pretty, red-haired sister, Mary Cecilia, had once exhibited on the ice of the Rox Arena. *Shusssh* went the skates as he sailed by us in an effortless run. I could see my father smiling. There was a glow of pride, maybe a touch of memory in that smile. Perhaps for him, as for both Eugene and me, skating was peace and solace, the perfection of the world put right.

My father respected my brother's choice to enter the clergy, and at such a young age too. He respected his studiousness and the fact that he read all those obscure books and was learning Greek. He liked Eugene's seminary friends—Mosslener and the others—whom he found amusing and so unlike the kids he coached in baseball. But in the end, he spent little time with Eugene, and the two of them found little in common.

After I finished speaking, there was no comment from Breslow, just the movement of his pen and the infrequent glance up from his notes. Sensing that he wanted me to continue, I began to tell him about Liz.

I cannot recall that my father ever tried to teach her how to play catch, which in those days was the most that the girls I knew did. We had no softball or Little League teams for girls, and most of us thought that it was physically impossible for a girl to throw a baseball very far anyway. "You throw like a girl" was a street insult that no self-respecting guy wanted to hear. My father did create a bowling league for fathers, sons, and a few daughters at the local Eagles Club, and Liz was on our team. Unlike my mother, he always referred to my sister as "Liz" and not "Sister," which seemed to cast her in a lesser, derivative light against her two brothers. Liz did engage in "girls' games" like skipping rope and playing hopscotch, but the dexterity and often high levels of coordination that these required were mostly overlooked. As soon as Liz was old enough, my father made certain that she could ride a bike; he oversaw her training on the sidewalk that ran the length of Amelia.

It can be said that he appreciated her intelligence and the fact that she was always first in her class and would graduate high school as valedictorian. From the nuns he received nothing but glowing reports about his only daughter, who was given the same rewards for achievement that we were. In a grudging way, he respected her independence and her toughness and her challenges to his authority, which led to mostly unspoken, but by no means concealed, hostility that often took the form of his long, hurtful silences. This simmering resentment would manifest itself in later years. Liz was gutsy, no doubt about it.

When she was ready for college—and there was no question that she would go—he found the money somewhere to send her east to Albertus Magnus, a prestigious Catholic girls' school run by the Dominican Sisters in New Haven, near Yale. She spent a year there but then decided for an assortment of reasons, both social and academic, that it was not a good fit for her, and she came back to Pittsburgh, where she attended Duquesne and lived, as I had, at home. Through his many contacts in the city, our father found her summer jobs, just as he had found them for Eugene and me, but otherwise he placed no work or financial demands on us that would have interfered with our attention to our studies. School was paramount. Where he and our mother—who was teaching middle school in the Rocks by then—found the money to help us was a mystery. For our part, we simply took all this largesse for granted, our just desserts for having so graciously agreed to walk upon the earth and breathe its air.

A special gift, at least as I saw it, was the cherished ticket Dad gave to her and to her alone, for game seven of the 1960 World Series. The game, one of the greatest in baseball history, was played at Forbes Field between the highly favored New York Yankees and the Pittsburgh Pirates. It was a slugfest, where a total of nineteen runs were scored, the lead changed several times, and there was not a single strikeout. There were many beautiful plays on that crisp October day, but, in memory, nothing would compare to Bill Mazerowski's walk-off home run in the bottom of the ninth inning. This gave the Pirates a 10–9 victory over the storied team of Mantle, Ford, and Berra. And Elizabeth Ann was there. She saw it all!

"That was quite a gift," Breslow remarked. "I remember that game myself. How the whole city celebrated."

But in the end, I told Breslow, she felt uneasy with my father, uneasy in his presence. When she revealed to the family shortly after her graduation that she was joining the Peace Corps, there was a combined shock and disbelief that spread from my parents outward to our near and distant relatives and my father's many friends. No one in the Rocks had ever done this, and Liz, who had shown little interest in travel or road trips or any form of adventure beyond the city limits, seemed an unlikely candidate for this bold move.

When asked by Aunt Agnes why in heaven she was doing this, Liz pointed to the next room, where my father was working on bills, and said in an angry tone, "Because of him!" Sister Agnes Louise would never forget this. Nor would she forgive Liz for having said it of her beloved brother.

Breslow listened to most of this with that impassive face of his, without asking me a single question. The only hint of interest was the meticulous note keeping that suggested a certain keen attentiveness to what I had said. When I finally fell silent, he began a brief summary and interpretation.

"So," he said, "your father did a lot for the three of you. They both did. They made sacrifices and with little gratitude, it seems." He paused for a few seconds to let what he had said sink in. "What they got in return was your performance. You all did well in something they valued. You were serious students, and you were willing to work, and your father, especially, seems to have admired that, though he probably didn't say much."

I nodded. We had, in fact, given them that much, though at that moment it seemed to me meager, a pittance. It would seem even more so as the years passed.

Then Breslow made an abrupt shift. "In your father's eyes," he said, "you were different. You loved something he really understood and cared about, and he spent countless hours with you outside the house, on all those ball fields. Eugene and Elizabeth must have seen that. There must have been resentment, even though they were given the same benefits you were."

He stopped there, and I told him I didn't see it; I didn't feel it. I was on great terms with both Liz and Eugene, and I loved both of them, and with Eugene I had had this long correspondence that spanned a decade and had ended only because we were both in the same city and could meet when we wanted.

★★★

Many years after my sessions with Breslow, my daughter Dana asked me in the context of a discussion on food and restaurants, "Dad, when you were young, how often did you and your family go out for fine dining?"

"Fine dining!" I laughed. "I think the answer there, Dana, is an unequivocal zero." She looked surprised by my jocular tone. I said, "Remember, Dana—when I was a kid, those were different times. People cooked. Ate at home. Eating out was rare. It was a big deal. A really big deal!" I lifted my eyebrows and smiled.

I told her we did go out once in a while, however, and when we did it was special. My father's favorite place was Sunny Jim's over on Camp Horne Road. There were the five of us (Aunt Gene, as usual, remained at home, an act of exclusion that none of us ever questioned), and we ordered chicken in a basket; my father ordered "philly of soil," as he called the popular fish, which

I once thought resided only in the Schuylkill River near the City of Brotherly Love. I remember liking their famous chicken in a basket, which consisted of deep-fried chicken legs and the best fries ever made. My father had a draft of Iron City, my mother had coffee, and the three of us drank milk. The place was crowded and noisy and welcoming, and I never objected to going there.

Sometimes on a Sunday night, the Tap Club in the Rocks had a spaghetti dinner put on by one of the churches, and my father would take the three of us there. He loved this place and the taste of real Italian spaghetti and the whole ritual of twirling the thick strands of pasta with his fork against a big spoon. He seemed to know everyone, and people would come up to our table and say, "Hi, Jim, how ya been?" And he would have them sit down, and we would each be introduced if they didn't already know us.

We must have gone to a few other places, like the Knights of Columbus, but we never went to Hyeholde in Coraopolis Heights, which is where my parents had their wedding dinner. It was far too expensive for our whole family.

Dana nodded and understood the situation. I was pleased by her question, just as I was always pleased when my daughters cared to ask me anything about the past.

***

In several of my sessions, Breslow suggested that it would be worthwhile if we devoted time to our family eating habits. He believed that these sessions could provide revelations about my father and about the family and how things changed over time. Unfortunately I can't remember how many sessions we devoted to this topic, but they were revelatory—I had no doubt.

With few exceptions, our dinners were eaten at home. They were regular—between five and six, whenever my father got back from work. The conversations, as I recall, were rarely animated as you sometimes hear about in other families. But, as Liz recalls, they were not silent or awkward either. Other than "food talk," which was of little interest to me, we shared information about our day at school, or my father's day on the job, which sometimes involved an unusual event like a disturbance on one of the trolleys or an arrest. My father would occasionally mention the cop downtown, the one who directed rush hour traffic at Penn and Smithfield and drew unusually large crowds by dancing and gesturing and spinning full-circle on his heels. My father found his antics amusing.

"I remember him," Breslow interjected. "He was a minor celebrity."

There were more topics of conversation when my mother returned to teaching at Hamilton Junior High. She often related stories about her new colleagues, especially Mrs. Halgis, who was beautiful and who had once acted at the Pittsburgh Playhouse, or her mentor, Mrs. Bitner, who acted as her guide to the perplexing and enigmatic folkways of young teens.

When my father spoke, Aunt Gene was silent, but the rest of us had questions, and my mother, as she went about her dinner chores, dutifully moving between the stove and the table, kept up the flow of chitchat and gossip. Ordinary days, ordinary dinners, like millions of others across the land.

"But things changed in our college years," I said to Breslow. "And in my memory, they changed abruptly. Liz says we became insufferable."

"That's a strong word," Breslow said.

"I mean, we still gathered for dinners at the same table and the same time as during our childhood. But our talk shifted to books and ideas. My father sat silently at the end of the table, mixing his usual gravy onto his mashed potatoes, pretending he was listening."

"That glazed look?" Breslow inquired.

"Glazed is right."

I can't remember the exact words, but a typical dinner conversation might have gone like this:

Eugene is talking about the famous first lines of *Anna Karenina.* "All happy families are alike; each unhappy family is unhappy in its own way." His arms are raised above the table, and his long fingers extend, parallel, in the air. "You know," he says, looking at me, "I think Tolstoy is trying too hard to define a principle here. A kind of law of physics like something you might find in Newton. But human nature isn't like that; it does not lend itself to these easy generalizations."

"I think you're right on this one, Eugene," I say, and Liz nods her head in agreement. "I've had trouble with that line since the first time I heard it in Lawrence Lee's class at Pitt."

"But Tolstoy has it right when he talks about unhappy families," Eugene continues. "They are all different. One man hits his wife; another comes in drunk every night, can't keep a job; in other families, it's the kids—they hate school, they join gangs, they rebel against their strict upbringing. They hate their parents. They're all miserable in their own special way."

And I say, "Sure, he has it right, but the same diversity applies to happiness. It depends on what you value or what congeries of values can be said to characterize a particular group. One family lives in impoverished circumstances, yet there is a pervasive hope, and the parents and children love one another despite the hardships all around. Another family is well off, and they enjoy their circumstances and find spiritual rewards in giving to others who are not as fortunate. They have a sense of civic duty from top to bottom."

"I like Levin and Kitty," Eugene says. "They were the only happy ones in the novel."

"I agree," I say. "And they could skate. I loved that scene. So peaceful. I even went back to skating after I read it. Out at the old rink at Bridgeville." I forget to mention Aunt Mary Cel, my father, and the Rox Arena. I forget that my father ever skated. And with such improbable grace.

Liz says, "I haven't read this yet, but I don't think happiness characterizes any person or family for all time. I'm happy some days; others I'm not. The same seems true of all of us." And she sweeps her hand around the table, where my parents and Aunt Gene sit impassively, with no hint of a revealing expression. Are they even listening, or have they just tuned us out? Dad is probably thinking, if he's thinking anything, *What in the hell do they know, anyway? Nothing! They've never even had to hold on to a real job.*

Another time we are discussing Turgenev's *Fathers and Sons.* My father is right there, a few feet away. He has been a real father for decades, but we act as though he has absolutely nothing of value to say on the subject. After all, he hasn't read the book. Or any book that we know of.

Eugene says, "I think Bazarov is a defiant, pseudoscientific bore, with his nihilism and complete lack of human compassion. Look at the way he treats the hapless Uncle Pavel. I was hoping Pavel would hit him square between the eyes with that pistol shot. I like to imagine Bazarov dead on the ground."

Liz says, "That's not very Christian of you, Eugene. What are they teaching you down there in southern Indiana? Isn't that a seminary?"

The three of us are smiling, and Eugene takes Liz's comment as an amusing bit of sarcasm. My mother is back in the kitchen fetching a warm dish of asparagus, and my father and Aunt Gene offer the slightest trace of a smile.

My mother returns, and I begin an uninspired defense of poor Bazarov, with whom I also have problems. "Look, Eugene, I think he was just feeling the sweet winds of change that were blowing through Petersburg at the time. Think how exhilarating that must have felt. I've felt it myself with everything that's going on in science and society as a whole. As for human compassion, look at the scenes with his own family, their absolute undeniable love for him and his obvious, if somewhat condescending, sympathies for them. He also seems, naively, to have given his heart to that cold, undeserving … what's her name? Odinsova, is it? I think."

And Liz, who was interested in Russian history, says, "What about the liberal revolutions of 1848? Those worked their way into every corner of society and probably into Turgenev's novel."

"Still," I say, "this guy's a true believer. I've met too many of these ideologues—beards down to their navels, offering up dogma on everything. In their hearts, they're never wrong. Really distasteful bunch!"

Our eyes are moving from one speaker to another. Meanwhile my father is slowly angling out of his chair, probably wishing he were already down at the Wil-Kar Grill propping his elbows on the bar with a good, cold Iron City in his hand. And Aunt Gene is nodding off, her head down and bobbing a little, her eyes closed, her hands folded neatly on her lap. Her wheelchair absolutely still. My mother, whose domain was literature, especially Shakespeare, seems to be familiar with *Fathers and Sons*, but she sits there silently until the end. "Is everyone full?" she asks. "Good, I'll start the dishes."

In later years, especially after our conversation, our beer, at Sunny Jim's, I began to realize what my father must have been thinking. He must have looked at me and thought, *What does he know? He's never been married. Never suffered what this life can do to you. All he knows are those damn books. He doesn't know a damn thing.*

Breslow must have found this historical reconstruction of mine mildly interesting. He asked no questions but wrote several pages of notes.

***

In the last of our sessions on the subject, I recalled for Breslow a somewhat memorable event at the table—memorable, at least for me! Breslow took a special interest in this because it seemed a confirmation of his initial hypothesis. It occurred at Thanksgiving, at a time when Eugene was away in Indiana. I was in my second and final year at Pitt, and Liz was a senior at de Sales. My mother had prepared her usual big dinner featuring a fifteen-pound turkey, stuffing, mashed potatoes and gravy, and peas and carrots. She had made an apple pie and a pumpkin pie, both with her light, flaky crusts that we all loved. There was whipped cream and ice cream for the apple pie, and freshly brewed coffee. We began dinner, as we always did, with grace: "Bless us, O Lord, and these Thy gifts, which we are about to receive. From Thy bounty, through Christ, our Lord. Amen." Before and after this prayer, we crossed ourselves in the traditional way. Then, as the gravy boat was passed and my father stabbed at the turkey with his fork, we began to eat.

I'm not sure why it happened, but throughout the meal, throughout this wonderful feast that my mother had spent two days preparing, my father and Liz argued. It was a low-key affair with no outbursts from either side, but it was relentless. On and on they went, exchanging insults—about what I cannot recall. It might have involved Liz's upcoming decision about college, or a verbal attack by my father on one of her high school friends. But throughout the meal, I felt increasing irritation and then anger.

Finally I blurted it out: "Why are you two doing this?" My hands began to tremble when I heard my own voice, and I felt my face burning red, the way it would burn before a street fight. Somewhere within me, anger was turning to rage, and rage to action. I reached out and grabbed the fine china dish on which the browned turkey was laid. And I stood up from my chair, lifted the plate with the turkey high above my head, and slammed it down as hard as I could onto the table. I saw the dish shatter into a hundred shards, and I saw the turkey leap upward and bounce off the ceiling. My rage could not be contained. I flung the chair aside and stormed out of the room, through the kitchen, and out the back door into the freezing November air. I had on only a white T-shirt and Levis, and I began walking as fast as I could through the empty streets of the Rocks. I was far down Chartiers Avenue, beneath the PC&Y trestle, when a stranger said, "Son, it's cold out here. You need a coat. You'll catch pneumonia."

But I hardly noticed him, and I hardly noticed the cold. I kept on walking. And before I knew it I was high in the bare, wooded hills above the railroad tracks along West Carson Street, looking down on the city of Pittsburgh. I sat on the ground with my knees tucked up to my chin, and for the first time I began to feel the cold. I rocked back and forth, trying to warm myself, but I could not. I looked down toward the Point, where the drab, gray rivers joined, and I remembered the night my childhood friend, McMullen, and I swam in the Ohio and then moved slightly to the right into the cold of the Allegheny and then to the left and the warmth of the Monongahela. Later McMullen and I climbed the crumbling shale of Mount Washington, dangling precariously from broken rocks above the rails and the speeding freights of the P&LE. This was near the very spot where I was sitting.

The slope of the hillside was steep. I slowly worked my way back down, my anger all the while subsiding, draining off into the winter cold. Along the streets there was nothing open, and I had no money anyway, so I decided to walk home. I don't know how long I had been gone, but it seemed like many hours had passed.

I entered the house from the back door, the same door I had left from. In the kitchen, my mother and Aunt Gene were finishing the last of the dishes. They said nothing to me. The dining room had been cleaned, and the table had only a white spotless cloth on it. My father and Liz were nowhere to be seen.

It was as if nothing had happened! And yet everything had happened. That evening, and in the days and months that followed, no one ever spoke of this event.

Breslow, after a few moments of reflection, said, "It was time for you to go. It was time for you to leave home, to leave the

Rocks, to leave Pittsburgh. The anger you displayed was directed at your father, not at Liz. There were all those memories stored in it: Mitzi being kicked, Eugene being forced to kick the basement wall, your deathly ill mother being subjected to those paint fumes. His insults and his failure to praise. His absence. That void he left each night."

"I don't know," I said. "I just know what I was feeling at that moment."

"There were years stored up in that," Breslow said. "You were making a statement and he understood. He never challenged you. And he never spoke of it in the thirteen years you had with him before he died."

I was silent. I didn't want to be in Breslow's office any longer. I was feeling claustrophobic, nauseous. Without a word, I got up and left.

Breslow's summary should have been enough to trigger a description of what happened at JFK. But it wasn't.

***

I was twenty-one the year of the blowup. It was the year of my graduation from Pitt, which I celebrated in my minimalist fashion by rolling down one of the steep lawns near the Cathedral of Learning and shouting joyfully into the traffic noise, "I did it! I did it!" There were no parties. No cards. No congratulations from the relatives. This was only a small step on my way to somewhere. In the fall, I left for Purdue University to study for my doctorate in chemistry.

A young family in the midst of an argument.

14

Conflict

Tensions rose over the years. There is no lasting perfection. We are lucky to have what we have, despite the gaps and gorges.

***

My conversations with Breslow were gradually exposing the strains and cracks that existed within what I had once believed to be our perfect family. They were also revealing that I had not exactly been given the gift of perspicacity, and that if I were to survive in this world, I would soon have to acquire some. I thought I had been reflective, had understood everything. Mine was not the unexamined life, the life Aristotle had pronounced not worth living. But in time, and through Breslow's council, I saw the flaws that were there. In some cases they were more than mere flaws; they were chasms and fault lines prominent as the San Andreas. My ignorance was apparent.

The natural division between my siblings and me turned on their perception that I had been favored by my father and possibly by the entire Green clan—Aunt Agnes and the others. If Eugene and Liz were allies in some real or imaginary family conflict, they chose my mother as a natural partner. Arrayed against them, they positioned Aunt Gene, my father, and me, even though they surely realized that a deep tension had always existed between Gene and my father.

Long after my father's death, and long after my time with Breslow, Liz and Eugene remained in close contact. She had settled in Columbus and he in Boston, and the two of them kept in touch with phone calls and frequent visits between the two cities. In those days—roughly the period between 1975 and 1989, the year of Eugene's death—Liz came to know his friends in Boston and Cambridge, where he finished his PhD. And she became close friends with Chris, with whom Eugene lived for many seemingly happy years in an apartment on Beacon Hill. Eugene, in turn, came to know Liz's daughter, Jessica, who found her uncle, Father Eugene, to be a heroic, cosmopolitan figure around whom an aura of saintliness and scholarly achievement took form.

Despite our deep friendship of many years, reified in a large collection of letters that spanned more than a decade, my own relationship with my younger brother grew increasingly distant. From the time we both departed Pittsburgh in 1975—he for graduate study at Harvard, I for an academic appointment in Ohio—we saw little of one another except for the regular gatherings with my mother. We rarely missed holidays with her in the Rocks.

Not that there was active hostility between Eugene and me. There was not. But for some reason we made only rare efforts to see one another or to call. And there were no letters of the kind we had once written. In those years after 1975, I might have visited Boston three times, except toward the end. And he came to Oxford, Ohio, once to visit my family. "Bill," he said with a big smile of approval, "this is the perfect house for a professor." He attended a college seminar I was teaching on plate tectonics, and even though he was not a scientist, he seemed to enjoy the class and participated with a few questions of his own. For a short time he was the sweet, loving brother I remembered from the Pittsburgh Oratory, and our daughters greatly enjoyed his presence and the informal, chatty dinner we shared while seated, as always, on the living room floor.

"He's a handsome man, Bill," my wife said. "Gentle and elegant. The girls love him. He looks like Richard Chamberlain."

But no sooner had he come than he was gone. He was off to the International Medieval Conference in Muncie, Indiana, where he was presenting a paper on the sermons of Aelfric, one of the great medieval orators he had studied. He would not come to our house again.

As for my sister, in those years she was making her way through the ranks of the budget office at Ohio State University. She and I saw one another with some frequency, especially in the years when my mother spent winters with Liz and her daughter in Columbus. During that period, it was my responsibility to pick up my mother in Pittsburgh, drive her to Columbus, and then, a day or two later, continue on to Oxford.

***

The signs of fissure could not have been discerned by a casual observer, but they were there. Liz reminds me today, with some amusement, that during his years in divinity school in Toronto, Eugene seriously thought of changing his name from Eugene A. Green to E. Lancelot O'Donnell. At the time, I took this as either the pretensions of a budding literary scholar or complete and utter lunacy or, more likely, a rejection of my father, as evidenced by his proposed adoption of my mother's maiden name. Possibly it was all of these. But it never happened.

Another source of amusement is the distant memory of a fit of anger Liz once displayed toward me—her version of the Thanksgiving turkey. It occurred when I was a senior at Pitt and she a senior in high school, a time in our lives when we really should have been too old for such things. The incident was brought on either by a sudden provocation or by the slow buildup, possibly over years, of unexpressed anger.

I am sure I deserved whatever happened. Something I said set her off one afternoon after school, and she picked up my physical chemistry textbook, the old classic by Gordon Barrow that I was using at the time, and without warning let it fly directly at my head. There is no question where she was aiming. She had a good arm—she was her father's daughter, after all!—and she threw overhand with exceptional velocity. I saw it coming, a speeding textbook about to brain me, and I ducked. I ducked and it splattered against the wall and the cover came off, leaving it a six-hundred-page paperback. Then, without a word, she stalked off, and we never talked about this episode again. I was left thinking, *What was that all about? What did I say?* To this day, who knows? All I know is that Gordon Barrow and his excellent book did not deserve this treatment. That ragged text still holds a place of honor on my shelves.

***

When my brother was forty-four years old, he was living with a man in Boston, had been diagnosed with colon cancer, and was now dying. My mother, Liz, and I went to Boston for the last time to be with him.

When we arrived, his partner, Chris, said, "I know the two of you have been estranged."

And I replied, "That's a strong word, Chris, *estranged*. I've never thought about it that way. It isn't true. We were just waiting … for the right time."

I thought of it as distance. I thought of it as something time and age would heal. I imagined Eugene with my daughters and how they would love him, and he them. I thought of our correspondence years ago, and how in some way, maybe with frequent visits and phone calls, those days would come again. I had no doubt that once this interlude of midlife questing and competing had passed, it would all be right again. I looked forward to our later years, the discussions of faith and the stories we would tell. My little brother, Eugene! He would always be that.

And of course someday we would discuss books, as we always had. He'd once said that his place on Beacon Street—the place where we now sat at his bedside—reminded him of Henry Adams. "You should read *The Education*, Bill." So of course I did, and over the years, *The Education of Henry Adams*, in all its stained-glass brilliance, became one of my favorite books. Eugene was seldom wrong in his literary tastes.

But after seeing him, after seeing his bone thinness and the empty sockets of his eyes, and after hearing the somber Gregorian chants he requested be played in his dying hours, I knew he would never come back. Whatever chances there had been for the two of us to reunite, to rekindle the pleasures of Cook Forest and Atlantic City and that magical summer on the lake—all of those chances were gone. On the last morning of his life, when he drew his final breath, I held his hand in the room that overlooked Boston Commons and the State House, and I felt the departure of my little brother's soul like a fine breath, an exhalation of time and memory gone swiftly off into eternity.

★★★

The famous W. Eugene Smith image—the one included in Steichen's *Family of Man*—that Eugene had once sent to Liz, showing two small children walking through a lovely arch of tall trees, was reminiscent of Cook Forest. Liz construed this postcard reproduction as the two of them—Eugene and herself—strolling lovingly, side by side, on the dappled wooded path. When I saw this image and understood its meaning, I realized that my brother and sister had made the right choices in life and had loved one another while there was still time to love. I had not.

***

But these were fissures, cracks in the fabric of family. The real chasm lay between my father and Aunt Gene. That relationship had awkwardness and pain already built in. It was irresolvable from the outset. My mother's parents had willed the house to Aunt Gene, and they had entrusted Gene's care, for life, to my mother. In effect, as month followed month, my father was buying the house from Gene. She was the bank. The thought of moving away was unacceptable to my mother. And so there they were: a proud man in debt to his sister-in-law and living in a household with two adult women, an arrangement that my mother was convinced could only produce instability. But what could she do?

From the time the three of us were fully conscious, it was clear that chilliness prevailed between my father and Gene. The lack of any but the most terse conversation, the seeming unwillingness on his part to help her physically, the flat tone in her greetings to him in the morning, and of course her absence from virtually every family outing … *chilliness* is probably too mild a term.

My mother's older sister, Aunt Mary Jo Shrode, cast this relationship in even darker terms. When I was in Washington for my first year of college, I often visited with Aunt Mary and Uncle Irvin in Alexandria. One day she took me aside and told me through pursed lips that my father was taking advantage of Gene. "She's a *maid* for you kids," she said. "She's a cleaning lady. And it's free. Your father isn't paying a cent. She might as well be your *servant.*" And then, muttering between clenched teeth, she laid out the definitive verdict on my father: "All he cares about is money. *Money*!"

Aside from a wedding photo, there is no picture of Mary

Shrode in my father's Blue Album, and there's not a single one of Irvin.

***

There are thirteen ways of looking at a blackbird, or so it is said. Mary Shrode had selected one, which I thought was narrow and indefensible. When I reflected on what I knew about my father and money, I saw it differently. There were too many counterexamples that opposed her claim. To begin with, my father was generous in his contributions, in both money and time, to St. Francis de Sales Church. His sealed envelope of cash floated each Sunday into the wire basket as it was passed around the pews. And not only his but also ours, which he distributed to us as we left for Mass. For his family, he provided vacations at a time when most people on our street stayed home for the sweltering months of July and August. None of us ever wanted for new clothing, including the annual Easter dresses and suits. These were items I could easily have foregone, and in fact I found our treks to Robert Hall, on the north side of Pittsburgh, among the more annoying rituals of the year. My father himself was not a vain man; he cared nothing about his appearance. On Saturday mornings, he would go down to the Wil-Kar Bar wearing a white T-shirt with Heinz ketchup stains down the front. My mother would say, "Jim, you can't possibly wear that out of the house," and he would just laugh and say, "There's nothing wrong with this shirt, Bunny," and out he would go.

When his brother, Jack, fell on hard times, my father gave him enough money to purchase two eighteen-wheelers so he could begin a trucking company. No one in the family, including Jack, had any trucking experience, and it seemed from the start a questionable investment. Not only did Dad provide money, but he also suggested to Jack, over my mother's strong objections, that he park the trucks behind our house, on the slab of concrete that once served as the floor of the West Park Car Barn. When my mother and our neighbors looked out their back doors, there they were: two unsightly flatbeds with their shiny bulldog hood ornaments, standing incongruously behind the house. Where these vehicles would have gone had it not been for my father's fraternal intervention is anyone's guess.

And then there were the tuition payments for Liz and me, and, for Eugene, full payment of his long-running expenses at St. Meinrad Seminary. If all my father cared about was money, these were odd strategies to amass it for his personal gain. As I view it, he seemed almost profligate in his desire to help those who were close to him, especially when it came to education. When he died, he barely had three nickels to rattle around in his pocket.

So my dear, elegant Aunt Mary, who had seen to it that my late application to Catholic University was expedited, made a completely spurious assessment of my father's goal in life. She was the polar opposite of Agnes.

★★★

Eventually it became clear that Gene would have to go. There might have been a proximate cause for her departure, but I can't be sure. There certainly were earlier ones. One involved Mitzi, our pure-white, pink-nosed, fluffy Spitz. Despite my parents' reluctance, I had picked her out at the pound. As she had been my choice, I took it as my responsibility to house-train her. Except for my father, we all had great affection for her, and Eugene and I often took her with us on snowy Sunday mornings to deliver the *Pittsburgh Post-Gazette.* She blended in with the snow and loved it, as though some vestigial memory were calling her back to the expanses of the Arctic.

Over time, she gradually formed an indissoluble bond with Aunt Gene. Nights, Mitzi slept with Gene in the bed across from Liz's, and during the day she sat or lay on the floor near Gene's wheelchair. It was Aunt Gene who monitored her comings and goings to and from the backyard and who made sure she was well fed. For Aunt Gene, Mitzi became a treasured friend.

But the dog had a mean streak, as my father had always suspected. With strangers, she would lower her tail and bare her fangs in a way that conveyed an unmistakable warning. Few people had the temerity to extend a hand toward her once that lip began to curl. With the family, she exhibited no such behavior unless we interfered with her meals. We soon realized it was foolish to approach her when she was bent over a bowl of food.

One evening when Eugene was in a playful mood, he made the mistake of getting on his knees to butt heads with her. This was a common form of play for us, and Mitzi seemed to enjoy putting her paws over our heads, gumming our ears, growling softly, and then rolling over on her back to be tickled. But this time there was food nearby and she was hungry. No sooner had Eugene butted her head than she exposed her gleaming white teeth and tore straight into his face. Before he could act, her claws had cut his cheeks and she had bitten into his lips. There was blood everywhere. Eugene leapt to his feet in pain and covered his face with his hands. He kicked the dog and she ran off. But the damage had been done. We took him to the emergency room, where he had thirty stitches put in his face. It would take him months to heal.

My father wanted the dog put down; she could not have been killed fast enough for him. But my mother would not hear of it. She argued that Gene needed Mitzi, and she promised that it would never happen again. If it did, she said, he could have his way.

So closely had the dog become allied with Aunt Gene that in my father's mind Gene was as culpable for the crime as Mitzi. Most families would not have tolerated this viciousness in an animal, and my father understood that. But he respected my mother's wishes, and the dog stayed on and lived to an old age.

The summer after I finished Pitt and was about to leave for Purdue, it became clear that Aunt Gene would have to move. And my mother, although she still felt the weight of responsibility that her parents had placed upon her for Aunt Gene's lifelong care, realized it too. The house had finally been paid for. In Washington, my cousins Jim and Bill Shrode had left home to begin their life adventures. Aunt Mary and Uncle Irvin were more than ready to take Gene in, to rescue her from her imagined servitude at 134 Amelia.

★★★

My memories of Gene during my last year at Pitt are nothing but pleasant. Back from a day of classes, I would read to her from Edgar Allen Poe or the short pieces of Benjamin Franklin. She was bright and articulate and understood everything. I realized that it had been a grievous and ignorant failure on the part of my grandparents to shelter her and treat her like a small child, and to keep her housebound as though she were an embarrassment to the family.

Together we watched episodes of *Route 66,* the popular television series that took viewers, with Buzz and Todd and their Corvette, across America and into the lives and problems of people from New Jersey to New Mexico and beyond. Through their eyes, Gene saw the country in its breadth and width, and she saw it on location and not as a Hollywood set. We discussed the moral dilemmas that the characters faced, and the black-and-white beauty of the land. She made us popcorn and drank strong coffee while we watched.

Sometimes when I had a paper due or was studying for my physical and inorganic chemistry exams, she would stay up with me until the early morning hours. I would say, "Aunt Gene, you need to go to bed. You're tired," and I'd offer to carry her upstairs, as I usually did. But she'd say, "No, I'm awake. You study." Soon she would be nodding in her wheelchair by the purring stove, her head would loll to the side, and she would begin snoring softly. When I had had enough and the Clausius-Clapeyron equation was growing dim on the page, I would carry her upstairs.

My sister also enjoyed her presence, and she often talked with her for hours at the kitchen table. Sometimes she brought her best friend, Zora, to these "kitchen conferences," and they talked with Aunt Gene about their lives beyond the walls of St. Francis de Sales High School. In the mornings, my mother and Gene chatted amiably in the kitchen over coffee, with an aging and becalmed Mitzi asleep at their feet.

And so it went. My father was cool and distant toward Gene, as always, but otherwise the house was calm. And in time—a year or two—she would be leaving.

That Aunt Gene herself might have had dreams and profound human longings occurred to no one. My mother thought of her as a child, not a woman. But she would soon learn that she was mistaken.

***

There were gaps, there were chasms and fault lines, but it was only after my father's death, only after my time with Breslow, that they became apparent to me. Breslow's thesis of Freudian struggle and competition may well have been true, but I was wary of any single explanation for all that had happened. Gradually it dawned on me that it hardly mattered. What mattered was that I was beginning to see my father as if for the first time, and I was beginning to refine my judgments.

My mother had always been a less difficult figure than he was. We all loved her and respected her for what she did within the family. Perhaps it was the case that she favored

Eugene, or that in habitually calling Elizabeth Ann "Sister," she diminished my sister's lively independence, her strength and intelligence. But I think she meant it when she said, "I love you all the same."

She was always easy for me to talk with. If I had problems with my homework, I would go to her. She read my papers and corrected the grammar. Sure, there were times when she annoyed me, especially with her knowledge of Latin. "I can't translate this," I would say, as I was reading Caesar and biting my lips. And she would say, "Here, Bill, let me help you." I would grit my teeth when I heard these words, but she would come over to the dining room table and sit with me and translate these sentences about Gallic warfare as though she were reading from *Dick and Jane*. "See Spot run, Bill. See Jane and Puff."

In college, when I was taking literature courses as an antidote to too much science and math, I would read her long passages from Henry James or Ernest Hemingway or anyone else whose style I found fresh and appealing. She was easy to talk with, and I often confided my romantic problems to her. She laughed often, and I could defuse any argument we might be having with a joke. I admired her intellect, but I also knew she had once played field hockey and was good at "catch" too. And in her younger days, after college, she had sailed to Old Havana. She had been a stylish, bright young woman with a sense of adventure, a love of the world, and big plans that once extended far beyond the confines of the Rocks.

About her, then, there was the sadness of dreams unrealized, and I think as we got older we all felt that. There was the occasional mention of the doctor she had met at Duquesne who had a practice in the well-off suburb of Mount Lebanon. And there were others too, but of them she provided only the slightest hints. To everyone in the family, she was a friend and a confidante, and her willingness to speak about matters of the heart or about the various paths we were each considering would continue until the end of her life.

I was finally coming to understand the family with whom I'd spent so many years. I attributed much of this understanding to Breslow.

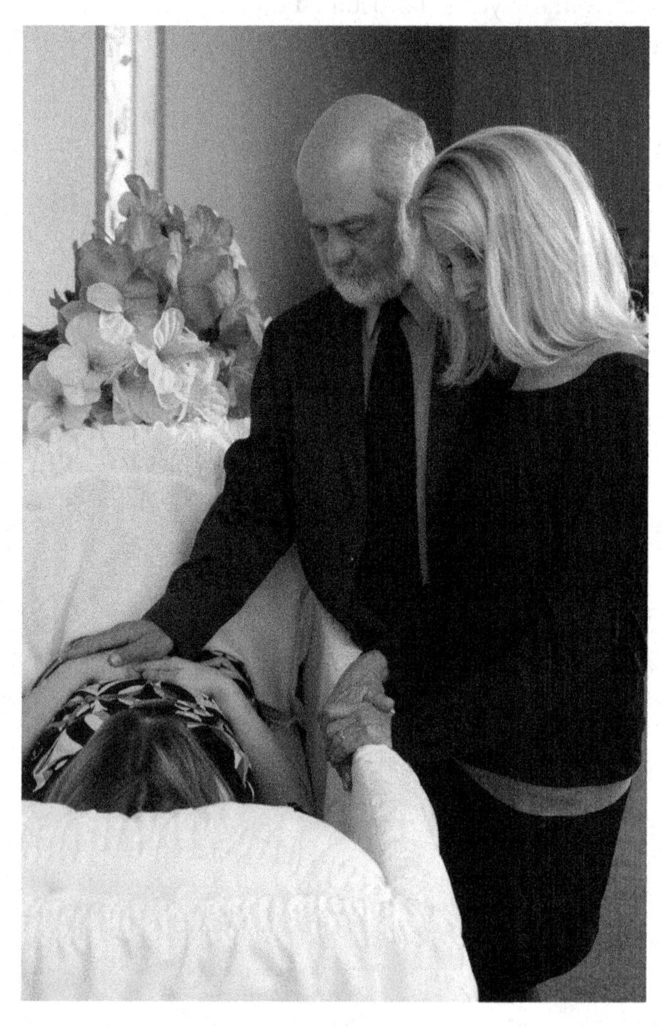

Scene at a typical funeral home.

15

DEATHS

I seemed unable to comprehend what was before me. Those who had been breathing at my side, those whose voices I'd heard coming from other rooms, now lay in repose. Forms stretched upon silk. And I had no idea what it meant.

***

I should have known death long before my father died in 1970. I should have known it intimately, but I didn't. Breslow wanted to know about earlier deaths in the family and how my responses to these were different from my response to my father's. I had said enough to suggest that that they were, but he wanted something more comprehensive. And so we spent several sessions (possibly in 1973) on this unpleasant but illuminating subject.

Uncle Jack, Grandmother Green, the others, had all passed cleanly in the 1950s and 1960s, without the lingering contrails of grief that I experienced when my father died. The grief following my father's death seemed as though it would never end. The most I could hope for was diminishment as the temporal distance grew.

The first to go was Jack. "Ah, Jack, he strong like bull," Mr. Danko, one of my paper route customers, said. "Strong like bull." And he was. I once saw him carry a bag of shingles up a ladder to his roof. It must have weighed two hundred pounds. *Christ,* I said to myself, *I don't believe it. No way in hell I could do that.*

Jack had the chiseled good looks of the young Brando in *On the Waterfront.* He was pure silver screen quality in my opinion.

When we had the big family Thanksgivings, he was always a hit. Not only did his appearance stand out, but his voice and his sense of humor animated the whole gathering. And he could bring the place to a teary halt with his baritone rendition of "Danny Boy." Everything stopped: the women grabbed their aprons, touched their eyes; everyone stared at him in awe. My god, Jack was something. When I remembered this in Breslow's office, I noted that I wasn't running from anything when I chose Belfast; I was running *toward* something—a myth, an ineffable Irishness that I had known from my earliest memories.

At these dinners, there were many of us: Jack and his wife, Aunt Peggy, and their adopted children, Johnny and Mary Margaret; and the Cookes—Uncle Frank, Aunt Mary Cel (my Dad's sister and erstwhile skating partner), and their children, Billy and Mary Frances. Aunt Agnes was there sometimes too. And from my mother's side, our cousin Mary Louise and her husband, Chuck Austin. And of course the six of us. The table extended from the dining room through the French doors and into the living room, and usually there was a separate card table for the younger children.

The women set the table and worked in the kitchen with their aprons on until all the food had been put out, and then it was time for grace, which my mother offered in her shy, barely audible public voice. The men drank Iron City Beer or Duquesne Pilsner, and the conversation, as I recall it, was jovial and never contentious or charged with politics. They were all Democrats, but they respected Ike for his leadership in the not-too-distant war. Everyone was Irish and proud of it, and there was talk of the Old Sod, as though they had all been there, cut and sculpted from the cliffs of County Clare. But who had ever been there—who had ever had the money? No one.

My mother was not a fan of these festivities, but for my father's sake she tolerated them and was a gracious hostess. From the time early in their marriage when my father left the house on Amelia Street and moved in with his mother and sisters up on Third, a few blocks away, she'd had an ongoing, unspoken grudge against the whole Green clan. He was away for no more than two nights, for what reason I can only guess, but the fact that they had sheltered him at all and had acted as coconspirators in this rash act of betrayal was enough to provoke a slow, steady burn that she never extinguished. To her mind, these things were not done; they were not proper!

***

Jack owned two big rigs. They were Mack trucks: the long-haul, heavy-duty classic with the red cab and the chrome bulldog insignia on the hood. For appearance and pure cachet, you couldn't beat them. But they were parked smack outside my mother's kitchen window on a slab of concrete. And there she was in the mornings, with her white apron on, staring right out at them with a discernible look of hostility. *What did I do to deserve this?* she was no doubt thinking.

But the business worked and the money came rolling in. Jack found drivers, but he sometimes wound up driving himself, over the highways into the Far West. It was wearing on him. At one point he felt he was being cheated by his best driver, Vaughn, and he had to lay the guy off. This meant more road time, more time away from the family, and more exhausting labor in the loading and unloading.

"Jack strong like bull," Mr. Danko had said. But there were limits. On one run through West Virginia, he had overloaded the rig. The weigh station was open that morning, and he had to bring it in. They found the extra poundage right away, and he had to help with unloading. This was hard work for a man who had just turned forty-four and was no longer as fit as he'd been at my parents' wedding. The exertion brought on a heart attack, and they couldn't get him through the mountains to a hospital in time. He died in the ambulance.

I remember the funeral only vaguely. There was sadness that he was gone, but, for me, there was no transmutation of this into grief. I was in high school, an altar boy filled with pious beliefs about heaven and the better life that awaited us above. I had no doubt that Jack was bound for a better place than this Earth, and I found solace in that.

I could never be sure how my father was affected. I never saw him cry—not for Jack, not even for his own mother. It was only in his later years, and through his many letters, that I became aware that there resided in him, in some far-off recess hidden from view, a deep sense of melancholy.

It could not have been more than two years after Jack's death that my grandmother Green died. I was eighteen, and I knew her well. Her house was the last stop on my paper route, and I often stopped by in the late afternoon to see her. My father was always quick to remind me that I should be spending as much time as possible with his dear Irish mother. So on Sunday mornings, when Eugene and I delivered the *Gazette*, we stopped for breakfast. When it snowed, we pulled our papers on a sled and took our white sled dog, the indefatigable Mitzi, with us. Third Street, where my grandmother lived with her daughter and son-in-law, Mary Cel and Frank Cooke, and their two children, Bill and Mary Francis—or "Francois," as my mother wrote in her letters, as though she had come from Provence or some arrondissement of Paris—was one of the steepest streets in the Rocks. Eugene and I would ride our sleds downhill in the brisk air and bright sunshine until we arrived at their door. We were cold and tired from a long morning of delivering the thick *Sunday Post Gazette*, and the sausage and eggs Aunt Mary Cel made for us were the perfect repast.

***

Weekday afternoons. The end of my half of the paper route. When I am in Grandma Green's living room and it is quiet with just the two of us—she's beginning to doze off—I look out the window across Third Street and see the roof of the Episcopal church. It is long, and to me it looks like a train. I am dreaming of where that train might go, where it might take me. I imagine landscapes that spread out in flatness, and there are small towns with Esso stations, and the guy comes dressed in a uniform and cleans my windshield and fills the tank. And beyond that, mountains with snow, and there are no trees like here, and I wonder what Grandma is dreaming about as her head lolls to the side. There are trains in her blood too, and in the whole family's blood, and maybe we're all dreaming the same dream. The dream of the clan. And I whisper, "Grandma, Grandma Green, I have to leave now. They will be expecting me soon for dinner." And she nods and I set off down the steps, down the hill, and stop for a minute at the bottom, at Kramer's Candy store. I buy baseball cards and a string of black licorice, and I play a few rounds on Kramer's pinball machine—*ding, ding, ding,* lights blinking on and off. But as usual I have no luck.

Grandma was a stocky Irishwoman whose maiden name was Sue O'Rourke and whose original clan hailed from County Meath, just north of Dublin. As firstborn, I was held in her favor, and I enjoyed her company for these short drop-ins. At dinner, my father always wanted to know the latest on his mother, and I'd give him whatever information I had. As she aged, there were long silences and she seemed confused; she wanted to know about Gerard, which was the name she'd given Eugene. To our knowledge, there was never anyone in the family named Gerard. Who knows into what past she was slipping.

As she had been in decline for a while, her death came as no surprise. She was laid out in her casket at home, in the very living room where she and I had talked, and I remember candles and flowers and public prayer offerings and kneeling beside her, whispering my own Our Father and Hail Mary in remembrance of our days together. The whole family was assembled, but there were neighbors too, like the plump Mrs. Mulkeen, whose voice, with its Irish brogue, boomed above the crowd.

After the solemnities, there was a big dinner with ham and potatoes and plenty of drink. It was a typical Irish wake, with lots of laugher and stories and a general celebration of my grandma's life. The wake was a grand send-off into the other world, which we all knew awaited her. It would be a better world.

Late that evening, I left with my cousin Billy Cooke for Amelia Street, and within minutes we had a near accident with an oncoming car. The driver was a kid from the Rocks I intensely disliked, and the feeling was mutual. We emerged from our cars, and I said there was no damage done and we might as well call it an evening. But he called me a name that went beyond fighting words, and it was clear he wanted to have at me. Years of working out in Benny's basement gave me all the advantage I needed, and when I had him on the bricks, I let my fists fly until his face was oozing blood. I could hardly stop myself. It was only Billy Cooke's voice that brought me to my senses. I let the kid go, and he ran for his car.

I told Breslow about this in one of our sessions. I told him I had felt little emotion at the wake, only sadness that she was gone. But on the street, something happened: something in me snapped. I was filled with rage.

And Breslow said, "It's all about loss. Loss has many ways of expressing itself." I knew he was thinking about my father and what had followed his death. But I had not connected these dissimilar events, which were separated by nearly a decade. Not until Breslow joined them for me.

Grandma died in 1960, but I did not think much about her final days until my years with Breslow.

***

There were other deaths that predated my father's. Irvin Shrode died of a brain tumor in the suburbs of Washington, and this finally precipitated Aunt Gene's departure from 134 Amelia. Mary Shrode (Aunt Mary Jo) came and got Gene, and they took Mitzi too, and the few possessions Gene had. Not long afterward, Mitzi died, and there was grieving on Gene's part that her most faithful companion on this earth had left her, dying in a distant corner of Mary Jo's yard without the slightest audible whimper. Dying alone is the way of the world, even if you are a white Spitz with a curly tail who has brought joy to some and inflicted pain on others. Not long after that, Mary and Gene decided to move back to Pittsburgh to be closer to my parents and to Mary Louise and the remainder of the O'Donnell clan.

They found two places that were attractive to them. One was very near to McKees Rocks, across the Windgap Bridge, about three miles from Amelia Street. The other was in Gibsonia, a town about twenty miles north of Pittsburgh on Route 8. Both houses were wheelchair accessible and pleasant suburban properties. My mother, of course, hoped they would choose the Windgap location, since she envisioned frequent visits with her sisters, both of whom she loved and to whom she craved proximity. She had not been in the same city as Mary for decades, and she still thought of Aunt Gene as her confidante and ultimate responsibility. But after careful consideration, Mary and Gene chose the property in distant Gibsonia, a cheerful, spacious place with rooms on a single floor and a large, flower-filled backyard that could be seen from the picture windows in the kitchen and living room. It seemed to Mary that this was the perfect house for Gene, particularly as it would allow easy access to the outdoors, something she had not enjoyed in our house on Amelia.

Arrangements were made, the property was paid for with cash, and the distance allowed my mother to have weekly afternoon visits with her sisters. Mary had a British-style tea service, and the afternoons were spent over tea and cakes in a manner meeting my mother's approval. Mary hired a maid service, something she and Irv had become accustomed to in Washington, and they hired a gardener to tend to the lawn and the lovely flower beds. The gardener, whose name was Albert, came highly recommended by our cousin, Mary Louise, and so many of the burdens of everyday living were lifted from Gene and Mary's lives. It could hardly have been better.

Even my father, whose duty it was to chauffeur my mother to Gibsonia (as a young woman, my mother had driven smack into a large oak and at that point called it quits) seemed relaxed at these afternoon "soirees," which I sometimes had an opportunity to attend.

It was not long, however, before Mary developed a deadly form of stomach cancer, and within six months she was gone.

Mary's possessions at the time of her death were not meager. They included not only the house and a considerable savings account, but also the valuable parcel of land Irvin had purchased near Manassas National Battlefield Park, and the rights to a popular mathematics text that Irvin's brother had left to him. Mary had left Gene in prosperous circumstances.

As you would expect, Gene needed care; at the very least she needed someone to look in on her on a daily basis. This became Albert's task, and, to his credit, he stopped by faithfully. He lived only a short distance away on a rural property in an open field. One day Albert and Gene discussed the possibility of him moving into her house, into Mary's former bedroom. There was plenty of space, and that way she would have his attention whenever she needed it. As a divorced man, he would of course be free to come and go as he pleased, and to be with whomever he wished.

News of this arrangement was eventually brought to my mother by Mary Louise, who also let it be known that she, Mary Louise, was pregnant with Albert's child. This was in the spring of 1976, long after my father's death and after my departure from Pittsburgh. My mother was living alone and savoring, at the age of sixty-six, her first real taste of independence.

But Mary Louise's news from far-off Gibsonia was too much for my mother to bear. One July afternoon in '76, Mother began having chest pains, but instead of going directly to Ohio Valley Hospital, she lay on the living room sofa and hoped they would subside. My wife and I had gone on a short vacation to the mountains of Virginia to visit Virginia Tech, where I had gotten my PhD in 1969. From the old hotel where we stayed near Blacksburg, I called my mother to see how she was doing. I was expecting our usual pleasant conversation, but instead Liz answered the phone and broke the news. Eugene, who at the time was teaching in Pittsburgh, was also there, and neither of them could convince our mother that she needed to see a doctor, and fast. They thought it was a matter of dignity, that she was too embarrassed to have them call 911. As was usually the case, they respected her wishes, irrational as they were.

My wife and I drove all night on the snaky roads of West Virginia and Pennsylvania and arrived in Pittsburgh the following morning. It is not clear what happened, but I think in a private moment, when Eugene, Liz, and I were out in the kitchen, my wife said to my mother, "Mrs. Green, they are very worried about you. There is probably nothing wrong, but for the sake of your children, please, please let us call emergency."

Mother lay there, pale and sick, her chest aching, and thought about this for an hour. Then in a barely audible voice, she said, "Yes, all right."

She wanted her thinning hair brushed, and she wanted Liz to

get her a clean robe for the ten-minute ambulance ride up to the hospital. In no time, the ambulance squad arrived, placed her on a stretcher, and took her out. Liz, Eugene, and I followed behind in our car and waited anxiously for news from the cardiologist.

The news, when it came an hour later, was not good. She had had a heart attack—curse of the family—and was resting comfortably with an oxygen mask over her face. They kept her two days for observation. No stents. No bypass surgery. No prescribed exercise regimen. Nothing. Just talk of drugs and frequent visits to the cardiologist.

Within a week, Liz and I had left Pittsburgh. Only Eugene remained to check in with our mother on a regular basis. We made sure one of us called her every day. Her reports gradually became more positive, and her sunny nature soon returned.

Slowly my mother came to accept Aunt Gene's situation, which likely included a suspected, somewhat vague relationship with Albert. Gene, after all, was not a child. By this time, Gene had moved to Albert's farm. My mother's last Polaroid of her, taken two years before Gene's death, shows her in a wheelchair in a field outside a trailer, with several cows standing a few feet away. She is wrapped in a blanket and looks old and sad and weary of a world she seems only too ready to depart. Not at all the brilliantly sunny Gene of my youth.

***

I was in Antarctica when my mother wrote me that Aunt Gene had died. For a few days, in the valleys and on the frozen lakes, I could think of nothing but her. I felt guilty for having visited her so infrequently in her later years, for having written so little. I had never written her a letter of thanks for the beautiful friendship we shared throughout my childhood and my college years. I remembered all she had given me—my pretty, black-haired, impossibly stoic Gene.

In time, though, these feelings of loss diminished, as they always did.

★★★

As I write this, it occurs to me that people have many reactions to death. My mother died nineteen years after my father. At the cemetery, Liz tried to fling herself into the grave—fling herself into the open grave, along with the dirt. It took many hands to restrain her. For my father, there was barely a reaction from Liz; I don't know what she was thinking. From the altar, Eugene had that ghostly vision of my father's presence. Nothing more. When my mother went, Eugene was, of course, already gone.

As for me, I thought my mother and I had understood one another, had spent our days together well. Initially I reacted only with the usual sorrowful thoughts that she would no longer be there. But then one day a year later, when we were clearing out the house for sale, I stepped into the downstairs closet, where there was only the long, tan winter coat that she wore to church each Sunday. I could smell lilac. I pulled the door closed and I wailed. I wailed and I could not stop myself. It was loud, and it echoed through the closet and the emptiness of the house. Then it became a sob, and it went on and on in the darkness of the closet that smelled of lilac and of her. Then it was over. And I never cried again.

ABC (1969).

16

ABC (1969)

It was such a tiny thing—a gold pendant she wore on a chain around her neck—and it was so unlike him to give it. And why the letters *ABC*? He could have chosen others: *T*, or *M* or *G*. But he didn't. He played it simple. Played it beautiful. There was art in it.

***

By the time we reached our mid-to-late twenties, Eugene, Liz, and I had a collective net worth amounting to some significant negative value, which registered as a big red number on the accountant's balance sheet. This would be the case for at least three more years. None of us could pull into the curb at 134 Amelia with a top-down Corvette or an MG, or even a car we had paid for. If my parents had expected that some wildly opulent scion would one day spring from their midst, they must have known by now that this was unlikely to happen. This was lightning that would never strike.

Had money been my father's principal concern, as our redoubtable Aunt Mary Shrode claimed, he would have viewed our activities as fatuous diversions from the real mission of American life: the getting and the spending, the competitive accumulation of wealth-unto-death, the ostentatious display of earthly goods and, of course, that richly appointed home in the suburbs. Ah yes, green lawn. Intricate gardens. Circular drive. Capacious garage. Polished vehicles. Lawn implements of every kind. These were what mattered. But apparently they did not matter to my father.

All of this became clear on the day in 1969 when Eugene drove into the Rocks from the Pittsburgh Oratory, walked into the house, and was greeted by my mother, whose adornments included a pendant on a golden chain, nicely displayed, that fell smartly across her blue dress. After giving her a warm hug, he stepped back and said, "Mother, that's new! Where did you get it?"

And she said, "Your father gave it to me. Do you like it?" She removed it from around her neck and handed it to my brother. He examined it carefully and said, "Three gold letters."

***

I wanted to relate this story to Breslow, as I thought it might in some way help account for my prolonged grief, might in some way reveal my father's largesse and the full dimensions of his heart.

It was Valentine's Day 1969.

Gene was gone. Liz, Eugene, and I had all left Pittsburgh. And there were just the two of them left in the Rocks. It was the same house in which they had spent all their married lives, but in our absence there had been a reflorescence in their marriage, and a new playfulness had emerged that could be easily discerned in their letters and travels. This was in the last three years of my father's life, between about 1967 and 1970.

We were surprised to receive letters and cards from the Bahamas, where they played the slots, nothing more, in Freetown and Nassau. My father went to the Tigers' training camp in

Florida, where he was greeted as the regional scout from Pittsburgh. And together they traveled to Dallas for the big Elks' convention and to San Francisco just to see the city, its famous trolleys slowly climbing the steep hills. There were local car trips too, to Williamsport to view the Little League playoff games and to Atlantic City for strolls along the boardwalk and for taking in the evening's salt air, which they both loved.

All the distant travel was by train or ship, since my father had a morbid fear of flying. Neither of them had ever taken a plane. When my father died, they were planning a trip to Belfast—they'd travel by train to New York and then on the *QE2* to London and eventually Ireland. They both enjoyed the languorous pace of the rails. And an ocean voyage, after their Caribbean adventure, did not seem at all daunting. These were their savored years of liberation.

***

Eugene was the first to learn about the gift when he came to visit my mother one day in 1969. The pendant she wore when she greeted him seemed so atypical, coming as it had from my father, who in all his years had never been demonstrably romantic. But there it was, gleaming on a gold chain around her neck. It was a large, gold heart, and beneath it there were three raised letters: *ABC*. She told Eugene what the pendant meant, even though its significance was immediately clear to him. The heart was obvious. It expressed in silent symbol what he had felt for her from the day they first met all those years ago. But the letters expressed something unexpected—pride in what they had done together as parents. For in those days, as now, children's lives were taken as reflections upon their parents, upon the values they had passed along in the common, day-to-day rituals of the home: the laughter; the conversations; the dinners—even with their awkward silences and our occasional pretentiousness; the

Sunday Masses; the summer vacations and morning coffees; the talks around the kitchen table. All of these, and the prominence given to learning and piety and truthfulness and the dignity of work, had made their mark.

★★★

The *C* was my father's way of denoting the country where Eugene was pursuing his master's degree in divinity at the University of Toronto. Eugene had decided upon this course of study not long after his acceptance as a novice at the Pittsburgh Oratory. The Congregation of the Oratory, which traced its origin to Cardinal John Henry Newman, was a self-governing group of priests and novices who ministered to Catholics at the nearby University of Pittsburgh and Carnegie Mellon University, as well as to the people of Oakland and the larger Pittsburgh area. Its leader was the highly regarded William Clancy, who had once been a professor at Notre Dame and then editor of *Commonweal,* the intellectual Catholic magazine based in New York.

Clancy, who became my brother's mentor, encouraged his budding scholarly interests and arranged for him to apply at Toronto, where he was awarded the master of theology degree in 1968. My father, who had virtually no interest in this subject beyond the Apostles' Creed, found Eugene's achievement at Toronto a wonderful testament to his faith and intellect. "I always knew that boy had it in him from the time he was a little kid," he remarked with obvious approval.

This was more than he expected. Had he lived a few years longer, he would have seen his son graduate from Harvard with a PhD in English and go on to teach and write books on medieval literature. When his mentor died in 1984, Eugene honored him with a book, *Times Covenant: The Essays and Sermons of William Clancy.*

Even though he did not live to see Eugene's ordination

in 1970, my father (and of course my mother as well) enjoyed attending the Pittsburgh Oratory services at Heinz Chapel and the big breakfasts and conversations that followed. Bill Clancy, in his relaxed and lighthearted way, welcomed my parents into the company of priests and parishioners who gathered in the cozy, well-managed house that stood on the hill overlooking the campus at Pitt. Eugene once said to me, "Dad is so comfortable in this company. It surprises me. It is so different from what he knows in the Rocks—the Elks, the Eagles, the Knights of Columbus, Little League. But people love him here. And they love Mom too."

I think this association with the Oratory only heightened the pleasure my parents took in those last years together. For him, it was a new world to explore; for her, it was something more elevated, something she considered more appropriate to the station in life to which she had always aspired. Added to their travels to cities and islands she had only read about in magazines, and to the new freedoms that she found in a house that was hers and my father's alone, their time at the Oratory gave these years a golden aura that I could sense in her letters to me.

★★★

If Eugene's work in theology seemed to lie along an intellectual continuum that had been established at a young age, Elizabeth Ann's decision to join the Peace Corps after college appeared as a sudden break with her past. My sister—high school valedictorian, history major at Duquesne University—had been content, despite the rough spots, to spend her college years at home, and had never in all our conversations expressed even a hint of wanderlust. Her summary announcement in 1966, given without consultation with my parents or any other family member, that she had been accepted into the Peace Corps, came as a shock. She was off to

Vermont for a training course and then to Brazil. The general family reaction to this was, in brief, "What! Liz? Not possible."

But it was possible, and before long, after learning enough Portuguese to get by, she was on her way. As surprised as I was, I considered this a really brave move. It was something I had thought about myself, but the most I'd ever done about it was visit a few recruitment tables set up in some university hallway and listen to the pitch made by the young, wide-eyed recruiters. *Maybe when I have more chemistry under my belt,* I thought, *I'll do it.* It was high on my list, but by then Liz was there.

The young Peace Corps was still feeling its way in the world, and my sister was unceremoniously dropped off in a rural area not far from an old town in the state of Goias, without so much as a letter of introduction to the mayor or anyone else. There she was, with no assignment, with her field partner, Lois, walking in the baking sun down dusty, horse-trodden streets under the gaze of the locals, who saw only two pretty, unfamiliar young ladies who were probably wondering, *What are we doing here?* For Liz—a kid from McKees Rocks, who had never set foot in a foreign country, whose only travels had consisted of family vacations arranged by my father, including that memorable trip to California—this was terra incognita. It may as well have been the parched plains of Mars.

Being resourceful, Liz made it her first order of business to contact the mayor the next morning. She and Lois sat in his office, a dusty reflection of the outdoors, and after appropriate introductions, asked him in their broken Portuguese what they should be working on. When he learned that they were college graduates in the humanities and not scientists or engineers or agriculturalists, he suggested they consider a project related to the woebegone institution that passed as the town library. This seemed to please them, as they both knew books better than any of the more practical arts that the mayor might have favored. But these were the late '60s in America, and idealism and romantic visions of the world were everywhere, especially on college campuses, and the Peace Corps in those days consisted mostly of liberal arts graduates guided only by a high sense of purpose.

Liz knew her books, and she'd always had an inchoate sense of how accounting worked. With this combination, and with Lois's gifts of organization, they were able, over time, to bring a fresh vitality to the reading life of the town. Books that had been famous only for collecting dust began to find new life in the hands of readers. The library became a place of quiet and solitude, a place to dream of what lay far from the town square.

In time, when the library was running as smoothly as it ever would, she and Lois were able to travel. They headed south for Argentina and Chile, and since both of them missed the cities of their youth, they sought out Buenos Aires and Santiago and stayed for a week in each. On one of her sojourns, Liz met an enterprising young man, George Hart (whom my father, in his letters, would habitually refer to as "Geo"), and the two them, through letters and meetings, as their schedules permitted, became increasingly close. Shortly before their departure for the States, they married in Rio de Janeiro.

My father was aware that somewhere in Brazil, the honorable Justice Cercone from McKees Rocks, Pennsylvania, was vacationing with his wife. My father found out that he was in fact in Rio, and through Western Union telegrams, he arranged for the wedding ceremony to be conducted in that city by the justice himself. And so it happened that, as the capstone of a two-year adventure, Liz left Brazil a married woman. In this way, the letter *B* found its way onto my mother's pendant.

***

I doubt that in 1968, anyone in my family would have predicted the origin of the letter *A*. It came about in a manner that involved the unlikely coincidence of several unrelated events in Blacksburg, Virginia. In that year, I was living in a trailer court, obsessively working day and night in the lab to finish the experiments for my PhD. It had only been five years since I completed my bachelor's degree at Pitt, but graduate school felt like endless purgatory.

There came a time, though, when a hiatus in my research was required by the need for some professional glassblowing. Fortunately, the chemistry department had a glassblower, named Claus. He was on site and was able to reconstruct the gas solubility apparatus I had inadvertently destroyed in a single clumsy move. Everything in the lab came to an abrupt halt. It was at this point that Roger Hatcher, one of my trailer friends, asked if I would be interested in doing some research in Antarctica. "Just for four months," he said. I said, "Let me think about it. I'll have to talk with my adviser, Paul Field, too."

In two weeks, after gathering all the facts and permissions, I said, "Sure, Hatch, why not?" I thought of it as a one-time adventure, a desirable combination of physical labor and possible discovery in a highly exotic land I knew hardly a thing about.

I was there from mid-August until mid-December, 1968, first in the perpetual darkness of the austral night, and then through the long sunrise into the spring and summer. We divided our time between McMurdo Station on Ross Island and the strange landscapes of the McMurdo Dry Valleys, with their glaciers and permanently ice-covered lakes and mountains, whose peaks reached up to four thousand feet into an intense blue sky. It was otherworldly and beautiful and unlike anything I had ever imagined. If it is possible to fall in love with a landscape, I fell.

★★★

When December came and I had to leave Antarctica and put on civilian clothing back in New Zealand, I learned that nothing fit. McMurdo Station, with its four cafeteria-style meals a day, its chili dogs and ice cream machine, its hot chocolate and marshmallows on call anytime in the Biolab, was too much for any impoverished graduate student to resist. The field, with its tents and Coleman stoves and bitter cold, only made these gustatory delights more appealing. So I ate and ate and ate some more and gained twenty pounds and waddled self-consciously back to civilization.

I got to National Airport with a ticket to Pittsburgh in my pocket—purchased, I'm embarrassed to say, by my father—and not an extra cent to my name. I was prepared to spend the night on an airport bench, when I began a conversation with a young lady. She was lovely, and she had the kind of euphonic voice I'd missed in the male-only monastery of McMurdo Station. She had booked a motel room nearby and invited me to spend the night with her, which I gladly did. She told me she was engaged and was planning to marry in the spring, but this commitment to some distant fiancé seemed hardly to register with her. Her kindness was not uncommon in those years, and I accepted it with gratitude.

***

It was not until long after my father's death, long after my last appointment with Breslow and his successors, that I came to understand that my father "talked" in symbols. To none of us did he ever utter the words *proud* or *love.* These were not part of his vocabulary. They were not part of his generation's vocabulary. But the ball in a game of catch was more than just a white, stitched sphere being tossed between a man and a boy; the crack of a bat in the springtime signaled more than a call to practice and perfection; and money—the tuition, the debts paid, the tickets purchased—was more than the medium of a fiduciary transaction.

Likewise, the pendant he gave my mother that Valentine's Day was far more than just a heart and a string of letters. In the language of signs, it registered the forecast for his children's lives. He was probably telling Mike Zavidny and Joe Vitelli and Bill Marm and Red Schlentner and all the guys he drank with down at the Wil-Kar Grill that his kids—that penniless, indebted, pompous band of dreamers—had written to him last week. His elder son was never going to play second base for anyone; that had been pretty definitely established. But "you know, he really likes what he's doin' down there at the South Pole." He always said I was at the South Pole, even though I was thirteen degrees north in the McMurdo Dry Valleys. But hell, what did thirteen degrees of latitude matter to a bunch of sloshed drinking buddies at a bar in the Rocks? And besides, people had heard of the South Pole, but in 1968, who in the hell had ever heard of the Dry Valleys? Really, who's heard of them now?

As for Eugene, he was only a year away from ordination: July 1970. For an Irish Catholic father, that was pay dirt. From all appearances, Eugene was a budding academic too: "He got that degree in Canada, and he's teaching college." And Liz, well, who knew exactly? But he foresaw big things. He told the guys, "She's so smart and she's got guts too. The Peace Corps!" That was Kennedy's creation, and he thought that Kennedy, the first Catholic president—and Irish too—was the best.

What transpired at that bar I learned at McDermott's Funeral Home and in conversations around the Rocks after he'd died. But of course he never said these things to us. To us, he spoke only in the silence of signs. In the silence of the three letters: *ABC.*

Arise! Come to your God.
Sing out your songs of rejoicing.
Psalm 100

Eugene Green
Born: September 3, 1944
Ordained: July 3, 1970
Died: February 8, 1989

17

Letters on the Road to Belfast (1965–70)

The words bring them back: my parents, Agnes, Eugene. I can hear their voices and see their faces. I can feel their presence.

*****

The Blacksburg years were, in a way, the beginning of everything, the onset of what would become my life. And the letters, especially my father's letters, are in part my memory of those years and of the people who wrote them. Letters are eidetic; they keep you honest in all your reveries as you move along the laid thread deep into the past.

A little history:

After California, after my pleasant, revealing spring with Eugene, I returned to Purdue for the summer and for an uneventful fall semester. During the fall term, my research adviser, Alan Clifford, announced that he had accepted an offer to chair the chemistry department at Virginia Tech, in the mountain town of Blacksburg. Some of his advisees chose to stay at Purdue; others, like myself, decided to move to Virginia. I wanted a new adventure and was intrigued by Clifford's description of the small energetic, department with big dreams that had enticed him to leave the more prestigious program at Purdue. My assignment would be to precede him and go to Tech in January to work with a young professor, Paul Field, who had just received a National Science Foundation grant and needed "a pair of hands" in the lab.

It wasn't long before I decided that I liked Field's project on molten salts, and, moreover, I liked Field. I just liked the guy—his acerbic wit, his lack of pretensions, his craftsmanship in the lab, his not infrequent praise of my ideas and my abilities with equipment. "You do nice work," he often said. "If you like, you can make the molten salt project your doctoral research." It took me no time at all to decide. Paul Field would be my mentor. "Remember," he said, "you're not working *for* me. You're working *with* me." And he said that word again, *with*, so I couldn't miss it—and I liked it. This would be a collaboration. It would be a mission, a quest. I felt a wind at my back, my sails opening to a soughing breeze.

***

But in Blacksburg there were many deviations and distractions from the course I'd set for myself. Those included self-doubt, which drew me at first toward a degree in English or toward the lesser achievement of a master's degree in chemistry, and the romantic impulse, which turned my rational mind to mush and led to an ill-advised but mercifully short-lived marriage to a lovely girl of nineteen. Laura, a bright, sultry blonde formerly from California, immediately reminded me of those flaxen, unattainable girls I had seen at the dances in Ontario when the air was soft and I was a shy sixteen. I was smitten instantly, and it did not take long before we were speaking of wedding dates.

In small part, I think, the attraction rested on the fact that I viewed life, at its best, as a continuum, a kind of Ariadne's thread, which if followed back through time and thickets would lead into the flowered fields of childhood and beyond. With the pert, adorable Laura, I could not imagine anything but a life of unalloyed happiness—but nothing went as planned. At this stage, however, I feel no need to revisit those days, and I hope only that Laura went on to a good life.

After the divorce, the call to adventure—and, more important, the opportunity—took me away from my doctoral thesis for four months and focused my attention instead on the great, pristine wilderness of Antarctica, its ice-covered lakes and a whole new world of research possibilities.

★★★

All my peregrinations were revealed in the early '70s to Dr. Breslow, who was languidly, endlessly formulating his hypothesis, which still centered on the theme of escape. I read him the letters from my Blacksburg days, and during some of these readings, he appeared alert and pensive, his head bowed and barely moving. He was listening closely, or seemed to be, selecting and underlining certain passages in his mind and discerning certain themes. Themes I had not seen.

Breslow told me how impressed he was that the family had kept such a steady flow of correspondence alive, even though it depended on the time-consuming means of handwritten letters. Looking back on this time from the present age of e-mails and tweets, texts and cell phones, these longhand letters seem like exhibits for the dust museum of buggy whips and stage coaches, quilled pens and telegraphs. Could these Palmer-perfect masterpieces even be deciphered today? And yet …

Yes, I thought, as I sat there in Breslow's office, the words in all their curlicued, cursive distinctiveness, *mattered*. They would always matter. Beyond the flatness of photographs, recording the mere surface of things, the words, in their riverine, flowing movement, seem somehow memory in the round. Holographic.

The words, the sentences, probe deeply for some distant truth and, in odd ways, may even find it. I pay attention. *"Don't you wish we could go back?"*

***

In January 1966, I wrote to my parents that I had arrived in Blacksburg. It was a small southern town: woods, shaded pathways, on old cabin, and, in the distance, the endless mountains of West Virginia. The chemistry building was down in a shallow valley off across the drill field. I thanked my father for a present he had sent and for a loan of thirty dollars. I signed it, "Love, your son, Bill."

I have a letter from March in which my father speaks of my erstwhile teammates Rudison and Talerico, guys from the California team. Highlight of my unlived life. How he had gotten them jobs on the "cars," the red-and-white, smooth-gliding trolleys. He is proud of them and he writes, "It makes a fellow feel good when he sees you kids whose character he helped to mold do good …" He reminds me that I owe money to a physician in Covina, California, and he thanks me for money I sent him as a first payment on something. *Jesus! Covina.* I'm still paying off California? And he's still reminding me of my unpaid debts. I feel like a real screwup.

Then he says of my epistle: "Was glad to hear from you but I had to wait until your mother got home to interpret it for me. Too fancy for me …"

I focus on the Covina reminder. I feel incompetent, stupid, and unable to handle the outside world without his pointed, demeaning reminders.

***

Breslow seemed to love everything Eugene wrote. His letters were heartfelt and deeply troubled, as though he were searching for answers, parting the tall reeds as he walked through life toward some imagined clearing, some great expanse of openness where he could finally see the light. There is a letter from early April 1966 in which he talks about our imminent homecoming. He worries about telling my parents that he is planning to pursue a master's in English at the University of Kentucky. He has a full ride, but it's a secular university. "If you arrive home before me," he writes, "please do not give any hint about your knowledge of my plans for the University of Kentucky. I think they would be offended."

I can feel the stabbing pain in his stomach, a deep knife wound. The worry that he will offend our parents—our mother especially. He will do anything not to offend her.

In August, he writes, "The intense physical pain has left and I am able to work again without great distress." Then he talks about the two of us, our temperaments:

> It's too bad, Bill, that we cannot change places. I'd like you to fight my battles for me and let you give me your battles to fight … I could use some of your breadth of spirit and air of freedom; you might in turn profit from my myopia. We both have a long way to go toward perfect balance.

Perfect balance. Oh dear brother, dreamer of dreams!

Eugene writes again in October. He has told our parents. He has gone off to Lexington. But there is no freedom, no lightness. It is as though his whole being is wrapped in a small, tight skin. "But, Bill, please understand—I have a problem. My vision has become blurred; my world has become a microcosm; my person has shrunk."

I want to hug him. Today, as I write this, I would hug him, if only he were here. I would tell him, *It's okay, Eugene. You will become the man you wish to become. But it will take time. We are both so slow.*

***

Breslow was intrigued by Sister Agnes. On the one hand,

it seemed to him, she was concerned with my well-being and happiness; but on the other, she was not unwilling to dispense with advice and criticism.

On December 4, 1966, Agnes wrote of Laura's visit to the Rocks. Laura and I had known each other a scant three months, and already I was inviting her home.

> It was nice having Laura home with you. She seemed to have enjoyed her visit. Is she willing to come back with you some time again?
>
> All of us like her.

Breslow said, "Your relationship with Laura was of great interest to Agnes. Hmm. I wonder why?" During the Blacksburg years, she could not let the subject rest. Agnes liked Laura, liked her immensely, and thought that one day she would be a welcome addition to the family.

"About someone you have known only a short time," Breslow said. "Agnes's judgment seemed rash. Untrustworthy."

"I agree," I said. "Things were beginning to feel rushed. A kind of blur."

★★★

The correspondence in '67 centers on my upcoming wedding with Laura, scheduled for June. I tell Breslow, "Look, I met this girl in September of '66; in December she dropped out of college. She went back to northern Virginia, where her family lived. During that period we visited each other a few times, but mostly we kept in touch by letter."

Breslow asked the obvious question: "Why did she drop out of college after one semester? Were her grades awful? Was she homesick?"

"To be honest," I said, "I have no idea." And I didn't. At the time, I just took it as something she wanted to do. "Not everyone likes college. Papers, equations, requirements—you know, this stuff isn't for everyone, no matter how intelligent you are. And believe me, Laura was plenty intelligent."

"So you began planning for a June wedding soon after she left? Did that seem wise to you?"

"Things had been set in motion," I said. "It all felt ineluctable. There was no consideration given to wisdom." *Wisdom!* I think. *What in the hell is that?* My wisdom had been turned off at the switch. But other switches had been turned on.

Agnes wrote in April,

> Excuse me for intruding. Your mother and dad are quite disturbed over the wedding. They really want you to get settled. They don't want you to be hurt; don't want you to hurt Laura. They want you to be honest. Perhaps you have a fear of settling down. If you proposed to Laura then you must be honest with her.
>
> I feel that you have been very dependent on your parents, even though you have seemingly been on your own. You always know they will come forth …
>
> God bless you.

I showed this masterpiece to Breslow sometime around 1973. Even though I had discovered the cache of family letters shortly after my father's death, it was not until much later in my sessions with Breslow that they became the subject of analysis. This particular letter arrived two months after my twenty-fifth birthday. I knew it reflected what my parents were thinking but would never say; they would never be that blunt. The old tropes were there—*You cannot be married to books. Settle down*—as if twenty-five were just too old to be rattling around single. The ancient, befuddled bachelor of twenty-five! Without wife and family. How could this possibly be rationalized? And then the nib of Agnes's pen stabbed right in my gut: *I feel you have been very dependent on your parents …*

Breslow, that coconspirator, the guy I was paying sixty bucks per session twice a week, actually agreed with this last point. "Yes," he said. "I think your aunt was right here. She saw how your father had been hovering, looking over your shoulder, making sure you were not going into debt. He even went so far as to come to you in California."

***

There were growing doubts all around. What did we have in common, Laura and I? Did she like books? Or sports? Did I give a damn about money, the way she and her family did? Did she ever show the slightest interest in my research? Was my friend Stewart right when he said, "Man, you ain't ready for this. I guarantee you it won't work. She's nineteen, for Christ's sake. Nineteen! And you, I don't know how old you are. Sometimes I think you're brilliant, and other times I think you're a complete jerk. This is one of those other times. Call it off. Screw the invitations. Screw the gifts. They can all be returned. Man, just bail."

I didn't bail.

***

My father wrote within months of the June wedding. He sensed trouble, but he kept it upbeat.

8/26/67

Dear Bill and Laura:

I sit here in the cellar at the middle desk, these desks which I believe were instrumental

> in helping to form and bring success to three children through education. I think these desks were part of the foundation and to me bring many pleasant memories. I now use them ... for my accounts ... I suppose you took our advice & took out life insurance and hospitalization ...
>
> Love and best wishes to both of you,
>
> Dad

The desks. He was so proud of the desks. Not only for the workmanship, but also for what they represented. He wanted children who would, in some measure, succeed. In his mind, these desks were instruments for their success. He had designed them, set the project in motion. But at this point, I was not exactly succeeding as he had planned. I felt I had let them all down.

Agnes wrote often to Laura and me. Sometimes she wrote with warm advice. But to no avail. Within months, we were seeking counseling. I never divulged any of this to Agnes or to anyone. Maybe it was all part of the adjustment period, when two people are trying to merge their lives, their pasts, their temperaments. We would have to see.

***

The divorce was issued in Las Vegas in the summer of '68, a little over a year after the wedding. At least we'd made it a year. Great success!

Since there were no children and no debts to speak of, it is difficult to imagine a cleaner break in the legal sense. But emotionally I felt drained, wrung out. I was a man torn with self-doubt. A failure.

For weeks I lived in the rancid backseat of my Dodge Polara like a penniless vagrant. Cheese and crackers, stringy fries scattered around the floor. Peanuts. Candy bars. Discarded cheeseburger wrappers. I had met guys like this on the road to California and in the orange groves and at the Commercial Hotel. Now I was one of them. I just wanted to get laid, but I was living in a dumpster, and I probably smelled like a dumpster—like a half-eaten banana, a bag of wilted fries.

Once it became obvious to the family what was happening, there was no discussion of why the marriage had failed. Silence. This failure of mine, by some unspoken pact, was never to be mentioned again, unless in some positive way. I liked that.

From Saint Basil Seminary in Toronto, Eugene wrote a lengthy, brilliant letter filled with the arcana of church law. In it, he advised me on marriage annulment. He would direct the process, he said. He knew exactly how to get this done; he knew what I should say. In the eyes of the church, it would be as though the marriage had never occurred.

But by then I had decided to avoid the complications of annulment. I considered the matter closed forever.

My father wrote an encouraging letter suggesting that this might have been an important learning experience for me, that it was best now to look toward the future. To my knowledge, there had never been a divorce in the family. Despite that fact, there was no criticism of either of us. What had happened had happened, and neither my father nor Agnes said a word. To my surprise, my father seemed more concerned about my progress toward the degree, the coveted PhD on which I had set my sights after Pitt.

1/17/68

Dear Bill:

Received your letter today and was glad to hear that you are meeting with much success on your project, for any success any of you have brings much happiness to_your Mother and I, for at our age it's all we have to look forward to.

> Your poetry being accepted must have made you feel real proud but as I have told you many times its good and relaxing to the mind to get away from the books for awhile, I know your trip to California should have helped some …
>
> I am doing pretty good with my diet and am still losing a little weight which is good for me …
>
> Love,
> Dad

Breslow asked me about the lines concerning my poem, about my father's claim that any success brought much happiness to him and my mother. And I told him this was completely unexpected, especially my father's dark revelation that at his age there was not much to look forward to. He was only fifty-eight! He was not an old man. Why was he talking like this?

As for the poem: "It was a small poem," I said to Breslow. "It was published in a little magazine called *Maelstrom.* It wasn't much. It was called "Meeting At Pittsburgh," about two lovers. I liked it, but I remember only a few lines:

In the bridge-silvered dawn
Among rain and the wet-scented stones
We met where the rivers met
At the concourse of days.

"In the larger scheme of things it wasn't … well, you understand?"

"It meant a lot to him," Breslow said. "Everything that you did meant a lot to him. He saw those desks that he made, he saw himself and his efforts, both in that poem and in your research."

I nodded and smiled a little. "I guess."

"And maybe it meant something to you," Breslow continued.

"It's set in Pittsburgh. At the Point. Were you thinking of anyone special?"

"Possibly," I said. "Possibly."

***

August, 1968

Dear Mom and Dad,

It has been a long flight. The C-130 was far from comfortable—noisy, crowded, hot. But everything around us—the endless Pacific, the sky, the ice shelves and vast stretches of whiteness—was beautiful.

I should tell you that there won't be mail in or out of Antarctica until sometime in October. This will be my last letter until then.

I hope you are both doing well. And at the risk of sounding repetitious, I want to thank you once again for the wonderful vacation in Atlantic City. Eugene and I loved it. The boardwalk. The hucksters. The tangy smell of the sea. It all carried me back.

Love, Bill

***

January, and I am back in Blacksburg. This is the year I am determined to wrap things up. No more distractions. I focus on the spinning gases moving swiftly among a swarm of ions.

1/3/69

Dear Bill,

I am sorry I was not more company to you on your visit here but I was really not up to it on account of my illness but someday we will

> have to have a good bull-shit session and a couple glasses of beer about old times and maybe a few good suggestions about the future. I am enclosing a check for $140.00 for you to use for tuition in case your South Pole check from Benoit is not there. If it is just return the check to me. I am also enclosing a check for $25.00 made out to Mrs. Wilson for your June rent which I want you to accept as a gift from your Mother and I.
>
> Love,
> Dad

I ignore anything with a dollar sign in front of it. So I owe money to someone; I'm probably in debt in three states and two foreign countries. In my copy of *Crime and Punishment*, I find a warning from the jewelry store where I bought Laura's engagement ring. I shake my head. *Marriage! What was I thinking?*

I read my father's apology—"sorry I was not more company"—and think, *No, Dad, no need for that.* I wonder what time and the recent events of his life—the illnesses, the job, the new management—have done to him. How these have humbled him. He is not the same cocky guy who wrote to me at Catholic University eight years ago, the man who could take a team of bat boys and mold them into a championship ball club. The man with the fungo bat who yelled, "Off to the left! Backhand it!"

But what is more important, what matters most, is the passage about a "good bullshit session and a couple glasses of beers …"

Breslow says, "He wanted to talk to you man-to-man. He understood that you *were* a man now, in his opinion, with your own life, your own experiences, your own successes and failures. Much like himself. He felt he could reveal himself to you, in ways you would understand. He was according you respect."

I nod and purse my lips. "Yes," I say.

★★★

If Breslow appreciated the sincerity and hints of darkness in Eugene's writing, his deep appreciation for culture, he found Liz's letters to be a relief, a source of both information and wry amusement. She wrote mostly to my parents, assuming that eventually her brothers would get the full story, though not in her precise words. Somehow, though, her letters found their way into my collection, and she expressed no interest in having them back. "You keep them, Bill," she said. "I don't want to remember." Maybe it was all too painful, the way things hadn't worked out between her and George. Maybe there was something else too, something darker that I knew I would never hear about.

June 24, 1969

Dear Mom and Dad,

We just arrived here in Goias about three hours ago from our two-week sojourn & I am ready to collapse. But I can't do that yet because I have to take a shower first & I can't take a shower because the electricity is off & the electricity is off because we didn't pay our bill for the last month & we didn't pay our bill because we're lazy. So if I collapse in the middle of this letter its because we're lazy. That plus the fact that I haven't written for awhile & you're probably cursing my very name by now.

Well, we didn't get to Buenos Aires because … we're lazy. We went to Sao Paulo & ate all the hamburgers & milk shakes we could stuff in for one day & then caught the bus to Porto Alegre, which took 22 hours …

Well, I'm going to collapse now. I'll write more later.

Write soon and take care,
Love from the Dear Ones,
George and Liz

Breslow—being a man of context and wanting to know as much as possible about the family—read every word that Liz and Eugene wrote.

"She's really funny," he said as he folded the letter and handed it to me across the desk. "And fearless too, travelling the whole continent by bus."

27 June 1969

Dear Bill,

Yesterday brought me to the Oratory at Birmingham (England) and so having freed myself of the seductive embrace of Lady Paris (and having shunned the allurements of London), I now find myself in a position and a state of body, mind and spirit better conducive to writing you of my experiences thus far.

Just to give you an overview from New York on: You did of course receive my air-written letter en route to Frankfurt. Well, I only spent about an hour there in wait for a plane to Paris. But I used these few moments to pay what little tribute I had time to pay to the German Republic. I did, obviously, purchase the stamps necessary to get your letter into the mail. I then perused the airport shops and studied the German manufacturer of various clothes and leather goods. I then sent only a few postcards, rushed into the coffee-shop-bar and toasted Germany and finally dashed to the news stand to purchase the principal Paris newspaper to read in flight. The Lufthansa flight was rather amusing because the German stewardess did not know whether I was German, French, or English—but since I knew just enough German to order the various drinks that I wanted I was able to keep her bewildered.

I arrived in Paris quite fatigued because the day was hot, the Paris airport rather uncomfortable and because the five hour time change had done strange things to my metabolism. But I cannot begin to tell you all that I did so I shall only attempt to tell you something of what I saw—but I do tell you in advance that I love Paris—that it is poetry in its structures and music in its people. But on with it! My first evening, I walked the banks of the Seine and stood breathless before Notre Dame (unfortunately the faith which built this cathedral no longer spiritualizes it).

There was so much theater to be seen and I managed to get in a respectable amount. I went to see Goldoni's "Le Menteur." Goldoni is a Renaissance and 17th c. Italian playwright who is now translated into many languages—for instance I saw another of his plays in Toronto in English. He is rather like Moliere in his comedy—and this play was an absolute riot with superb actors. The performance was given in the courtyard of the Hotel d'Aumont which was built in the 17th c. as the home of Michel Scarron whose wife was one of the mistresses of Louis XIV and who was also involved in black magic circles with La Voisin and others (read some of Montague Sommers on black magic and its history in various countries for good bedtime stories). Another night I attended a production of two No plays—these are Japanese ritualistic dramas which involve only a limited amount of voice work. The final theater which I had occasion to see was at Les Halles, the singing of Monteverdi's Orphee—really a breathtaking piece of baroque music—also held in the courtyard.

Well, perhaps that must be all for now. Next letter I shall have more to say about places I visited and people I met—but either category would take too long for tonight. Also by then I should have more to say about the Birmingham Oratory—which at the moment is still a bit of a blur to me since I am here only slightly more than 24 hours and suffering the shudders of cultural shock from being so clearly back in the 19th c.—architecturally, culturally and (I suspect) theologically.

Do take care of yourself, Bill dear friend, and let me have a word or two from 1969 and the world of science if you can find a free moment to write your time-machined brother.

Love,
Eugene

Oh god, I think, *Eugene is still balled up, knotted, sweating, despite that cool, copacetic, cosmopolitan front of his. I love this brother of mine. I want him to find the balance he once wrote about. I want him to find his way. Jesus, he will soon be ordained. Maybe that will help. But I doubt it. He is searching for something more. We all seem to be.*

6/19/69

Dear Bill,

Thanks very much for remembering me on Fathers Day. I was sorry I was not home but I had started a ping-pong tournament & had eighteen fellows to play Sunday afternoon at the Elks, then I had to go to work at 6:00 pm to load busses for the mayors convention in Pgh. The tournament was very successful & we have another one the 29th of June to run for three successive Sundays. Had a letter from Eugene in Paris, he apparently is very inspired with the place and said he is getting along real well using his French, also has seen some interesting plays, the only play I liked was Captain Video. I have interesting brochures on Ireland and if you can you can wait until you come home to line one up. But don't borrow any money from the banks down there for you see the high interest now, 8 per cent. Harry suggests we lend it to you from the building fund.

Love,
Dad

Okay, Dad, I think. *Captain Video. Why the hell not?* I liked *Captain Video* too. I had my decoder ring. I watched every episode, Aunt Gene sitting there in her wheelchair.

***

It seemed like years since I had corresponded with Estella, but in September of '69, she wrote a congratulatory note that seemed to open up new possibilities in our long-standing time together and apart. It had been ten years since we first met at Westinghouse Labs. Ten years! And we had not forgotten.

9/2/69

Dear William James Green (Ph.D.)

Hi, I have many thoughts of you that I can't put into words—need you to help.

Cryptic. *Once again beyond my comprehension,* I thought.

> Spoke with your mother when I was home last month—heard about Belfast. Good for you ... So you had enough travel to the Antarctic? I'm proud of you—a Ph.D.—always knew (sort of) that you would (ever since Westinghouse). Now you'll have more time to get out that poetry that is in you. Have a good time in Belfast. (How long?) Keep in touch if you can. Wish I could talk to you but am not certain would say my mind then ...
>
> Estella

"What did she mean about saying her mind?" Breslow asked.

"I don't know," I said. "Maybe she meant we needed to talk. Talk about where things were headed. Ten years is a long time. But we'd been too busy—she with her master's and the beginning of a career, and me with the doctorate in chemistry. But I'd always wanted to travel, see the world. I'd been desperate for that. And with the offer in Belfast, I couldn't resist."

***

The family letters continued during my months in Ireland. Right up to the end, to my father's death. I read some of these to Breslow.

> Dec. 15, 1969
>
> Dear Bill,
>
> First I must start out by wishing you a Merry Christmas and a Happy New Year. We sent you a box on the 11th, which we hope you receive for Xmas. Eugene is going to preach his first sermon Sunday Dec. 28th at the Episcopal Church at the corner of 3rd

and Broadway, that is the church Mrs. Edel belongs to. I want to go and hear him. I started to get out my toys for Christmas, George will probably think I'm nuts. But that's what keeps you young.

Love,
Dad

I had to explain the toys to Breslow—the bear, the guy with the lit cigar, and all the other mechanicals he had stored in the attic. Breslow gave a rare, barely audible laugh at hearing this. I also had to explain the significance my father placed on the prospect of having the neighbors hear his son preach. He was so proud of Eugene, and so was my mother. But she would not attend an Episcopal service. Never!

January 2, 1970

My dearest Bill,

George and Sister arrived at home at almost the same time as you did last year from Antarctica. We had a rather exciting time and became better acquainted with our new son-in-law. Certainly your engaging personality and delightful repartee were sorely missed over the holidays. Your absence surely dampened our spirits at a time when most things seemed to be in fine shape. Perhaps another time, another day, will find us together again … Sister is now working in the Clerk of Courts Office in Bloomington. She has to be deputized and also bonded. Before Christmas she worked part time and liked it very much.

Happy New Year and please write at great length and tell us the news.

With lots of love,
Mother

"She is sweet to you," Breslow said, "but so demanding. So insistent that you write, and write at length. Did it annoy you?"

I shrugged. "Not much. I got used to it over the years. I even found it flattering that she wanted to know everything that was happening in my life. She's always had a broad interest in the world. Always wished she had travelled. So of course Ireland fascinated her, and Europe even more."

4 January 1970

Dear Bill,

... I write you now—at least to tell you how much I think about you, how much I enjoyed and appreciated your letter to me, and to wish you this new year of a new decade (and the beginning of the new century's fin de siècle) the best of surprising gifts that Lady Life can produce from out the many folds of her long and glittering gown.

As you may already know, the structure of my life this past term formed itself around the courses I was doing at Pittsburgh Theological—all three of which were helpful. But in addition to that I have made (over the last six weeks) a beginning on my thesis. I have decided to write something on John Donne's handling of various Christological issues in the ten volumes of his sermons.

This term has involved some travel—a few trips to New York—the last of which included the rare treat of a dinner at Bill Buckley's Park Avenue apartment (prior to the debate in which Fr. Clancy pretty much slaughtered him)—but it was a memorable night. There was also a visit back to Toronto—the sadness of which can be explained only in a full-length novel. And then a few weeks after that I visited D.C. and C.U. and my friend Steve there and all that was quite pleasant. The past weeks have mostly been rather predictable rounds of Christmas activities—before and after—with the same yearly round of occasions and responses, etc., etc. and I am eager at the moment to get on with life in the months to come—with the hope that they may prove more encouragingly fruitful.

Interesting how at times our psychic gears seem to shift and send the vehicle of our lives whirling off into some distant space, circling around a cold and dark sun—the planet of lives, growing daily more unrecognizable, while the flowing streams of our days turn to ice and the gentle flowers of our nights fade away and die off. And yet we can opt for a radical hope-perspective in life—foolhardy as at times that may seem—and trust that another galaxy of circumstances will send, by another violent shift of our psychic gears, the planet of our lives back into the orbit we know to be our own—the one we know to be a succession of days and nights, a mixture of light and darkness, and a passing from warmth to cold and back again.

Liz and George, as you know, were home for Christmas and my time with them was pleasant but with, of course, the disturbances that newness always produces. With Liz one must become reacquainted and in George one must try to find a new friend. He, however, is difficult because a rather sullen and unexpressive person. But I find his interiority fascinating and hope it suggests years of captivating mystery—it could suggest nothing more than simple dullness, but I think not.

I preached my first sermon last Sunday—but not in a church of our own tradition. An Anglican priest-professor of philosophy, who is a friend, asked me to take his services for him so he could have a few days to vacation after Christmas. I agreed and so preached at St. Timothy's in McKees Rocks and a church in Mt. Washington. Dad, Liz and George came to the St. Timothy's service. (Mother, un-liberated, post-Tridentine Catholic that she is) refused to hear me till I appeared in a Roman pulpit. It did strange and wonderful and beautiful things to me to watch Dad out there in such rapt attention and to provide my reflections on the meaning of Christ for the thought of Mr. and Mrs. Edel. The experience was a good one for me and has made me, despite the terrible and almost nauseating responsibility I feel attached to preaching, lust all the more after a ministry whose words and whose message are now more than tinsel wings of hope flying in the face of life's hurricane winds.

Forgive my not asking about your commitments—but I hardly know enough even to ask an intelligent question. Do write with details. By the next letter, I should have more definite things to tell you. Till then, I leave you with the expectant echoes of the new decade's new bells still sounding.

With love,
Eugene

Breslow nodded slowly, hinted at a smile, as though he might be recalling some fragment of his own academic past. And he took note of "Tridentine-Catholic," especially in reference to my mother. "He signs his letter 'With love,'" Breslow said, with obvious approval. "But he does seem dubious about Liz's choice of a husband."

January 5, 1970

Dear Bill,

We had a nice Xmas here at home with Liz here for a week and Eugene running in and out but we missed you. The girls across the street were here, also Don ... We are very happy to hear that you are doing well with Dr. Ivin & that he has recognized your ability as I did that you were a 2nd baseman, also that you have made some other friends which will help to make your stay there more interesting. Now that we know you are going to stay in Ireland until at least July we may look into & make plans & make a boat trip over. Let me know if you get your Xmas package. If you run short of cash let me know and we may be able to send you some. Let us know how the project was that you were to have completed by Dec. 17th. Tell the Kennedy girl we hope her operation was a success. Also say hello to Mr. Cavanaugh, your friend Norman Lyle & his parents ... Keep us informed of your trip to Germany.

Love,
Dad

"The girls across the street?" Breslow said, looking puzzled in that Breslow-puzzled way, glasses slid down to the tip of his nose. "Who are they?"

"I don't know," I said. "They're Liz's friends. Cez and Wanda. I think they came from Lithuania. I've seen them but have never actually spoken to them. I find the younger one very attractive, almost like one of those Eastern European models you see on the cover of *Vogue*—tall, thin … you know? They seem to appear only on Sunday mornings on their way to church. Big, outdated dresses from another age. I've never exchanged a smile with either of them. Maybe someday I'll stop over at the house and see if anyone answers the door. It looks pretty formidable."

Breslow was bent like a big question mark, sitting across from me.

"A really mysterious family," I continued, "with lots of rumors swirling around the neighborhood. You know, the mother does roofing. *Roofing, Jesus!* Shingles and all that stuff. And she cuts down trees with a chain saw. And the father, 'Russian Pete,' speaks a polyglot language of German, Lithuanian, English, and who knows what else. No one can understand him. But he's a great businessman, they say."

Breslow nodded and gave an awkward smile when I mentioned "Russian Pete."

I told him, "Liz says I'd enjoy talking with Wanda. There's a touch of the bohemian in her. And she has a great voice when she plays the guitar and sings the familiar folk songs and some Old English ballads. She smiles a lot and seems smart and happy."

January 10, 1970

Dear Bill,

Receiving a letter from you is such a joy. You make everything sound so rosy and pleasing—not a care in the world.

Writing back to you is rather difficult—especially when we cannot use words and phrases as you do. Accept me as I am—or no more letters!!

We have missed having you home again this year at Christmas time. Did you receive your Christmas gifts from your parents? They get much enjoyment out of preparing your packages. Your package was the only one they had to send this year.

Liz, George and Eugene were home to open packages together for a change. The living room looked like years gone by. I was in the day after Christmas and all the gifts were still around the tree …

Liz and George look better than when they returned from Brazil. They went back to Indiana on New Years Eve so no party at either the Greens' or the Cookes'.

I think you are very wise in traveling while you are in Ireland. Of course, it does take money. Maybe this small gift will help buy a meal or two while journeying. Can you save it that long? This is really your Christmas gift. Don't worry about saving it!

Good luck on all your undertakings! Keep smiling! We all love you.

Love and prayers,
Aunt Agnes

"A kind, loving letter," Breslow said. "Since the divorce, the PhD, and the journey to Antarctica, Agnes seemed more deferential. She respected what you'd done. Had your own, sometimes painful, experiences. The experiences of a grown man. Successes and failures. She'd probably been talking with your father."

"Yes, I sense that too," I said. "It came as a surprise. Agnes is such a good, thoughtful person. A saint in some ways."

***

I was thinking how much the letters had changed. How a stratigrapher might have noted the passage of years, a mere decade recorded in the thin laminae of language, one year stacked seemingly imperceptibly upon another. Yet that same observer of words would have seen here the workings of time, its weaving, binding and enfolding, its drawing us inexorably closer.

1/18/70

Dear Bill,

I am watching TV & right now the gym teacher has 3 boys climbing ropes remember when you and I went up to the Hi school for your practice rope climbing. I am sending you a box with tobacco in it for your smoking pleasure. Liz has a Political job in Bloomington & is doing very good. Eugene is still attending classes at Pittsburgh Theological Seminary and stops down home about twice a week. How is your lab work coming along, also how is Cavanaugh and Norman and I hope you haven't forgotten Norman's mother being so nice to you when you were sick. Write to Eugene.

Love,
Dad

"Yes, the rope climbing," Breslow said. "That effort he made to help you with your dreams of West Point. He seemed to remember all the details of your past together. He even compared your research work with Professor Ivin with your skills as second baseman.

February 1, 1970

My dearest Bill,

Yesterday we had Christmas in January instead of December when your lovely gift arrived from the "Old Sod." It is really beautiful and we surely appreciate your thoughtfulness. The shamrocks made it seem more Irish than the words "Irish Linen" stamped on it. Again thanks from both Dad and me.

The letters seem to be coming at a rather slow pace but now they have stopped completely. Maybe your trip to Strasburg has prevented your writing but I do hope we'll hear from you this week from the continent.

Eugene spent last weekend at home and we certainly enjoyed having him here. Then on Monday he was asked to teach at Carlow College. The one course is in Biblical Theology. The other is a three-hour seminar. The offer made him very happy because he felt he was becoming mentally stagnant since he hasn't been teaching. Of course he is still continuing his work at the Theological Seminary.

Try to write soon and tell us what you are doing. It seems so long.

With lots of love,
Mother

2/9/70

Dear Bill,

We can't understand why you are not getting our letters for I have written two and Aunt Agnes one, hers had a $5.00 bill in it for you. We received your Xmas gift and it was real nice, thank you. Father Clancy and Eugene were here for supper last night, they did not stay too long for Fr. Clancy had to give instructions to a couple who wanted to become Catholic. Fr. Clancy sure loves your Mother's dumplings and you should see him eat. We read in the paper where the bricks are flying again in Belfast. Glad to hear you had a nice trip to Germany. Eugene is to be a guest lecturer at Duquesne University on Wednesday. He seems to be much happier since he started teaching at Carlow. I think before he had too much time on his hands, it was getting the best of him. I hope your interviews are still going OK. Please write a little more often, we like to hear from you.

Love,
Dad

Breslow said, "Clancy seems an important figure in Eugene's life. Your father and mother regard him highly. They almost revere him, with his New York past, his intellectual gifts, and his obvious admiration for your brother. To say nothing of your mother's dumplings." Breslow had to smile at his own touch of humor. Maybe there was even a silent laugh.

2/19/70

Dear Bill,

Received your long awaited letter today, we thought you had forgotten our address ... Eugene likes his job very much at Carlow & just yesterday Dr. Darcy told him he would like to have him back next year for a full schedule, he probably won't be allowed to accept this. Liz and George are doing OK we hear from them a good bit. Aunt Agnes is talking to your Mother on the phone as I write, she says hello and don't forget to write. We have had a real bad winter, snow pretty much every day making the streets & roads real bad but not a heavy accumulation. Now that you are back on schedule we will expect letters more often. Mother gets off the phone and is now on her back her favorite position. I suppose everyone is getting ready for the big day over there March 17th. I sent you another package of tobacco if there is anything else you would like to have let us know. Write to Liz and Eugene.

Love,
Dad

"Shades of Catholic University," Breslow noted. "I thought he was about to give you their address."

I had to laugh at this. Breslow was becoming quite the comedian!

February 22, 1970

My dearest Bill,

After a seemingly interminable wait your letter finally arrived. Why did it take you so long to write? We wanted to hear so many things about your trip and all the places you visited and things you saw. How long did you spend there? When one has never visited these countries, one keeps wondering about all the interesting and fascinating sights you might have seen. Perhaps at a later date you will find time to write at greater length …

Eugene just called and said that he finally managed to contact you. It sounded so wonderful. We were delighted to hear that you sounded so fine.

Your visit to that little country church must have been a delightful treat. How was the attendance there and what kind of people formed the parish? How did you travel to Donegal? Do you know someone who drives?

Dad has had a rather hard winter because whenever we have an overnight snow (which is quite often) he is called out at 4:30 or 5:00 in the morning. Sometimes he doesn't even take time for lunch.

Please try to write soon and tell us all the news because we do enjoy hearing from you.

With lots of love,
Mother

Hard winter. Overnight snow. 4:30 or 5:00 in the morning. When I read this in Belfast, it meant little to me. But in Breslow's office, after my father's death, I recognized that these words might be linking his death to his job. He was older and heavier than he should have been. He was unaccustomed to working odd hours under such inclement and harsh conditions. And his diet of fats and salt had not changed. All of these factors, in retrospect, seemed to me conducive to heart disease.

March 16, 1970

My dearest Bill,

Since your call a short time ago, I have been unable to regain my composure. As a matter of fact, I still can't believe it. The phone had rung shortly before and it sounded as if I were getting a bad connection locally. Then I decided to hang up, so that whoever it was could ring again. Your voice sounded the same, but I couldn't believe I was hearing from you, especially at 6 pm. It was truly wonderful and made me so very happy …

Isn't it wonderful about Sister and the new baby? I knew you would be happy to hear this news. They naturally are very happy and I certainly know how exciting this time can be.

As I told you, the pictures you sent were delightful. You really look fine. Aunt Agnes said you look like a "professor." So maybe you will be one next year, that is, this year.

Aunt Gene was so happy to hear from you and she never fails to ask about you. Of course, you were really "tops" with her. Aunt Agnes was down over the weekend and she, as well as the others, wanted to know what we had heard from you. Francois, Joe, Bill and Tina always ask about you.

I am enclosing this map and hope that you have visited Donegal, the home of the O'Donnells. Let me know about it.

Try to write soon and tell us all the news. (Love you for that call.)

With lots of love,
Mother

3/27/70

Dear Bill,

What great pleasure you gave to your Mother and Dad last week! They were so happy with your call. A voice from heaven!

I am going to the Oratory with your Mother and Dad on Saturday for the Easter Services. They had thought of going to Indiana but feel they will go later.

Hope you like my picture. Show it to all the Irish.

God bless you. Keep the faith.

Love, Aunt Agnes

This was among the last pieces of correspondence of the decade.

I was struck yet again by how little the divorce had mattered. There was no mention of it in any letter that arrived at Queens University. Had there even been a marriage? A divorce? Sometimes I doubted it. The erasure was as complete for them as it was for me.

Photo of blackbird in flight.

18

BLACKBIRD

There are more than thirteen ways. The ways might be infinite for even the simplest thing: the raindrop on the windowpane, the arc of the rainbow. Once a stranger told me that every time she saw a rainbow, she remembered her father's death. And it gave her hope, she said, that he spoke to her from the heavens through the clouds.

***

The letters could be seen in their sundry ways, from many points of view, with their various themes and repetitions and with the occasional evolution in points of view. In the letters and excerpts I showed him back in the early '70s, Breslow had seen exactly what he saw in my memories and dreams: my father's protective presence, his concern with my payment of bills, my social life, my obsessive (to him) attachment to books.

My father had not been subtle in his letters about what was owed, what should be repaid. He seemed to know every cent I had not reimbursed some bank, some book club or agency. Even his most wistful, poignant letter might have dispersed within it a monetary duty I had failed to discharge. It felt like he'd stuck a shiv in my chest each time he reminded me of an unpaid debt.

And each letter contained a reminder that there was someone—an aunt, a friend, Eugene or Elizabeth—toward whom I had been negligent in my correspondence. And for my mother and him, the words were never enough. Another letter should be in the mail. An insatiable appetite for words seemed to run in the family. And while I can now see this familial tendency as well-meaning and as evidence of the love that passed between and among us, back then I saw it as among the principal sources of my discomfiture.

If his own words were not sufficient to inflict the requisite sense that I had failed in my correspondence and expressions of gratitude, those of his sister, Agnes, with whom he was in constant contact and who reflected his views and could put them effectively into the form of incisive "sermons," more than sufficed. She was far more explicit than he about how much he had given and how much he was owed.

Dr. Breslow, rocking back in his black chair and peering at me from across the desk, asked, "You see why you had to escape, don't you? It seemed like the perfect solution to your problems. But there was no place distant enough." His analysis was entirely consistent with the Joe Vitelli School of Barroom Psychiatry: "Jim, you gotta let him go."

"Sometimes," Breslow said, "love holds us too tightly."

***

Later I gathered the letters in one place; I read them in two days. It was such a simple act of organization—taking what pages I had and arranging them as I might have done with a collection of baseball cards. I could hardly have expected to be, in any measure, edified. But I was.

I had not remembered that my father had written so much, had not remembered that he had recalled so much: those seventeen years; that rope in the gym at Rocks High; the high-gloss desks in the basement; even the poem that I published in Virginia.

He had not seen it all, but he had seen enough to know that he had raised three children who had not let him down; who had, in some broad measure, carried out his wishes and who moreover understood what he had given them.

He had seen his eldest—despite all the divagations associated with California, the "South Pole," the divorce—complete his doctorate, and had recognized that achievement with a passage, bought and paid for, on the *QE2*. His son was not a quitter after all. In life, he had not lollygagged as he had once lollygagged down the first baseline that evening in the Rocks.

And he had seen his second son preach at the Episcopal church, and must have witnessed in Eugene's sermon the power of his priestly voice, his hard-won erudition. For Eugene had labored long in the vineyards of the spoken and written words and could hold a crowd spellbound if he chose. It was clear that someday he would become the scholar he had always wanted to be.

Liz was pregnant, and our father respected motherhood, pure and simple, as its own great achievement. But he could forecast—from her letters, her easy sarcasm, her years on her own in Brazil, her willingness to engage with the arcana of budgeting—that she was on her way to something else. He saw the potential there, even though he could not have foreseen that she would go from accounting for the measly thousands of dollars in the Clerk of Courts Office in Bloomington to overseeing, as budget director, literally hundreds of millions, possibly billions, in the vast system of departments, divisions, research institutes, and hospitals that comprised the Ohio State University. But he knew something like this was on the horizon for his only daughter. What he could not have predicted was the humility with which she handled it all, seeing fit as she did to praise her brothers more than herself, when in retrospect it was her accomplishments, her boldness and fearlessness, that stand out.

I think my father could see on the map of his later life the lines he had begun to trace for the three of us, and he had imagined their continuance through time. The *ABC* pendant, cast in gold, said as much.

Neither for him nor for us, nor indeed for our dear mother, did success have much to do with wealth or worldly recognition. It had to do with dreams, with images of the kind Henry James wrote about in *Portrait of a Lady:*

> I call people rich when they are able to meet the requirements of their imagination.

***

Through all the overseeing ("the meddling," as Breslow called it back in the '70s), there was an unveiled pride in what we had done. When I dedicated my dissertation to him and my mother in 1969, in words that now appear to me far less effusive and heartfelt than they should have been—

To My Parents
James and Elizabeth
As a
Token of Gratitude

—my father immediately made three copies, one of which he passed around at the Wil-Kar Grill for his friends and patrons to see. In their letters and conversations, Eugene and Liz had similarly expressed their gratitude to my parents. Whatever else, they knew they were loved.

***

Wallace Stevens's poem "Thirteen Ways of Looking at a Blackbird" captures in thirteen stanzas, each a kind of haiku, the richness of possibility in our experiences of the world. In one stanza, the eye of the blackbird is the only thing moving among snow-covered mountains; in another, the blackbird whirls "in the autumn wind"; in a third, it is merely a shadow; and in a fourth, the blackbird whistles.

***

In the letters, I see my father's vulnerability, the illnesses, the weariness, the apologies he writes for not being able to come to the phone. I see the worry that came to him when I was a *brasero* in the orange grove; when I was in Belfast with the bricks and bombs and guns; when I began college in the distant city of Washington. His casual mentions of heavy snowfalls, which he must have known posed a threat to his health, hardly registered with me for years. I said nothing about them to Breslow and offered no expressions of concern. Certainly my mother worried about him, as her letters and later conversations revealed. "Bill, sometimes I think you need to be hit over the head with a brick," she would say. When I reread the letters, I think she was right. I was sleepwalking through much of my self-absorbed life.

***

The blackbird whistles; his eye moves among snowy peaks; he whirls in the wind. There was more than what Breslow had inferred: more than anger, more than the need to escape, more than the joyous, senseless tune that passed my lips at JFK. There was the awful, lasting sadness—call it grief, as my dear brother had—that came with his sudden departure. The guilt that I had not really gotten to know him, had not shared in his moments of triumph, his teams, his Exalted Ruler medal at the Elks, his Man of the Year award. Nor had I thanked him for those long hours, those evenings on the ball fields of the Rocks, when those unspoken bonds were forming amid the crack of a bat, the smell of linseed oil, the long metal arm of the pitching machine tracing its silvery arc through space.

I had written him about some abstraction, some academic nonsense ("too fancy for me," he'd said), rather than inquire about his work on the cars, the bitter winter on those terrible streets, the white sore on his tongue he discovered in Dallas, the small defeats that were wearing him down toward his decision to retire. "Don't you wish we could go back?" "Someday we will have to have a good bullshit session and a couple glasses of beer about old times and maybe a few suggestions about the future." From me, there was never a reply.

***

The other letters are cast in a softer, crepuscular light. The few letters I have from Aunt Gene amaze me simply by existing. How had she learned to write? Who taught her? Was it my ever-watchful mother? The letters, in their brokenness and sheer physical effort, bring to mind what Gene had meant to me: the afternoons McMullen and I spend with her after school at the kitchen table—her laughter and wisdom, the creak of her metal chair as she turns to bring over a new jam she has opened. "Try this," she says as she carves out the waxen seal. She drinks her coffee black, unlike the rest of us, as she reaches down to touch the white dog at her side. Her speech is perfect, like my mother's. In speech, there is not the burden of cursive, the neatly formed letters. There is no encumbrance of spelling. Only the effortless flow of words crossing through air in waves of sound. Gene's sweet voice.

Aunt Agnes, in retrospect, is among the most thoughtful people I have ever known. Cards for every birthday, every holiday, every graduation—no occasion is ever missed; each is celebrated and blessed by her words. She marks the year in the liturgy of symbols. And the letters are so numerous, so prayer filled. Even when they hurt in their preachy way, I understand them now as well-meaning in their concern, both for myself and for my father.

She wants the Lord of All Things to bring nothing but blessings upon our lives.

When Gene died and when Agnes died, I was nowhere to be found. As always, I was away in some inaccessible valley—the Wright, the Taylor, the Miers—the glacier-carved lands of Robert Falcon Scott and his team. There was no way I could get home. No way I could even get word that their lives had ended. The city of my youth seemed barricaded somewhere on a distant planet. But still, I felt I had failed my dear aunts, who had cared enough to write me and advise me and (in Gene's case) stay with me through the weary night hours as I studied and fretted over equations and formulas long since forgotten. I had been derelict in my duty to honor them.

Eugene's letters, continental in their formality, seem a gloss over a troubled soul in quest not only for a cultured world, but also for itself. His identity lay shrouded, exposed to me in part only through innuendo ("Bill, you must read Isherwood's *A Single Man* or Mann's *Death in Venice*"). There was much he would not speak of directly, and given the Irish Catholic family he grew up in and loved, it is clear why. My father's expansive understanding of human nature made him—Jim Green—a perfect candidate, unbeknownst to Eugene, to hear him out. But my mother, whose rigid interpretation of faith allowed for only the narrowest latitudes in belief, stood as an impediment to Eugene's candidness. Eugene knew this. So it was only in Boston—at a comfortable distance from Pittsburgh—that he could be free. If he wanted, he could even speak there at an Episcopal church without feeling like a pariah.

Reading his letters today, I see my own failure. I see what I missed in not knowing this lovely, gentle man for who he was. And I lament his early death. As with my father, there is a dream: Eugene's hand extended through the open window of the train, stretching back toward me. But I cannot reach it. He is gone into some unending Midwestern flatness. Only his typed words, fading on that worn onionskin paper, remain.

"My dearest Bill." All her letters begin the same way. She is positive, inquisitive. She wants to know what I have seen, where I have been. If Agnes often preaches, my mother rarely does. If my father seems obsessed with each nickel, she is not. Money is of little concern to her. She seems to assume that all is well and that, like the rest of them, I will muddle through. God will provide. If only I would write every day, preferably twice a day.

***

It came after my father's death, but my mother insisted on going to my doctoral graduation. It was 1970. I was not planning to attend—I never attended graduations—but she would not hear of that. She wanted to be in Blacksburg, Virginia, for the formal conferring of the degree upon her son. So we drove there, the two of us. I wanted her to the see the Blue Ridge Mountains. We drove the parkway, where she looked straight ahead through the tinted mists but would not look off to the precipitous sides.

I wore my gold-and-blue robes, and she took pictures with her old Polaroid. Or we had friends photograph us by the gray war memorial or the library or Davidson Hall, where I had finished my research. She would remind me, until the day she died, how much she loved this journey south.

Liz's letters become better reading with time. There is always the humor, always the sarcasm, the irony, whether she is writing from Goias or Bloomington. She wrote more about her travels through South America than she will ever talk about. I have always doubted it, but she has never wavered from the story that she just can't remember her time there. So I am keen to read what she has written, to read it again after so many years.

Nor does she speak of Bloomington—as if here time there is somehow appended in memory to Brazil. And indeed it is, since she spent it with George, a man she later divorced. I see in rereading the letters how she, as a history major at Duquesne, became an accidental accountant, a manager of budgets small and, finally, prodigious. I see how, on a personal level, she and George struggled constantly with finances, with rents, with car payments and with travel expenses that are the bane of graduate students everywhere and for all time. I see how they struggled with George's paranoia, his schizophrenia, his refusal to take his meds.

In the letters, everything is understated, even the birth of her first child. I know this feeling: to become excited, to be demonstrative in any way about anything is to invite disaster. Do not tempt the universe to strike you down with its iron hand. Is this the atavistic reservation of a once-conquered people? Is it pure and simple knowledge of how the universe, fickle and unpredictable, seemingly bereft of concern for the individual, for the species, operates? Or is it only the three of us who feel this way? Children of the same parents—the same household—under the influence of a hidden strife.

★★★

There are so many ways to see the blackbird. Each day, each hour, the eye of the blackbird shifts among the snowy peaks. And the peaks themselves are not the same moment to moment, cloud to scudding cloud, and wind to wind, the way one wind lifts the snow and lets it fall refulgent in showers of crystal and another wind crowds it upon the barren slopes. Not thirteen ways, but a multitude of ways beyond reckoning—an infinity. So too is it with memory.

JFK Airport circa 1970

19

JFK (1970)

The small things we barely notice often shape the world.

***

It was near the end of my years with Breslow when I finally decided that what had happened at JFK on my return from Belfast might, in fact, have mattered. It was so short-lived that for years I thought it inconsequential. But one evening in 1974, entering Breslow's office from the dim hallway, I began my brief, guilt-riddled revelation as soon as he asked, "Well, what have you been thinking about?"

"I've been thinking a lot about the plane coming in that morning from Heathrow. The way it glided straight in and seemed barely to touch the ground. It was a beautiful landing."

He looked at me as if he had forgotten Heathrow, JFK, my homecoming from Ireland, the early revelations. He looked thoroughly bewildered.

But I ignored his confusion and continued. "We were in the concourse," I said, "and I had collected my luggage. I would soon be boarding the flight to Pittsburgh. I was aware that I was returning for a funeral, that it was my father's funeral. Everything at home would be sadness and tears. Holding the office phone in Belfast, when Eugene called, I had felt all that."

Breslow began to nod, as though everything were coming back to him.

"But no sooner had I begun to walk through the airport than a kind of lightness came over me. I had no idea where it was coming from, but it might have been from some distant place. I wasn't exactly floating, but with each step I felt that I might lift into the air."

Breslow's eyes were covered with his right hand. His head was lowered. Slowly, he uncovered his eyes and let his hand drift upward as though it were rising on a gentle updraft. A quizzical look came over his face. Then there was silence. The silence seemed to go on and on. It was unusually long.

"Do you remember what you were feeling at the time?"

"Yes," I said, "vaguely. It was several years ago. Nearly four years, but I do recall how I felt."

"Describe it for me," he said, "and take your time. We've already made a lot of progress here. This could be important."

"Well," I said, "it came as a big surprise. I noticed as I moved through the terminal that my pace had changed. My step had changed. I seemed to be almost skipping. I caught a view of myself in a window I was passing. There was an unmistakable smile—not a broad smile, just a relaxed one, like you'd have if you stepped out of your house on a spring morning. You know."

I stopped talking for a few seconds. I looked down at my hands. They were lying on my lap, my fingers interleaved. I raised my head and saw Breslow, his pen poised above his notepad. He was waiting for more.

"Then what?" he asked.

"The next thing I knew I was whistling. Or humming. I don't quite remember. I think I was whistling."

"Whistling what?"

"It wasn't a particular tune. Not that I know of anyway. But it was light and breezy enough to send me skipping or dancing or just walking with more exuberance or excitement than usual. Nothing you would ever associate with a funeral. Certainly not your father's funeral."

"So you were feeling this lightness in your step," Breslow said as he wrote without stopping, without looking up at me.

"It was lightness. But it was more than that. It was *euphoria.* I felt it in every cell and muscle and joint in my body. It was like that day in California when I stood on third base, hardly believing my good fortune.

"But then I caught myself. *Oh my god,* I thought. *This is mental patricide.* This was some fantastical dream of patricide, as though I myself had murdered my father. As though I had done it with my own hands."

Breslow looked shocked. He stopped writing. He stared at me—just stared. Behind his owlish glasses, I could see his eyes open wide. I felt like I needed to say something; I needed to break the awkward silence. But it was Breslow who spoke.

"Why didn't you say something about this? It's been four years."

"I didn't think it was worth my time. Or yours. It shot by in an instant, and then I caught myself."

"But an instant can contain multitudes," said Breslow, in a biblical way. "What was going on in that instant? In your mind?"

"I'm not sure," I said. "Maybe I'm making this up, but memory tells me I was thinking of how all my life he was a constant presence, a keeper of records and debts, of payments not made; of how he doubted that I would ever grow up, that I would ever be able to hold my own in the world. Now he was gone, and all these things were gone with him. I felt free."

"You felt free," said Breslow, "but for that you have paid a terrible price. You felt intense guilt, and as we've said, guilt can manifest itself in frightening physical symptoms, of which you've had plenty. It was a costly freedom you won for yourself."

This small moment amid the crowds of JFK that morning obviously meant more to Breslow than I had expected. Perhaps this was as revealing as anything I had told him in our four years together. Perhaps I had helped to further illumine those early days: the memory of the dark forest; the memory of being unable to breathe. ("We have to go, Jim. We can't stay here with him like this.") The prophetic words of Joe Vitelli: "You've got to let him go ..." The dreams of flight and the release they provided, the momentary sense of freedom from that eternal, omniscient presence.

It was the last time I saw Breslow—in 1974, before I departed for Jersey, for my first college teaching job. I felt a deep sense of gratitude for this humble, quiet man. I told him I'd make an appointment to see him when I was next in Pittsburgh. I thanked him for all he'd done. I almost wanted to hug him, but instead I simply shook his hand and walked out the door. But as way leads on to way, I never saw him again.

Modern day Tucson skyline

20

UNFINISHED BUSINESS: TUCSON (2013)

In the evening and morning hours and over the years, I had plenty of time to think again about the letters, plenty of time to consider what Dr. Breslow had said in the dusky past, plenty of time to gather my own thoughts, to focus on the whole arc of my father's life.

***

What I have written here and in later chapters is from the perspective of 2013. In part, these chapters look at the past, turning it slowly as though it were a many-sided crystal with revelations yet to be discovered. In part, these chapters examine what I learned from my research in Tucson, Dallas, and elsewhere—seemingly disconnected cities that nonetheless provided new insights into my father and his times.

***

Breslow had seen my father's mild sarcasm at work, especially in the letter he wrote to me at Catholic University reminding me of the address of the home where I had lived all my life, as if somehow, in my few months away at college, I had gotten too big for my previous life, had forgotten everyone. Breslow had focused on my father's comment that he needed a translator, needed my mother, to interpret what I had written. *(Who is he trying to impress? Big words. "Captious"? What the hell does that mean? Who cares?)* While I considered these jibes benign measures of my father's sense of humor, Breslow, with his glasses slid down to the tip of his nose, took them differently. *Ah, pertinacious Breslow! That was nearly forty years ago, and to some degree I'm still refracting reality through your crafted lenses. And will, I think, until I die.*

Breslow noted too how Aunt Agnes's letters seemed designed to induce guilt. She praised my father as a selfless, caring man who gave far more to his family than anyone she knew; whose sacrifices, whether in work or in unremunerated community service, redounded to the benefit of us all; and whose love and admiration for his three children was succinctly expressed in the lines "He idolizes the three of you. I know he expects nothing in return except love, respect and obedience."

I recall Breslow leaning back in his soft chair, letter in hand, and looking at me somberly. "Those words placed a heavy burden on you—on the three of you. He made you carry those burdens for years."

He fingered the letter—from across the desk, I heard the crinkling paper move in his hands—and exclaimed, "Obedience! What do you think Agnes meant by that?"

And I said, "He expected success. In whatever we chose. He did not want us to waste time. He had done his part. Had paid the freight, as he put it. And he expected that in some way we would triumph." Breslow had nodded in seeming agreement.

Breslow did not miss the reference to the three desks. How could he? In a way, my father's words—"I sit here in the cellar at the middle desk, these desks which I believe were instrumental in helping to form and bring success to three children through education"—suggested that we had already done what he had wished we would, or that we were well on our way, at least. But Breslow noted the date, August 1967, and commented on how not long afterward I had left for Antarctica.

"Apparently," he said, "you thought he wanted more. A PhD wasn't enough. You had to prove yourself in some other way. Perhaps you knew he expected something more manly, more physical, less cerebral and abstruse than chemistry, something he could understand as viscerally as he understood the double play."

Breslow liked to take dramatic pauses even though he rarely spoke above a whisper, as though someone in the waiting room might hear us through the thick, soundproof doors.

"You knew he liked and respected work in the outdoors. He knew working in snow and ice was hard, from his own winter experience, but he enjoyed it nonetheless. It was a *man's* work. You knew he had no knowledge of what you did in the laboratory. But Antarctica was different; he understood. He knew the snows of Pittsburgh. He knew ice and hard physical labor. He could tell his drinking buddies about that."

Breslow couldn't stop his summary, the collection of all the straws and pebbles I had given him over the years. "And you knew he felt proud to be Irish, so you later took what was available in Ireland, even though it was Protestant Belfast. Still, as your mother said, '"it's the Old Sod."'

He gave that little smile of his. "The pressure was always on you. It was on you from the beginning, on the ball field when you were a kid, in the tournaments, in Williamsport, in California, on Saturdays around the house, at Christmas with the train layout. You could not escape."

Aunt Agnes's words—"I really feel you have been very dependent on your parents even though you have seemingly been on your own"—struck Breslow with the same force that they struck me. "You *were* dependent," he said. "You can see that everywhere, in all the letters that mention money and unpaid debts. He wanted to know every aspect of your finances. He wanted to control them. You felt that someone was always looking over your shoulder."

Silence and more silence. I felt as though I should be lying, eyes shut against the world, on Freud's sofa in old Vienna. Breslow let his words sink in, and he looked at my face for a sign that they had. Then he continued with his précis, his reiteration of JFK. "It was only when you knew he was gone that, at last, you felt some relief. When you could whistle and finally taste what freedom is like. And you hated yourself for that. You still hate yourself. It expressed in real life what before you could only express in dreams."

The blackbird whirls in the wind. He will always whirl in the wind. We will see him turn in a thousand ways.

***

There was a sudden impulse that came one day: I wanted to experience some of what my father experienced. So in the spring and summer of 2013, forty-three years after his death, I set out on a short journey involving a couple of cities I hadn't seen for a while.

My first stop was Tucson, Arizona, and the Center for Creative Photography. It seemed an odd place to be visiting, since our road trip from California in 1965 had not even included this place. I knew it as the city of brilliant stars, of heavens full of galaxies spiraling above the desert; of treeless mountains that reminded me of the naked Asgards of Antarctica. It was the city of Kitt Peak Observatory and Biosphere II and the towering saguaro cactus, finger-branched against the dry, azure skies. But in addition, it was the repository of W. Eugene Smith's remarkable *Pittsburgh Collection,* the largest assemblage of black-and-white photographs ever taken of my hometown, of my father's flourishing city in its heyday—the 1950s.

It was nearing nine o'clock in the morning, and already the temperature was approaching ninety degrees. The doors of the center opened exactly at nine and I entered the stark, Bauhaus-like foyer. Only the staff was there at that hour. I was taken upstairs to the temperature- and humidity-controlled room where Smith's photographs were catalogued. They were expecting me, and the cart was already positioned with ten boxes of Smith's pictures, negatives, and letters. It was a Friday, and I was thinking how I would never get through these in a single day without my eyeballs turning to jelly. But I had to.

The curator brought me a box of white gloves and said the photos could only be handled with these. The notes and letters could be touched with fingers, but never the photographs. This was precious material. No pens were permitted, only pencils. Aside from an assistant, I was the only person there. There was absolute, research-library quiet, an inhuman stillness. I was alone with W. Eugene Smith, with whom I felt a kinship. It was just the two of us, plus an incorporeal presence that only I could sense.

I knew all these places in the photographs. I'd walked these streets, but I'd forgotten the names. My father, who was present to me like a spirit, knew them all. He had worked every one of them for years.

There seemed to be no organizing principle to the collection, no movement from the center city outward to the working-class neighborhoods like McKees Rocks. It was random, and my mind recorded a mosaic of scenes. Smith seemed fascinated by Mellon Bank, in the heart of downtown, and had shot it from many angles. In one shot, the tall buildings of the city are reflected in the curved surface of a glass sphere that stands before the marble stairs leading to the columned temple of Andrew W. Mellon.

In the next packet, there were photos of a cop directing traffic on Grant Street near a coffee shop. He was that one, the *famous* cop. In profile, he looked like my father. And I thought I could feel my father looking over my shoulder, nodding his head and smiling. He remembered too.

In the '50s, the celebrity cop still directed traffic by dancing, by spinning 360 degrees on one leg as though he were my father at the Rox Arena. He held a whistle in one hand. Smith photographed his motions in close-up: first the whistle in the cop's upraised arm, then clenched between his compressed lips. There is a skater's joyousness in his movements as he sweeps through Smith's lens, through the acrid air of Pittsburgh at rush hour.

My eyes focused on the street itself, on the cobblestones, on the gentle curve of the trolley tracks as they turn down Grant. On the back, Smith had written, "Magnum Photos."

In the next group, girls in floral dresses are seated in Mellon Square. It might have been noon of a spring day. You could see the fountains breaking in spray high above the marble. Smith was fascinated by fountains; he was fascinated by water, and by the lovely ordinary girls assuming different positions: seated, turning this way and then that, standing, looking down in conversation with a friend, a coworker. There was no story written on the backs of these pictures, so I made one up for each photo as I moved through the collection. My fingers were beginning to turn gray, and I hoped I was not stealing away the print. I was a thief in the Center for Creative Photography in the desert city of Tucson, looking at midcentury Pittsburgh, industrial heart of an America long gone.

From the tall buildings on Smithfield, from the twentieth floor, Smith looked down on the tops of passing trolleys making their way slowly through the morning streets. In his lens, you saw prosperity. The woman in the white dress and white hat walking across the street looked like my stylish mother in her early years. I imagined my father nodding behind me. It was 1955. His time.

His moment. His year. And this was the woman he'd loved all his life, caught in Smith's photo.

In the Hill District, Smith photographed a black woman with a small child cradled in her arms. She is handsome and dignified, and he captured that. She appears strong standing against a wooden porch railing, looking off into the street. He photographed her in many positions and with many facial expressions. Sometimes the child is folded into her arms, and you cannot see its face. Then an older woman appears—the grandmother?—and the three of them are together against the railing of the small porch. I had been on this street; maybe I had walked past this very house. I think it's near the Crawford Grill, famous at one time for jazz and for sponsoring the Pittsburgh Crawfords in the Negro League. My father said to me long ago, "You should know all about the Crawfords, Bill. They were something: Josh Gibson, Cool Papa Bell. Great ball players. They were Hall of Fame great. They should have been in the Bigs. Except for the prejudice."

★★★

I took a break from the photos. My eyes were turning into little gelatinous balls. Where did my eyes leave off and Smith's images begin? Where did Tucson end and Pittsburgh begin? I was ringed by naked mountains, telescopes perched on arid peaks, a brilliant sun, and the bluest skies on earth, and yet the cop gesturing and turning on Grant Street moved in the deep haze of Pittsburgh smog, and the girls in white dresses were seated on cool marble near the splash of fountains. The girls reminded me of California, of the lawn party on that fragrant night before the tournament, of my first wife when I met her long ago. Time blends and bends again in the convexities and concavities of memory. As Ciaran Carson wrote, "Where am I coming from? Where am I going?"

***

My white gloves were off and I was paging through Smith's notes, but I had no context for them. What were they? Letters? Reflections? Smith typed on thin, transparent sheets, like my brother Eugene once did, and made corrections in pencil. I transcribed the words:

> The marks of my fists are against the sky, are blunted into shadow. Fury demeans me in my wrath against continuing transfusion to a vampire. Pittsburgh is well built but am I? The tight wire is fraying thin—I am cramping.

And then farther along, "Terrible urgency; respectful hesitation."

And below that, "I cannot speak of Pittsburgh, even briefly, the volumes are too long."

I was beginning to understand: Smith was *possessed* by this city. It cut deep into his personal life, his marriage. Through Smith, I sensed why my father, despite the attractions of California and Florida—the sunshine, the baseball—could never leave.

It was nearing a hundred degrees outside as I returned after my break. Christ it was hot! I lurched forward into the cool bath of the center. I put on the white gloves. On roll E-1, Smith had photographs of Oakland. The Cathedral of Learning at the University of Pittsburgh rose in its dark sootiness. The black carbon had rained down on the light-colored stone, years of mill-borne carbon unburned. At Phipps Conservatory, Smith had photos of children walking among exotic orchids and pitcher plants. I colorized these in my mind. I imagined line spectrum intensities of yellow, blue, and violet.

***

Looking at these pictures, I was thinking of a question: *How many hometowns are like this?* Hometowns that you know you've got to leave, you just can't wait to leave. Your heart becomes a plangent note each time the sky blots out the sun. Sometimes, as Breslow once said, you have to get so far away no one will ever find you. Ends of the earth! And then you find out, too late maybe, just what you've left behind. And maybe in some cases it wasn't much, and you haven't the slightest hint of regret. But in other cases it was abundance, a horn of plenty, replete with childhood friends, relatives, your own family. The lost world of the city spilling out to form a giant tapestry of objects, dreams, memories, and the people you loved. The lost world of the past.

File E-2, Rolls 50–55: the corner of Federal and Plush, the Fort Wayne Hotel. Plush this was not—it reminded me of the Commercial Hotel. I wondered if Smith had stayed there when he was going broke. Then the reading room at Carnegie Library, with all the daily papers—the ones threaded through bamboo so you read them standing up—and old guys standing in a row, wearing crushed hats. Outside in the park, there were hot dogs for twenty cents, wieners and kraut for fifty cents.

Rolls 96–100: South Side. The spires of the ethnic churches. There were pictures of women on a Heinz assembly line—pork and beans. More cobblestones, red bricks, trolley tracks. No asphalt anywhere. Rolls 80–85: kids at play. They were a ragtag bunch, chasing one another up in the hills above the smokestacks. It looked like Belfast. But these were kids playing, having fun, smiles on their faces, a big field spread in verdure across the hills. In the distance, Smith captured the dark incline as it inched up Mount Washington. You could see the rectilinear slash of windows as an opaque whiteness.

I couldn't see enough of Smith, but it was getting late. I'd a plane to catch.

***

Dr. Breslow, who was probably in his early fifties at the time of my father's death, had lived through much of the same history as my father. In one session he asked me whether I had ever dreamed about the city, and I told him only in the most peripheral way. I had not dreamed of racing with pounding heart through its streets or alleyways, or being chased through empty weed lots, or being in some grave danger at the point of a knife. But I had had other dreams with the city as a backdrop that Breslow, I recall, found significant in his analysis.

There was that recurrent dream of flight, so common and so familiar to most of us. In one version, I was walking on what appeared to be Liberty Avenue, one of the main arteries of the downtown. It was crowded, and I was in a dense group of people who might all have been on their way to work. We passed the coffee shops—some dim, some brightly lit—but I hardly noticed. My body was gradually becoming lighter; it was becoming like helium, a gas I knew well and had worked with. When I placed a foot on the ground, I ascended a little as though I were defying gravity. Finally, I took a step that propelled me into the air. Suddenly I was high above the crowd, looking down on them, and they were looking up at me, startled. I realized that if I extended my body horizontally I could swim through the air; I could move effortlessly, and I could swim upward like a seal ascending from the dark depths of the sea. Eventually I could soar. I could pirouette and somersault. I could play with the air like a great, speckled monarch, and the crowd became nothing more than a collection of dots far below me.

I said to myself, *No, this is not happening, this is a dream.* But then I corrected myself and said, *This is surely real, this is happening. I have this special power.* I told Breslow I felt such great joy in this dream. I was a spirit cast upon seas and mountains and rivers, upon the eternal whiteness of polar snows, upon the atmosphere itself.

I convinced myself it was real. How could it not have been real?

I did (and still do) this often. If the dream is pleasant, if it brings to me someone I want to be near, if it confers upon me a special power or brings to life someone I've lost, then I know I'm not dreaming. My skepticism melts away like so much candle wax, and I am in a state of ecstasy. And even when I awake, when I pinch myself back into the waking world, I feel a glow around me for having seen what I've seen, been where I've been, felt what I've felt. This dream—reorganized, rationalized, turned in an instant into a story—is as real as rain, as sunlight on my shoulder.

Breslow was fascinated by this dream. He had been furiously taking notes. He wanted to know if there were others like it, and I told him there were too many to recite them all.

"The flight dream," he said, "is a dream of escape." He tied it to my father, of course, and said the crowd that I was leaving was the uncomfortable, claustrophobic environment of my father's house. I wanted to escape him. I wanted to gain distance. I wanted to be anywhere but in that city, knowing how wonderful I would feel if I were no longer in his presence.

★★★

"Happy families are all alike," Tolstoy says in the first line of *Anna Karenina*. "Every unhappy family is unhappy in its own way." We lived in a happy family—Eugene, Liz, and I and my mother and father and Aunt Gene. I was once so sure of that. I carried this belief through my callow teens, and it was never really challenged until my father's death. Until Breslow, that "destroyer of worlds."

Leo Tolstoy, had he been around, would have seen our family for what it was. My time with Dr. Breslow in the early '70s revealed this, dream by dream, session by session. If nothing else, Breslow compelled me, in his gentle, bespectacled way, to see the strains within our home and to see my father as a man from whose abiding love an escape was required.

Smith's work, tucked into the vaults of Tucson, brought them all back: my father, my good psychiatrist, and the anonymous crowds and structures of the city. Smith defined a world that is gone, just as the world of my father is gone. "Not people die but worlds die in them."

Modern day Dallas skyline

21

Dallas (2013)

The city of Dallas was important in my father's life, as were the Elks, and both of these were now important to me. So I was in Dallas to do some research.

***

I got to my room and lay on the bed. I needed to be out at the Dallas Elks Lodge the next day at eleven. Lodge 71. This was a new lodge, if you consider forty-two years new.

I'd already talked with the people there by phone, and they seemed friendly. As soon as I told them my father was exalted ruler at the lodge in the Rocks, it was as if I were one of the family. "So he was Exalted Ruler," the administrative assistant said. "And where is McKees Rocks?"

"Right next to Pittsburgh," I told her. "You can't tell one from the other. At least I can't."

"Okay," she said, "I've never been there. But then I haven't been to many places. Texas, Oklahoma. Nowhere in the East."

It is 2013, and I still hear this a lot. Some people stay put. And as I've come to know, that isn't a bad thing.

In the morning, I set off for 8550 Lullwater Drive, home of Lodge 71. My father and mother seemed to enjoy themselves out here at the Dallas convention back in '68. The Garmin guided me nicely to Lullwater, even though I made ten or twenty wrong turns along the way. But the female voice never yelled, "You freakin' idiot, you screwed up again!" She was very understanding of human failure. When I got out of the car, the first thing I saw was a fine bronze statue of an elk, symbol of the Benevolent Protective Order of Elk (BPOE).

I was remembering some words from one of my father's Christmas letters, the one where he talked about bringing out the toys, by which he meant this comical mechanical man that smoked a cigar with a lighted tip, and some other improbable stuff. If Liz's husband, George Hart, thought my father was nuts, he also thought he was the greatest, most uninhibited guy he'd ever met. The words of my father's that I'm thinking of are these: "The Elks Christmas party is next Sunday and I expect to take a couple neighbor kids." The Elks organization was important to him in his later years, after his coaching days were nearly done.

Inside, the assistant was just as friendly as she had been on the phone. She was proud to tell me that she was an Elk herself. It had only been fifteen years since women were admitted to full membership in the organization. She handed me some literature. "Here is a yearbook for 1994," she said in that pleasant, slightly syrupy Texas accent. "And here is the *Dallas Lodge 71 Elks Press.* It's just out this month." I thanked her and she said, "You can keep them for your research."

I asked, "Can you tell me some things about the organization? Any oaths, for example?" I was thinking of that scene in *Peggy Sue Got Married* where Peggy Sue visits her grandfather's lodge—comprised of a group of time travelers from the fifteenth century called the Order of the Golden Dawn—and was wondering if my father conducted rituals and wore tricornered hats when he inducted Bill Rudison and the others into the group.

"Sure," she said, "the oaths are simple. You swear you're a citizen, you have never been convicted of a felony, and you believe in God." I can't quite define the way she said this, but I realized how much I like regional accents, even my own, which is distinctly Pittsburgh despite the fact that I've lived in places that should have obliterated any trace of an accent long ago.

"Good," I said. "I think I can meet those requirements."

She smiled and said, "Are you thinking of becoming an Elk?" And I stammered out some kind of nonanswer, because I was not quite sure about that last criterion. I might be an agnostic—until, that is, the chips are down. Then I'm relieved to talk to a kindly priest and receive Communion as a kind of Pascal's hedge against eternal damnation. I didn't know how this would go over with the Dallas Elks. I doubt that Pascal was an Elk.

I asked her about the big bronze elk out front, the one I'd already photographed. She told me a long story about how it got here. The elk was about ten feet tall, with an impressive rack of antlers. I kinda liked this elk.

There were not many people around on the morning of my visit, but fortunately the lodge secretary, Frank Krejci, stopped in and asked if I would be interested in a tour. I was, so we set off to explore. There was a lounge, a breakfast room, a kitchen where occasional dinners were prepared for the members and their families, and an impressive ballroom, which was used mostly for karaoke. Frank talked about the popular spaghetti dinners, and I recalled that when I was a kid, we attended these whenever they were held, and that even my mother seemed to enjoy them, possibly as an evening away from the stove.

Frank wanted me to know about the charities that Elks Lodge 71 supported, and it was a generous list: programs for the homeless, a camp for kids, assistance for the hearing impaired, college scholarships, a hoop shoot contest, and help for veterans in need. My father used to say BPOE stood for "Best People On Earth," and I never knew what he meant, but after listening to Frank for fifteen minutes it became clear.

I also had the feeling that, if you wanted, you could build

much of your social life around the activities provided by the lodge. Bingo, dinners, breakfasts, card games, dances, and occasional lectures were all part of the calendar of events. Frank seemed justly proud of his organization. The only note of sadness entered in when I asked about trends in membership. "Well," he said, "we're having problems there. Our membership is down to four hundred fifty. It was over seven hundred once."

"And the average age?" I asked.

"It's seventy-one," he said. "We don't seem to be drawing in the young ones. People are just too busy these days, with both husband and wife working."

"Maybe the scholarship program will help," I said. "You seem to have selected some pretty bright kids for those awards."

"I hope so," he said, "but society seems to be moving in a different direction these days." Then he smiled. "Are you going to send us a copy of your book? Maybe the book will do some good."

"Sure," I said, "assuming everything works out."

I went back to the office and said good-bye to the kind woman who had set up my visit, and then Frank saw me out to the car, where I had another chance to photograph my friend, the stately, benign elk.

At the hotel, I decide to write a little and give some thought to what I'd seen and not bother with further travels in Texas. I was beginning to see the appeal the Elks had for my father. Out at Lullwater, I felt like I was back in the 1950s in the Rocks. In the May newsletter, Esteemed Leading Knight Marion McDaniel wrote, "Let us all share and give to those who are not as fortunate as we are … Not just the charity of alms, but the higher and nobler charity of thought, word and deed. CHARITY IS THE GREATEST OF ALL THE VIRTUES." And there was sincerity, an absence of irony, in the directive of Brenda Taylor, who wrote, "In every organization, there is work time and playtime. Look around the Lodge and ask someone what you can do to help." A pride of association permeated her list of former Elks, just as it had registered in Frank's words too: Roosevelt, Truman, Kennedy, Ford, Clint Eastwood, Mickey Mantle, Vince Lombardi, Ben Affleck. With a few minor changes, and with the help of my mother, my father might have composed this newsletter in 1969.

I tucked away *Elks Press* Volume 25, May 2013, in my luggage for my upcoming flight. There were two more places I had to see again.

Rails (2013)

22

RAILS (2013)

It was the rails, the silvery rails, that ran through my father's life. They are embossed on my memory, my dreams. I can see them rolling out in long, straight lines from the fiery mills of Pittsburgh onto the streets of the nation. The world.

***

In Santa Monica, California, there is an old motel on Main Street where we often stay when we visit our daughters. It's clean and simple, in that '50s, no-frills way. What the place may lack in amenities, it compensates for in its location and the friendliness of its owners. Up the street there is a Starbucks and, not more than a few hundred yards away, an Irish pub. The pub features live music, Harp and Guinness on tap, and, for me, more than a few memories of 1970 Belfast, a city I gradually came to love and for which my affection over the years has only grown. A city I so hastily left behind. I go to the pub on Main and I think of Small and Jameison. I think of Gladys Kennedy, who was too young in those days to drink. I can smell vinegar and feel the oily paper outside the dance hall at night. In spring, Lord Kelvin stands in the fragrant gardens at Queens.

On the wall of room 8 is a poster that I'll bet no one ever

looks at. Hell, why would they? It is so ordinary, so unassuming, so dull and faded in its hues that it is unlikely to garner so much as an upward glance. But it captures my attention immediately. One Christmas my daughters bought me a copy of it and had it framed and glassed, and I hung it in my study back home.

At the foot of the Santa Monica Mountains and the bohemian enclave of Topanga, down where the Pacific Coast Highway wends its way south from Malibu, the tracks hew close to the barren hillside. Along the berm of the PCH, old parked cars stand at odd angles, as though released by a powerful magnet; then it's shrubbery, chaparral, and beach sand down to the breakers. In the foreground, a red-and-gray trolley makes its way south, and below that are the words: World's Greatest Electric Rail System / 1000 Miles Of Relaxing Trolley Lines /2700 Trolleys Scheduled Daily. All these rails once existed in the mad freeway tangle of LA!

When I look at this poster, I think of the Great Cities of America once imprinted with a circuitry of rails, and the rails with their silent-smooth steel casting, connecting town with town.

And across prairies and mountains, along the winding banks of rivers, through tunnels of pure granite or limestone upon which forested peaks sit timeless in sun and rain, the rails stream on the worn stone and then suddenly roll off into the desert. And this vast landscape was once all joined by these parallel threads of metal—the dining cars, the glass-domed observation coaches set high above the tracks, the domes like speeding observatories racing along through the dark Dakotas under the fresh-lit stars. And again, E. M. Forster says in my mind, "*Only connect.*"

"I want this back," I imagine my father saying, *"I want this all back. Don't you wish we could go back?"* And I imagine he is looking at what once was: The rails in the black-and-white photos of W. Eugene Smith, embedded in the ancient gray cobbles of Smithfield—the old Smithfield Diner, where the men are seated

in their work hats at the counter with coffee, pie, and scoops of ice cream, cigarettes in hand. And the rails join the whole city of Pittsburgh, even as they once joined LA long ago and even, on a grander scale, the whole majesty of America itself.

★★★

At home in Oxford, Ohio, beneath this very same motel poster, I found my father's wallet. My mother gave it to me not long after his death; somehow it had survived, like the letters, in the basement of our house. I opened the wallet one day and saw my name, William J. Green. It was printed on a license, but it could not have been my license. I looked at the date. It was 1937. Expired February 28, 1938. The address was given as 914 Third St., McKees Rocks, Allegheny County, Pennsylvania. It was my father's address—that is, my grandmother Green's address, the place where her body lay in the silk-trimmed casket, where we drank and celebrated her life and her soul's return to God. It was the driver's license of my grandfather, whom I knew only as the man with the blue engineer's cap, seated high in his cab in the P&LE yards; the man of stone silence; the man after whom I was named.

My father's license was there too, and there was an Elks card reading James W. Green, E.R. It was stamped with the President's Award and the insignia of the Dallas Grand Lodge. There was a card for Sam McDowell Enterprises, with McDowell's phone number. I imagined the tall, slim kid I once played ball with, imagined him with that fluid motion to first base that could catch you dead unawares; then, later, the fireball strikeout king of the Cleveland Indians. And I imagined him now, striding through the Legends, his own retirement community in Florida, striding as lord of the manor among subjects and admirers, all of whom knew the story of Sudden Sam.

Another card, with a struck medal of St. Christopher, read:

"St. Christopher Be My Guide." There were drawings of a Union Pacific diesel locomotive and a great ship, perhaps *Cunard*, on an ocean voyage straight to Southampton. Finally, a card: "In Case of Accident, Illness or Need please notify Mrs. J. W. Green." By happenstance, I found life and death in a thin leather wallet half a century old.

There were only two photographs: his sister and confidante, Agnes Louise, Sisters of Charity; and his feisty, sometimes maddeningly independent daughter, Elizabeth Ann.

★★★

This had been a parlous psychic journey, but I was beginning to see where all the longing of those years, the grief, had come from. Breslow had it half right: the whistling, the near-dance steps in the JFK concourse, and the need—like rail lines streaming through the night—for distance. My eyes searched the vast imaginary heaven above my head. "Breslow," I said, "wherever you are in this unimaginable universe, you got it half-right. But, dammit, man, I remember every word you ever spoke."

★★★

My recent visits to Tucson and Dallas helped clarify who my father was and what his life had been. Through the lens of W. Eugene Smith, I saw the rough-hewn city of bridge builders, trainmen, conductors, steelworkers, shop owners, barkeeps, churchgoers, mothers of small children, assorted celebrants in the ample gardens and parks—the whole cast of a rising America, with whom my father had rubbed shoulders, manifested in the city he knew.

In Dallas, I understood what it meant for him to be a member of the Benevolent Protective Order of Elks. The Dallas Elks Lodge felt like another era, the one he had known, as though I had stepped back into a time when people knew their neighbors, when there was more trust, when families stayed close and weren't dispersed across the land; when a president of the United States could address a letter to a bunch of insignificant kids playing baseball games in the dust and clay of Ontario, California.

Sunny Jim's Tavern. Photo courtesy of Sunny Jim's

23

Sunny Jim's

The past is never dead. It's not even past.

—William Faulkner

***

I round the bend in Camp Horne Road and there it is, all of a sudden, much as I remember it, standing against a copse of maples and oak in its own shadowy space. The front is the same, maybe a paint job and some repairs. I notice, though, that there is a wheelchair ramp leading to the door, and I think of Aunt Gene and there is a wire connecting us—her and me—through the ages, and I can only think how we left her and left her again in what now seems a cruel abandonment.

But I will not mention Aunt Gene to him unless he broaches the subject; nor will I mention the dog, the way he treated Mitzi even before she tore into Eugene's face. There will be no questions about the Thanksgiving turkey. About how he just let the matter die in the melancholic silences that were deeper than oceans. I will not say the word *love*, even though it is on my lips and I want to say it. I desperately want to tell him, but it is not our way. Nor will I ask about his absences. His silence. The mask behind which he hid from us. "Who is this man? Who is this man with whom I sit each night; to whom I pass the steaming potatoes, the gravy; whose looming presence defines me; who has helped craft me into something I was not at birth?" No. Nor will I ask if he was offended by my long absences, by the distances I kept. Maybe he didn't even notice. Maybe it was only Breslow who noticed, after those years of talk and dreams and letters. To my father, I know now, family mattered more than anything. So I cannot tell him that, like Liz and Eugene, I needed to get away from him. We all did, desperately. The three of us, all seeking the "geographic cure," as a friend once called it.

And I cannot tell him Eugene had not even *liked* him, despite the vision he had at church, and that Liz was ambivalent at best. "He made those desks to display his trophies," she once said to me. "He only *said* he made them for us."

About the evening there is haziness, like a pool shimmering off in parched sands. I remember a few details, mostly mundane, and around these I try, for myself, to construct something that makes sense. They are like the femur and incisor found embedded in the newly exposed clay of a riverbank, from which the paleoanthropologist arduously tries to build a once-living creature, a diet, perhaps an entire civilization. I am that anthropologist, digging amid the stratum, carefully sorting out the stones and pebbles from the precious treasure of bone. And all around I feel a fog descending, enshrouding me at ground level. What was once visible is now concealed. In the chill, my hands begin to stiffen as though arthritis has set in. Still, there is a desire to speak, and this desire will not be quieted. Quotidian as it may be for some, for me a conversation of length with my father is as unusual as a comet transiting the night sky.

***

When I arrive he is already there. I can see him sitting at a table off to the left, in the darkness, not far from the long bar. He's alone, as I expected he would be. This place is big, bigger than I remember, but it is not as crowded. We're in hard times. And there's a deck way off at the other end. That's new. I'll bet the little creek runs right under it. My father loves this place and so do I.

I walk up to his table. He raises his head and puts down his beer. He has a big smile on his face, but he is not getting up to greet me. He remains seated and stretches out his hand. Just as I remember it: large, soft, no grip. I notice three cigars in his shirt pocket, El Productos. I guess they still make those things. And even though they're wrapped, I can smell them, just as I smell the scents of chicken and beer heavy in the air of Sunny Jim's.

"Hi, Dad," I say. "I've been looking forward to this ever since you suggested it in your letter to Blacksburg. Remember? A couple of beers and some good bullshit?"

He nods his head and smiles. "Sure, I remember."

"Well, I'm ready for both. No better place than Sunny's," I say. "For old time's sake."

"Best fried chicken in the world. And the 'philly.' You know, that breaded fish they make? I always liked it."

"You did. How could I forget?"

The waitress stops by and slaps down two menus. "What would you like to drink, hon?" she asks me.

"Iron City. I think my dad needs a refill too," I say, glancing over at him. He nods and hands her his empty.

"I'll be just a minute," she says.

We both look at her as she leaves. I like the way she walks, that exaggerated sway of the hips. My dad nods his head with a subtle wink of approval, like he used to when he and Joe Vitelli were together at the bar. I can see Joe grab his wrist. "Nice, huh Jim?"

My father looks across the table at me. He fingers one of his cigars. He seems perfectly relaxed, even though there are only the two us. No baseball, no bat. No TV. Nothing but words or silence can possibly pass between us. "How's everyone?" he asks. "How're you? You look pretty skinny. You were a lot more muscular back then." He flexes his arm. "Up here. Good biceps."

He seems genuinely poised to listen, maybe even talk, although I think he's anticipating a second round of Iron City. "Pittsburgh piss," they once called it. Maybe it's gotten better.

Ah, the waitress is back. The bottles have that cool, nacreous sparkle to them, and I'm thirsty as hell by now. She has the glasses covering the tops of the bottles. They clink when she removes them and sets them on the table. I remember these glasses from the Wil-Kar Grill. I used to clean them by the thousands. Soapy water, a special brush, and then the cloth you had to work hard and twist around down into the narrow bottoms. This was all before I jumped into the front of his orange truck, with its radio's awful rolling-gravel sounds. Driving off to calculus at Pitt.

The waitress wants to know if we've made up our minds. My father points at the fish on the menu, and she writes on her green order pad and says, "Good choice." She looks down at me and I say, "The chicken and fries look great. I'll have those." She flips the page and writes it down. "Won't be long, hon," she says smiling. "Be back soon." And she turns and sways off toward the kitchen.

I ask him if he's ever heard of a photographer named Smith. "He was working around the time you were at Craft Avenue," I say. "He shot a lot of street scenes, rail lines, trolleys." He's listening, looking at me. I can see the veins in his face. "Those old trolleys, Dad, the red-and-white ones. They were beautiful things, works of art. Smith knew it too, and photographed them. But you never took a picture of the trolleys. Never put them in your Blue Book. Why?"

He had an El Producto out of his pocket and was fingering it, crinkling the cellophane wrapper so that it sounded like leaves. Then he laid it on the table.

"Well, you know, Bill, in the end, there were bad things that happened. I broke some company rules because I thought I was right. I wouldn't give up on my principles. They hit me hard for doing what I believed in. I lost my office at Craft Avenue. I was no longer a supervisor. I once had my pride, and then it was gone. I worked harder—physically, you know? They made sure of that. I got the message. They called me out on every one of those snowy mornings, even if it was four or five o'clock. It was then I knew I had to retire. I began to hate the Port Authority. It wasn't my old Pittsburgh Railways Company. I really missed the PRC. They knew how to treat a guy."

"I remember hearing something," I say. "Eugene told me in one of his letters. But he didn't know much. He said you were keeping it close to the vest. And as usual, I didn't think to ask you for details. God, there was so much I didn't think to ask you! The silence in our family. Jesus, we were all afraid to speak."

He doesn't respond to that last statement, just lets it hang, lets it hang there unexplored. He finishes off another glass of Iron City and pours the last drops from his bottle. "Where else did you go?" he asks.

I tell him I've been to Dallas and his eyes widen. He says he's liked the city from the time he was a kid, riding the rails for kicks. Liked it even though his hero was killed there.

"Yep. I visited the Dallas Elks, Dad."

He looks surprised. He's probably thinking, *Why in the hell would he do that?*

I say, "I always meant to ask you about the Elks—what you did there, why you liked it so much, how you became exalted ruler. What that ER position meant. I was going to ask several times during our trip up through Texas and Oklahoma that gorgeous spring, but something else always popped into my head and I forgot."

"Your mother and I used to say you thought too much," he says. "You needed to have more fun. You're only young once. Then it all goes away and it goes away real quick. Gone before you know it." And he snaps his fingers, to make a point. "One minute you're chasing down a fly ball, you grab it, do a few somersaults, get up and throw a perfect strike to second. Next thing you know, you can't even imagine doing that. Your knees stiffen, your joints ache, your gut expands, and you might as well be dead. Then you get that thousand-yard stare and maybe you are dead. Inside."

I let that unexpected wisdom pass without comment. "Anyway, they treated me well at Lodge 71. They were impressed you had been ER in the Rocks, and so they answered every question I had and made sure I saw every corner of the place. I could see why you loved it so much."

The food finally comes. I haven't had fried chicken in years, but it's damn good and we both order another beer. Both of us have a big side of golden fries. His fish looks nicely breaded and browned to a light tan; it's crunchy when he chews it. He eats with his usual gusto. He's always enjoyed his food.

I tell him I took the family to Honolulu for a whole year. "I spent a lot of time with the kids, the way you used to in Atlantic City. I remember you in Jersey—playing in the surf, having those festive pancake breakfasts, walking the boards with all those hucksters you couldn't resist."

"Ah, that was fun, Bill! That's what we were there for, to have a great time. Escape. Forget things. Act a little silly. Good to be silly—don't lose that."

"Well, you succeeded."

"I always told you, family's what matters. Family activities, no matter how corny they are, matter. And I guess I was corny. But once you get family right, you've got it all."

I nod agreement. "You must be so proud of Eugene, of his success at Harvard, of all his scholarship; and the same with Liz, what she does at Ohio State."

"She was always good with numbers," he says. "That girl was really smart! I never told her I thought that—didn't want it to go to her head—but it was true. And she didn't take any crap either. Not from me or anyone."

There's a little silence and then we click our glasses to salute family, especially the happy ones. They aren't so much alike after all. And we down some more beer.

"Anyway, Hawaii was magical, like that first time in California," I say. "By the way, we go out to California a lot these days. Our daughters both live there. Actually they're not far from Ontario and Pomona—you know, where I met you that year at the train station?"

I ask him why he never moved out to California. Never down to Florida. "Those were your dreams," I say.

I think, *South Florida. Dad wanted to go there to die, didn't he? Die among all the cool, green fields. Balls racing in flight. White contrails over distant walls.*

"No," he says in a low voice, as though he doesn't want to give too much away, get too sentimental. "I had my important dreams: your mother, you three kids. And I had some good friends too, and then the ball clubs and the winning teams and all. And for a long time I loved my work. I really did. I was the boss. Craft Avenue. I was *the* boss. Then the Port Authority came. Everything changed."

We have both managed by now to coax out a big red mound of Heinz Ketchup onto our plates. That viscous stuff is delicious once you get it out of the bottle.

I'm stabbing my fries into the ketchup, just as my father is. Nothing like hot fries at Sunny Jim's.

"By the way, Bill, what happened to your first wife, the attractive blonde? Where did she end up? I told your mother that girl just wasn't right for you."

"I don't know. I haven't seen her since my trip to San Diego in the winter of sixty-eight, when I thought we might reconcile. It never happened—not a prayer. In August I got the divorce papers. I signed them right away. Then I left for Antarctica the next day."

"Best thing for you," he says. "Best thing that ever happened.

Best it ended without kids. Or debts. You know how I always thought she was wrong for you."

He asks me about Stewart, my good friend from the Blacksburg days. I tell him I've lost track of him too.

"I remember he was a good southern boy and one hell of a carpenter," he says.

"He was. Like you and your old buddy Jimmy Pites," I say. "When I first got to Virginia, he knew where all the seedy, wood-frame houses were over in West Virginia. Some pretty girls over there, and they had some good stories too. It kept me interested."

He gives me a knowing look, laughs and shakes his head. "There might have been some other things over in West Virginia that were keeping you interested. Not just the stories."

"Maybe," I say. I laugh and settle back, throwing my arm over the chair.

He's different from how I remember him. The sullenness, the moodiness and melancholy are gone. He is the man from our vacations in Atlantic City, the man on the boardwalk; he is the man who handed Liz the ticket to game seven of the World Series; the man who bought me a berth on the *QE2*. In this twilight conversation, I am seeing, possibly through the clarifying fog of beer, what I have only dimly known.

"And I thought you always had your nose stuck in a book," he says, laughing.

I haven't seen him quite this jovial since our days drinking with Joe Vitelli. His face has that good Christmas glow to it, as it had when he came home at night with too much drink in him.

"Later, though, I learned there was plenty going on outside Blacksburg too. Radford College, Hollins, Sweet Briar. There were some sweet girls there. I wish I'd met any one of them before I met Laura. But that's ancient history now."

"You were doing okay," he says. "You were about to get that degree. That meant a lot. And to tell you the truth, it meant a hell of a lot to me and your mother."

"I think it did, Dad," I say, nodding my head, my eyes closed. "And you played a big part in it. You and Mom both played a big role. All your encouragement."

"You know," I say, looking down into the basket for remaining bits of chicken, "with that degree, I thought about quitting a lot. I thought about giving up, finding something in industry or in the public schools, finally earning a few dollars. I was so tired of being poor, being the eternal student. But I remembered how you hated quitters. You had some pictures of them in your album. Remember?" I quaff down some Iron City. I need it. "I never forgot the day you kicked that water bucket, pitched me upstairs like an old sack. And that was for quitting, for not giving it my best. Not running it out. I was twelve years old, and it stuck. It was the only time you ever took a hand to me."

He is sliding his fingers along the length of an El Producto. It is unwrapped now, and he puts it to his nose just to inhale the fragrance of the tobacco. He looks reflective. "I didn't know whether my anger meant anything to you. With you, I could never tell. 'Nonchalant,' I'd always say to your mother. 'He's so damn nonchalant.'"

"I guess," I say. "But I was a teenage boy, full of quiet rebellion that I didn't understand. Still, I thought you were a great coach, and I took whatever you said seriously. I tried to play my heart out for you. I even took your concerns about the minor leagues seriously; you know, broken-down buses and hot afternoons. Miniscule chances of ever making it. All those lost years. All those dreams that would probably have come to dust."

"Sometimes I wish I hadn't discouraged you. I wish you had given it a shot. You were damn good out there. Everybody who saw you knew it. I should have encouraged you to see what you had. Maybe put you in touch with a good batting coach. You really needed that. That might have been all you needed."

"It still feels a little like unfinished business, Dad. The would-haves and could-haves that haunt us. The roads we might have taken but didn't. There were so many roads to choose from, and they all branched off into unknown darkness."

"I know, but things worked out for you. The South Pole, I could understand that: the bitter cold, the hard physical labor you wrote home about. I *knew* physical labor. I understood it and I respected it. The chemistry? That was a different matter. Chemistry! Funny. Who understands that stuff, anyway?" He laughs when he says this—that closed-mouth laugh that comes mostly from his eyes and his flushed cheeks. He looked like he did the day I saw him step down from the train in LA.

"I know you respected hard work, Dad. You taught me to respect it too."

"That's why I framed the article from the Richmond newspaper, Bill. The one that had your picture in it, drilling ice out there on that frozen lake. It looked hard. I showed it to all the guys down at the Wil-Kar Grill. No one there knew anyone who had ever been to the South Pole. They knew people who had been to Europe during the war. But not where you were."

"I have the picture at home, Dad. I'm proud of it, and I'm grateful you did that for me."

He looks at me and nods his head, as if he's known all along that someday, when my mind was more open to the world, I'd appreciate it.

"And speaking of pictures," I say, "remember the great photo we had of your father sitting high in that cab, looking like he owns the whole damn thing: engine, cars, caboose, and all?"

"Yeah," he says.

"What can you tell me about him?" I ask. "What do you remember?"

"To be honest, not much, Bill," he says in a low voice, as though he's ashamed. "He was quiet. He worked a lot. He had a steady job. Always had that. Kept a roof over our heads, good food on the table. That's what a man did back then. I had great respect for him—we all did—but we never sat down like this. We never did get to talk. I never went out with him, just the two of us. Never had a drink with him or threw the old ball around, like you and me did all those times on the field or in back of the house."

I'm a little surprised, but not that much. *That's what a man did back then.*

So we talk like this through a few more beers, and we are both getting pretty looped in the skein of reminiscence. I don't press him on his own father; maybe that's all he knows. I think of Yevtushenko again. The Russian poet plays in my mind like a song that won't go away, will never go away:

We who knew our fathers
In everything, in nothing.

Small pebbles rumbling, rolling down a metal awning, then onto the pavement like rain. *In nothing. In nothing.*

It's been a good bullshit session, the way he wanted it. The way I wanted it too. No Tolstoy. No Turgenev. No Wallace Stevens. *Captain Video*, his favorite "play," was probably somewhere in our ramblings, but I forget.

Then, recalling one of our ostentatious twenty-something musings at the dining room table long ago, I ask him if he thinks youth is wasted on the young, the way they say it is, and he says he was once young and strong and smart in a certain kind of way. "I wasted a lot of that, Bill," he says. "No one could convince me school was worth anything. I should have flunked out, but they gave me a break. They let me finish in summer. Gave me a couple of special courses they knew were easy. I can't remember what they were.

"Later, in my thirties, I coulda been kinder to your aunt. She had it real hard with that polio. Real hard. Harder than Roosevelt. But I resented how easy it was for her to talk with you kids. And I couldn't. So I had to leave. Hit the bars, the Elks, the Eagles, anywhere to get the hell out of that house. I was jealous and angry."

He makes it clear to me that for all those years, those tortured years, he was an exile from his own home, his own family. Days he was out in the city, working; nights he was either coaching his teams, running a meeting somewhere, or drinking until all hours, when everyone else was asleep. *Hell of a life,* I think, *when you're a take-charge guy, like he was, and you don't feel welcome in your own home.* It may as well have been exile from the very place he loved.

"How did you tolerate it for so long?" I ask. "There were no arguments; no heated disputes with Mother about Gene; no talk of options, like having Mary and Irv take her in. I never heard you raise your voice once, with either Mom or Gene. And the house was small. You could hear everything that wasn't whispered."

"I never did," he says. "I knew what the O'Donnells expected. I knew it all going in. Knew it when I proposed, when I married your mother. I just didn't know how tough it was going to be. I didn't know how long, you know? It was so long."

He closes his eyes, puts his hands over his face, and I imagine him traveling through time, going back over the pained decades, the memories of the door closing and closing again behind him. When it opened, it opened onto absence. It opened onto silence. Onto a house that was dark and still. Where he did not belong. *It was so long.*

"I know," I say in a hushed tone. "I know. It was hard for a guy who loved family the way you did. It was hard all around. Just the whole damn situation."

He is still drinking and there is sweat rolling down the bottle of Iron City. Beads of sweat on his forehead. I want to take his hand and give it a little squeeze. But I don't.

"I was always so busy," he says, "always on the go. Didn't matter what—I had to get away. All those teams. I never slowed down. Never stopped to appreciate. You seemed to know how to do that, how to appreciate things. Little things. Even when you were a kid—looking at the stars, sending up those silly rockets. I remember you wrote that poem in college. It was about raindrops on cobblestones. Rain. Whoever thinks about rain, except as a nuisance? But you saw something in it. And in the train, you were up in the observation car, staring out at things. Looking at all that flatness. That emptiness. I could never understand what you were looking at. What were you thinking? Me, I just wanted to talk to people—tell them about our tournament, what we had seen in LA."

He's expressing regret. He's even telling me things he admired about me. Jesus! I am learning, but I hardly know what to say.

"And the South Pole," he continues. "I would have found that place boring, but you seemed to love it. The silence and all. You were so excited to be there." Something jogs a memory for him. "I saw you one day on the porch. It was fall—windy, if I remember—and you were watching the leaves come down, whole bunches of them. And you told me it was raining leaves. Raining leaves! Reds and yellows, out of the big maple. And I just shook my head and walked into the house. I didn't see the point."

I've never heard him talk like this, with this frankness, and it is strange and unexpected. He is reaching into the past, into sorrow. Even praising me. Admitting to me he hasn't lived with his eyes open. I can smell faint sawdust, like the confessional boxes at St. Francis de Sales.

"You know," he says, "there's something else. I never talked to you about girls. About what you should and shouldn't do. About sex, or any of that stuff." He seems a little embarrassed. His face reddens a shade beyond its usual florid hue. Jesus! I can't believe he's talking like this. "But I didn't know where to begin. To be honest, I was embarrassed. I knew you were shy and hesitant. That girl in Mexico, the really pretty one? You seemed afraid of her, afraid to put your arm around her, even for a second. I had to coax you. I was sure then that you needed a real talking to. And the girl on the train coming east—I knew you had your eye on her. You wanted to say something. I saw that." He shakes his head at the memory. "We should have had a long talk, the two of us. Like some of the guys I knew at the Elks had with their sons. But we never did. I don't know why."

It's clearly a confession now. I can hear the priest's door sliding open, hear the priest speaking: *In the name of the Father* … And my father responding: *Bless me Father for I have sinned* … and on and on and on.

"Dad," I say, "it's all okay. It worked out fine."

★★★

Without notice, he changes the subject. "I was always surprised the three of you loved books like you did. That was your mother's doing that made that happen. She was something, Bill, with that Latin. Who was it? Ovid? Someone like that? And some philosopher maybe? Some emperor? I never understood why any of that stuff was important, why it mattered. Poetry, philosophy, history … they were all beyond me." He looks at me as though he had nothing to do with any of it.

"Dad, I think you were involved right up to your eyeballs with our education. All of us knew it too, but we never told you. It was clear as one of those streams at Cook Forest what you valued."

A little insight flashes through my mind. My mother had thought of books as vessels, conveyances into the larger world. The travels of Halliburton, the journeys of Scott, the courage and endurance of Shackleton, the insane boldness of Hannibal—these were among her favorite stories, and through her we learned of them and of the world's breadth and possibility. But for my father, books were practical instruments of betterment, of respect and opportunity and, yes, a bigger paycheck. "Better make it by forty, Bill," he'd say. "After that, it's getting too late."

Reflecting on what he said earlier about the mistakes of his youth, he says, "It wasn't all mistakes. I have some good memories from when I was young. Lots of memories." He gives me a big, conspiratorial smile so I can see those "choppers" of his, the ones he'd put on the mantel at night to gross out my mother. ("Oh Jim!" she'd say in mock horror, with a hand over her mouth.)

All those rail trips west. I think I can imagine what he'd been up to outside the Rocks, outside the watchful eyes of his Irish Catholic family. My father was no candidate for sainthood.

I shake my head and smile at him, knowing there's a world in there I might never hear about. Or maybe someday I will. "Dad," I say, "you seem kind of tired."

He nods and looks around. The place is empty except for a young couple hanging onto one another for support at the bar. He says, "I think we're closing her down."

I look at him and wait till his head is up. I look him straight in the face. "You know, Dad, I probably never said this to you. I know I never said it." He is rubbing his forehead, looking down at the table. "But I need to … I need to tell you how much …" Then I stop. I can't say it.

All those things unspoken—the compliments we might have exchanged, the questions we might so easily have asked. They hang there, the festoonery of conversations past, frayed and worn to threads by time and neglect, dangling as memories, as reminders of some connection that could have been made had only the words, the courage, the will been summoned.

So instead I say, "I really appreciated all those letters. They were great. Straight off the top of your head like you were thinking out loud. No artifice. Nothing phony."

"I remember writing them," he says, smiling up at me. "I worked at them. Words never came easy."

"But they were great letters anyway. Direct and honest. I never knew where a sentence was heading. Always some nugget stashed in among the boring debts and receipts and financial advice. The money talk. If you know what I mean."

He nods. He knows I found the "money talk" insufferable.

"And those were wonderful family vacations," I say. "Cook Forest, Atlantic City, that one crazy, miserable camping trip where Eugene saved our ass. I never told you thanks." I pause for a second. "And I loved our whole family. We were all so different. We all had our different dreams. You could see the dreams waking in us, evolving, sometimes through a lot of fits and starts. A lot of pain." I'm thinking of Eugene. I'm thinking of his letters, of all those corrosive doubts about who he was and whether he would ever become what he'd dreamed of becoming. And I was thinking of Liz too, and how she needed to get far away to somewhere, anywhere, no one had ever heard of. Goias, Brazil! Jesus Christ, it was more obscure than the Dry Valleys. And that wasn't easy.

I'm feeling the slick surface of the cool bottle beaded under the dim lights of Sunny Jims.

I say, "As for me, I just had to get some distance for a bit. Things were too close as they were. Like Joe Vitelli said that night at the bar, I needed some room. You were a strong presence—a strong presence for all of us. Sometimes I felt suffocated. You understand that, don't you?"

He has a serious look on his face, as if he is pondering the past, remembering how he once was, his fierce silence and his sarcasm that made you feel small and stupid. So stupid and incompetent. Only Liz ever challenged him. Eugene and I kept everything bottled up, except for that one Thanksgiving.

He nods, and I know he understands. I continue: "You know the dinners, the TV shows, the picnics at North Park—they were great too. Even the rosary was okay. It was a time to slow down, to go into a trance."

He laughs. "Bill, I used to think you were in a trance most of the time anyway."

I find that amusing and have to laugh too. "So, Dad," I say, "what exactly were we praying for?"

He laughs again and says, "I don't know about you, but I was praying I'd never have to pray another rosary again." He tosses his hands playfully into the air as though he's throwing a pair of beads into the heavens of Sunny Jim's. "But there was this Catholic crusade going on: the family that prays together stays together."

"Well," I say, nodding, "it worked. Mostly, anyway. And, Dad?" I wait until he turns his face to me, until I'm looking him straight in the eye, above the redness of his veined, broad cheeks. "I ..." But again I can't say it.

He lowers his head. There's that faint, shy smile on his lips. He says nothing, but I think he knows. Oh yeah, he knows all right. He always knew what was what.

I signal for the check. "I got it, Dad. I have some money now. And maybe I owe you. Just a little."

He's laughing at this just as I am, remembering all those handouts. His red cheeks are swollen. He looks so Irish, like one of the guys in Belfast, or down at the Wil-Kar Grill. So full of himself.

On our way to the door, he says, "And what ever happened to your friend Estella? And to the girl across the street, the younger one, the one you really liked?"

And I say, "Wanda, you mean? Oh, those are long stories, Dad. They'll take some time. When we talk again, I'll be sure to tell you."

The air outside is chilly—early spring air, like practice time. And I can smell the trees and the creek that flows by Sunny Jims. I want to hug him, throw an arm around him. Feel that big, warm belly press against mine. But he only holds out his soft hand from a distance.

We shake hands, and he walks away, taking the unwrapped cigar and feeling his shirt pocket for the others. I know he'll light up as soon as he hits the car. When the car door closes, I see the flicker of a match. I think I see someone in the front seat with him. Her arm is raised as if she's touching her hair, putting the thin strands in place. But then suddenly it is dark again and there are shadows, and I can no longer be sure what I've seen or if I've seen anything at all.

***

That night I went back to the hotel where I always stay, in the heart of Pittsburgh. I took out a copy of the book I'd published in 1995 and turned to the page I once had such difficulty reading at my talk in New York City. I began,

> There are such dreams in daylight here! Everyone speaks of them. Long and slow moving, unfolding like cinema, a whole lifetime running through. In the stones of Bull Pass, I dreamed of my father. It was as though he were here … I saw his face through the window along the tracks disappearing into the night as we moved east. New York. London. Belfast. You could see the glow of the mills moving on the night sky like an aurora. It was the last …

I read and read, and my voice was strong, and I finished it out loud for the first time. There were no tears in my eyes. My voice didn't crack. I knew that night I would sleep. I would sleep without waking.

In the morning I would go down to the restaurant on Penn, not far from the old Smithfield Street Café. I would remember the tracks and trolleys W. Eugene Smith photographed and all the hard work he recorded: the buildings going up, the latticed bridges arcing the wide rivers.

I would remember the proud, lined faces in Smith's pictures. The streets tilted upward to the heavens.

All of this my father knew. For a man of the city is that city.

All of this my father knew, even when he dreamed—during those heavy snowfalls—of Florida and California. All of this he knew when he dreamed of the way the palm trees bent in the wind so you could hear their fronds as they clacked above the bat, above the *pock* of the ball in the catcher's mitt.

And I would remember Breslow and what I had not told him. What I had forgotten to tell him. What I had not known and could not answer. Absence defines—and there were many absences in our sessions. Many things I had not known about my father and I'd felt deep anger toward him, that he had not opened himself, had not talked as he did last night. And yet somehow, through the dreams and photographs, the voices that rose like waves from the pages of old letters, and the memories that came like film, as if from a studio in LA, the healing had begun. It had begun in Breslow's presence, in a faded office in Pittsburgh.

Why wasn't Breslow present now so he could hear how it all turned out? So I could tell him how peace and resolution had finally come? So I could remind him what Estella wrote all those years ago from Kansas—"I just love being alive." So I could thank him.

Even in Breslow's absence, in an old shop out of a dimly lit Hopper painting, I would sip coffee as the crowds moved swiftly up Penn. I would remember Sunny Jim's and what my father told me about Aunt Gene and her struggle to move through an ordinary day. About being an exile from his own home, an outcast from the family he loved. About never stopping long enough to marvel at what was small and commonplace and wonderful. And I would remember what he told me about silence, the granitic silence of his own father, of himself—the dense, unknowable silence of men.

I would remember the sweat on his forehead and how he said that words never came easily to him either, like those words that still reverberate down the years: *Don't you wish … Don't you …?* And in the end, I would remember his big belly as he stood outside Sunny Jims and fingered his cigars, and the feel of his soft, distant hand when we said good-bye. And I would recall the moist spring breeze—like all those scented spring evenings we spent together—as it flowed down among the watery tall trees and wet soils, touching the endless dark hills of Pittsburgh.

APPENDIX

More photos

Aunt Agnes, the Author, Grandma Green and Jim Green

The Rox Rams. Bill Green is at lower right. (1958)

My mother (on right) with her sister, Mary Jo.

Bill, Eugene and Liz stand behind our train layout.

"The girl across the street."

Formal portrait of Elizabeth O'Donnell Green.

Jim Green with the three of us at Cook Forest.

Jim Green with Bill, Liz and Eugene.

High school chemistry class. My mother is second from left.

Printed in the United States
By Bookmasters